THIRTY YEARS OF SHIKAR

Owing to the antiquity and rarity of this book, certain pages are regrettably absent, and readability is compromised due to the blurring of the original text. If you possess any insights regarding the availability of these missing sections, kindly inform us. Your assistance is crucial in ensuring the completion of this significant work for the benefit of future generations.

THIRTY YEARS OF SHIKAR

BY

SIR EDWARD BRADDON

K.C.M.G.

GYAN

Published by

Gyan Publishing House
5, Ansari Road
Daryaganj, New Delhi-110002
Phone: 011-47034999, 9811692060
E-mail: books@gyanbooks.com

Distribution Network
gyanbooks.com
India, USA, Canada, UK, Australia

ISBN: 978-93-6208-094-3 (PB)
First Published, 1858

2nd Impression 2024

Printed at: Gyan Press, Delhi.

THIRTY YEARS OF SHIKAR
Author: EDWARD BRADDON

THIRTY YEARS OF SHIKAR

"THE TIGER EMERGED NOT AT THE POINT EXPECTED."

Frontispiece.

THIRTY YEARS OF SHIKAR

BY

SIR EDWARD BRADDON

K.C.M.G.

WITH ILLUSTRATIONS AND A MAP

WILLIAM BLACKWOOD AND SONS

EDINBURGH AND LONDON

MDCCCXCV

CONTENTS.

CHAPTER I.

DAYS OF GRIFFINAGE.

CHAPTER II.

SPORT IN LOWER BENGAL.

CHAPTER III.

AMONG THE INDIGO-PLANTERS.

CHAPTER IV.

THE SANTHAL REBELLION.

CHAPTER V.

THE SANTHAL COUNTRY IN THE MUTINY.

CHAPTER VI.

THE DEOGHUR TIGERS.

CHAPTER VII.

THE JAMTARRA MAN-EATER.

CHAPTER VIII.

THE ELEPHANT IN TIGER-HUNTING.

CHAPTER IX.

A HUNTING CAMP IN THE TERAI.

CHAPTER X.

MIXED SHOOTING IN OUDH.

CHAPTER XI.

RECOLLECTIONS OF THE TERAI.

CHAPTER XII.

STATION LIFE IN OUDH.

ILLUSTRATIONS.

INITIALS.

TAILPIECES.

THIRTY YEARS OF SHIKAR.

CHAPTER I.

DAYS OF GRIFFINAGE.

OFFICE WORK IN CALCUTTA—FORT-WILLIAM STUDENTS—THE HAILEYBURY CIVILIANS—A DUMDUM SYMPOSIUM—A BORROWED MOUNT—FIRST JOYS OF PIG-STICKING—PIG-STICKING *V.* HUNTING—MY FIRST BENGAL BOAR.

FROM time to time the suggestion has been made to me by Anglo-Indian friends that I should write an account of my experiences in the wide field of Indian shikar. Up to the present time, however, I have always repelled this idea as impracticable, or at least unprofitable. Hitherto I have always been very chary of telling tiger stories *viva voce*, from a confirmed conviction that the most brilliant conversationalist could not make any such narrative palatable to his audience. Conversation nowadays does not lend itself to monologue; the anecdotal person is as much out of vogue as pig-tails on English heads; and the man who went about describing how he killed this or that tiger would now be regarded by society as an anachronism, intolerable as that princess of interminable tales —Scheherezade—would be in the present day.

But I have lately been encouraged to believe that the narrative which would be wholly unacceptable if administered orally, may meet with a more indulgent reception if it appear in print. Even in this age of hurry there are in the lives of most men odd hours of leisure, during which sporting reminiscences may afford a wholesome relief from the mysterious murder of the sensation novel or the intrigue of the French yellow-back, or the miscellaneous crimes of other branches of fiction devoted to the annihilation of the Decalogue; and for those leisure hours I write. I shall be no more autobiographical than I can help, and if I touch upon some of the doings of Anglo-Indians of a bygone generation, this ancient history will be, as far as possible, confined to the matter in hand—Indian shikar—or to subjects which, whether cognate thereto or not, shall incidentally suggest themselves.

And now that I try to conjure back out of the distant past the incidents in my sporting career, memory fails me save as to the most salient points. Phantasmal tigers, panthers, and other *fauna* of the jungle, pass in dim array before my mind's eye, a procession longer far than that of the ghosts which tortured Richard on Bosworth field, or the string of apparitions that Macbeth interviewed in the witches' cave. I say with the latter usurper—

> "Another yet! A seventh! I'll see no more:
> And yet the eighth appears, who bears a glass
> Which shows me many more;"

and oddly enough, the most conspicuous are the tigers I did not shoot. That bygone period seems to have commenced at a time as remote almost as those days when men measured the passage of the hours by the clepsydra or Alfred's candles; and, sooth to say, I have never cared to keep my memory in practice by recounting the bags made, or chances missed. Sufficient and very keen was the joy of pursuing the quarry, but deadly uninteresting that pursuit as the subject of subsequent conversation. This, I fancy, is very much the case with every man who has killed much big game, however thrilling the incidents that may have accompanied the slaughter.

It did not seem, when I went out to India to join the mercantile house of a relative in Calcutta, that very large opportunities in the way of sport would present themselves for me. My work consisted of sordid office details relating to Indian produce, and sale and barter; it was sedentary, save for an occasional run in an office *jaun* (carriage) to the Custom-house or elsewhere, and provided no occupation or thought beyond invoices, ships' manifests, fluctuations in prices, and similarly humdrum commercial items. It soon became revealed to me that this was not work after my mind: I had no desire to become a merchant prince,—my aspirations inclined rather to the career of leather-leggings than to that of Dick Whittington; and so the mercantile bonds, that were strained from the first moment of my wearing them, snapped in the course of a year or two, and I was let forth from the city of palaces free to make my way in the great beyond hazily known to me as the Mofussil. Heredity, not I, was to blame for this: my forebears had been sportsmen, good with the gun, the rod, and in the saddle, and I was no degenerate scion of my race.

Yet during my term of bondage in Calcutta I served in some sort my shikari apprenticeship, and made, with great pleasure to myself, the acquaintance of some notable pillars of every form of sport. Those Calcutta days were so long ago that a fair maiden who then adorned Chowringhee society, and claimed to be the original Becky Sharp, was still young, and still, I suppose, on the look-out for her Rawdon Crawley. And Calcutta was then a much more go-ahead place, socially considered, than it is at present. For in those good old days, when John Company was king and Downing Street an unimportant factor in Indian administration, the Haileybury civilians of the Bengal Presidency commenced their career by entering the College of Fort-William: I do not say they began active service by passing through that college, for in some instances they did not pass out of that institution at all,—one collegian, who was a hero in his day, although now forgotten, having spent seven years off and on as a Fort-William undergrad. and being then retired.

And these students, who by no means studied over-deeply, if at all, were many in number, accomplished in manly sports, admirable in the ball-room and cricket-field, and prized in the matrimonial market as good for £300 a-year dead or alive. As far as this mercenary appraisement went, it should be stated that it sometimes erred as to the value of the living collegian, inasmuch as he generally was worth many thousands of rupees less than nothing. For those were the glorious days when credit abounded and the shroff was ever ready with the loan required by embryo rulers of the land. Fine old times, when the young civilian could, and did, live at the rate of £4000 or £5000 a-year on an income of £400—making things go merrily during his collegiate days, and recking nothing of the years of sadness that should follow, when with slow labour and quick regret he came to pay the heavy cost of those Calcutta joys. All that has been changed: the latter-day civilian goes not now into a Presidency college to become a social ornament, but is drafted off promptly to some Mofussil station to learn his work; the money-lender in these degenerate times is coy in the matter of advances, and even the tailor looks to be paid in the course of a year or two.

But in the pre-Mutiny days the Haileybury civilians in Calcutta were towers of strength in the C. C. Club and the Calcutta hunt. Many a pleasant day have I spent on the smooth turf of the Calcutta Cricket Club playing against the garrison or any eleven that came to hand, when the victory that crowned our efforts was mainly due to the skill of the Haileybury men; and wherever the hounds met, there was to be seen a strong contingent of these unemployed, well mounted, and good for going while their horses or the run lasted.

Not very satisfying were those runs to the sportsman. I fancy that most of us engaged in them had to make believe largely, after the manner of Dick Swiveller's marchioness, that we were really enjoying the sport of kings. For mostly the pack, newly imported year by year on account of the climate, was in no condition for travelling: the jackal was, we found, a sorry substitute for the fox, and the country hunted was generally devoid of those features that delight the hunting man in England. I have seen the hounds dead-beat and brought to a stand-still in actual sight of their jackal. And as the climate of Calcutta has not changed, I suppose the Calcutta hounds are still newly imported every season, and that now, as then, a morning with the hunt does not always repay the hunting man for getting up in the night and driving in the dark to Dumdum or Cox's Bungalow, or wherenot. Many a one of the gilded youth of that old time has had a smarter burst with a bailiff behind him than ever he had with a jackal in front. For then the bailiff was, as Pope remarked, a mighty hunter, and his prey was man.

But we made believe some of us, preferring any apology for sport to pondering over the Bagho-bahar or Mahabharat in the company of a moonshi, or drawing up bills of lading with a Banyan's aid; and so we hunted *con amore*, and were as glad over it as we could manage. We were eminently hilarious one Christmas night on the eve of a meet at Dumdum (then the headquarters of the artillery in Bengal), when a dozen or so met in one of the gunner's quarters after mess, in view to making a night of it. We made believe that we wanted a roaring fire, and, fuel running short, some of our host's furniture was requisitioned. We caroused there by the blaze of table-top and chair-legs, and we finished up making a night of it some time in the small hours, when most of us had to get on to the roof to extinguish a fire that was burning merrily round the chimney-stack. Satisfied with this new form of house-warming, we retired to our couches for a couple of hours' sleep before starting for the meet. One of the revellers of that Christmas night was he who, not many years afterwards, made India ring from end to end with a shout of admiration at his heroism, and caused each British heart to mourn the loss of such a soldier when he lost his life in the British cause. He it was, the gallant Willoughby, who in 1857 blew up the Delhi magazine after a defence of five hours against the mutineers.

He is gone. Lives there yet, I wonder, the man (an indigo-planter) who lent me a mount one day at Dumdum? And if he survives, has he yet fully repented the wrong he did me by that loan? I had my own hireling hunter there, a discreet animal of mature age and much experience in the art of saving himself. He was good enough for the purpose of the day, however: he could be reckoned upon to clear the sunken roadways and ditches that intersected fields and the banks raised above them; he might be depended upon to jump into, if he did not jump over, the streams that here and there occurred; and, at any rate, he was as good a goer as the hounds. But there at the meet was this planter, a hail-fellow-well-met man of deceptive appearance, in that he looked guileless as the callow chick, and with him a string of splendid walers in tip-top condition; and there were placed at the disposal of such as chose to accept the offer a dozen horses. There was nothing in this liberality that necessarily excited surprise or suspicion: indigo-planters were known for their lavish hospitality, their open houses, and their love of sport. Who could regard this one as a Greek to be feared even when he brought gifts? I entertained no doubt of him or his stud: I chose a noble beast that looked like a flier, mounted, and rode off with the crowd, leaving my hired Rosinante to stroll back to town. Oh, what a time I had of it in that hunt! My steed was a flier, it is true, but the flight was whitherward that erratic beast inclined, and not where I would have had him go. Obviously the bit was an unknown form of torture to him, or he had a mouth of iron corresponding with a will of the same material, and when he was not occupied in running me into difficulties, amidst bamboos and so forth, he devoted all his energy (which was considerable) to bucking. Once he shot me over his head by the latter method, twice he put me down heavily by running me into timber, and it was only because time and opportunity failed that he let me off with those three spills. If at the end of that penitential ride any one had put to me the question of the courtly Chesterfield, "If man ever hunted twice?" I should have felt disposed to answer, "No man but a fool." However, nobody put this question; instead of it, I was asked by the perfidious planter whether that beast of his had carried me well. He had the effrontery to ask me this with an air of seraphic joy and artlessness; and when I endeavoured, out of respect for his feelings, to tone down the eccentricities of his animal, blandly informed me that it had never been broken, or, as far as he knew, had a saddle on its back. Ah, they were fine, free-spirited, open-hearted fellows, those Bengal planters, and (at all events this one was) generous with the ribs and necks and collar-bones of other people.

But I had not been long in Calcutta before, by a lucky chance, the joys of pig-sticking were revealed to me. If hunting the fox be the sport of kings, surely pig-sticking is the sport of kaisers—especially when the Bengal boar is the quarry. Well enough, as a substitute, is the boar of the Ganges-Kadirs, and thereaway; but he cannot gallop, and does not fight after the manner of his Bengalee congener, which goes like a greyhound for a few furlongs, when he elects to move, and dies fighting to the last, or, possibly, goes not at all, but opens the attack, and charges again and again, until, with a dozen spear-wounds in his sides, his life gives out. Splendid is the race for the first spear when the boar flies, and quick is the race when the gallant beast is young: cups are given to those who take most first spears in the Cawnpore and Meerut Kadir hunts; *kudos* is for him of Bengal the sole but sufficient mode of honour. But better even than the race is the fray that lasts while the boar can stand.

I have often heard the relative merits of pig-sticking and hunting discussed, and verdicts delivered that this or the other was the finer sport. But when men have argued upon this point in my company, they have always failed to convince me: I am not sure that they ever succeeded in interesting me in what I have always regarded as an insoluble problem. Except that horse-riding is common to both pursuits, pig-sticking and hunting are too hopelessly unlike for qualitative analysis. In no sense can pig-sticking be regarded as a substitute for fox-hunting. Both are admirable in their way; both appeal to the sportsman with irresistible force in different fashions; and I have no doubt that both would be pursued in India if they were both practicable.

Whatever the merits of any other form of hunting, it cannot be gainsaid that pig-sticking is a noble sport. It is true that a pig does not give one such a run as may be enjoyed with the Quorn or Pytchley packs: at the best it treats one to a burst of a mile or so; it may very possibly decline running altogether. But such run as it does afford is a race of the keenest between the following spears from find to finish—a race which is not necessarily for him who is swiftest, but to that one who, with a sufficiency of speed, can most closely follow the pig in its devious way and many doublings. Pace alone may, indeed, spoil him who pants for the first spear-pace, where the horse is not in hand—may take the ardent pursuer a furlong or so to the right, while the pig, having jinked, is bounding away in the opposite direction, close followed by the rider who, but a few minutes since, was a bad second in the race. Some few horses take to pig-hunting so kindly that they may be ridden with a loose rein and left to their own discretion in regard to following whitherward the pig may lead. Tartar, a Cape horse of Jack Johnston's, was a paragon of this sort; but the great majority of steeds require skilful handling and guidance by their riders. And he who follows the boar, while he seeks to come to close quarters so that he may deliver his spear-thrust, has to avoid, as far as possible, riding over the pig. It is not that this is a crime in venery equivalent to the enormity of riding over hounds: a man who does this is not howled at and made the object of opprobrious epithets, justifiable only as applied to him or the wretch who burned the Ephesian Temple of Diana. It is a blunder (not a crime), because a lively boar may very well throw its head up, and in that hurried action rip open the horse that is going over it; but it is a blunder that is often unavoidable, inasmuch as the horse cannot be stopped or turned in its stride at the moment when the boar, jinking at right angles, passes underneath it. But he who rides after the boar has something more than his horse to handle: there is his spear, which demands careful treatment lest it bring trouble to other than the pig. I have seen some accidents arising from mismanagement of this weapon. I have seen a man heavily thrown as a consequence of his running his spear into the ground; I have seen a rider spear his own horse; I have seen a rider spear the horse of a companion; and any one of these accidents may occur to the novice or to him who is inexpert or careless.

Nor, as a rule, is the ground over which one rides after pig such as tests the qualities of an English hunter. For the most part it is level country, totally destitute of obstacles such as the bullfinch, or stone wall, or wire fence, and kindred accessories of English cross-country riding; sometimes it is rough and tussocky; sometimes a blind ditch betrays a rider into an unpremeditated somersault. In Western India pig-stickers get into difficulties amidst the rocks of stony hills. But speaking generally, and for the Bengal side, the country is a flying one, and its worst difficulties such as are best taken flying.

The two difficulties that I have in my mind are (1) the gaping crevices—three to six inches in width, and two to four feet in depth—that intersect the dried-up alluvial deposits of the rivers, and convert the newly spread soil into a system of horse-traps; and (2) the sharp-pointed stakes left in the *ahrah* fields when the crop is cut (the *ahrah* plants having stems of an inch or more in diameter that are cut with a sort of bill-hook), and which convert the harvested field into an exaggerated *chevaux-de-frise.* Both of these are formidable enough in their way, the first threatening broken legs of horses, the second promising impalement of riders; and both are best negotiated at top speed, and best of all by an Arab.

But riding a boar is not by any means the whole or even the best of the hunt; there is the possible scrimmage after, or without, a run, when, standing at bay, or charging hither and thither, the boar defies all comers. Then is the sport sweetly savoured to the shikari by the spice of danger; for a boar in its prime is no mean foe, nor is it an enemy that nature has meanly armed. Quick and intrepid in attack, each charge it makes home to its object may leave a wound in horse or rider; and it is like an Englishman in that it does not know when it is beaten. When spear-thrust after spear-thrust has drunk its life's blood, its rage may be impotent and its thirst for battle idle, but the passion of war animates it until, the brave life having given out, it sinks unconscious upon the ground. I have seen one of these porcine warriors charge its foes when the spears implanted in it stood out in all directions and became weapons of offence against the spearmen who lodged them in the boar; and even then, when smarting from half-a-dozen wounds, the bloodshot eye of the boar has breathed defiance, and its champing teeth have seemed to churn out curses with the foam that flecked its chest.

My first interview with the Bengal boar at close quarters impressed these points upon my mind indelibly, perhaps because the quarters were so close. The boar was charging, or about to charge, as I galloped up, and, as became me in the circumstances, I pressed my horse on at its topmost speed to meet the charge. But we met not in the shock of battle, as I had devised; there was no shattering of spears to the cry of *à l'outrance* in that tourney. The lists were wet, and my war-horse slipped up, and I went over its head and found myself stretched out upon the sward *vis-à-vis* to the astounded boar. There we were face to face: for the moment the situation did not commend itself to me as one of unalloyed bliss, or such safety as prudent folks prefer; and then the matter was abruptly terminated by the pig leaving me (I suppose) in disgust, to have its quarrel fought out with another. The climax, so far as I was concerned, was bathos.

I think that incident occurred during my earliest expedition into the Berhampore country, when the chapter of accidents was fuller than usual. I cannot remember how many horses were out; but it was on that occasion, I think, that Johnston lost a valuable animal through a heavy fall into a blind nullah that broke the horse's neck; and a globe-trotter who was out with us speared his horse;

and one of our party was knocked over by sunstroke; and F. B. Simson had his boot ripped up by a boar. But it would require many more and worse mischances than these to prejudice a pig-sticker against his sport, and the sportsman who goes to India as a visitor with the purpose of doing the country is unfortunate if he does not see something of pig-sticking. The Prince of Wales had some fair sport of this kind shown to him in the Oonao district of Oudh by that brilliant horseman and polo-player, John Watson of the 13th Hussars; and, I rather think, the delights of Bengal pig-sticking were purveyed for H.R.H. by Archie Hills, the latter-day King of Spears.

It seems to me to be a matter of regret that some of India's notable visitors do not substitute pig-sticking for less innocent subjects of investigation, such as the opium traffic, representative government, and so forth. A very short apprenticeship would give them something like an intelligible idea of what pig-sticking is, or is not, and enable them to talk innocently, if inanely, of that sport thereafter. But apparently they do not care to bring away merely harmless experiences that at the worst only bore people: they prefer to devote themselves to inquiries for which they have neither time nor material. They dash into subjects of which they cannot hope to master the merest rudiments, and then they return to England to air their ignorance by shallow talk that is mischievous as well as boresome. Exeter Hall encourages perfunctory study of this sort, and Exeter Hallites, with the best intentions, occasionally conduct themselves after the manner of a Society for the Propagation of Error.

"Vis-à-vis *to the astounded boar.*"

CHAPTER II.

SPORT IN LOWER BENGAL.

"THE MIGHTY BOAR"—CALCUTTA TENT CLUB—GUN ACCIDENT—THE TIGER AND THE SHOE—JACK JOHNSTON—HENRY TORRENS—COLONELS' STORIES—THE HOWRAH JHEEL—SNIPE AT KANCHRAPARA—MIGRATION OF SNIPE—CAPRICIOUSNESS OF SNIPE—ENCOUNTER WITH A PANTHER—BOAR AND BEATER.

MANY were the songs sung by pig-stickers of Bengal in honour of the creature they hunted,—songs with a refrain that was generally to the effect that "the boar, the boar, the mighty boar" was blessed with all the virile virtues. Possibly in moments of enthusiasm and wassail this animal may have been over-praised. He has not a pleasant temper, his habits are open to unfavourable criticism, he may fail in his family relations—but he has plenty of pluck. He will fight anything that comes in his way; not even a tiger daunts him, and, what is more, the tiger sometimes succumbs to the terrible tushes of the boar. I have seen a boar bearing away from such heroic battle the marks — deep and frequent marks — of a tiger's claws, and that boar swam the Ganges in flood, — a sufficient feat for an unwounded animal, and one that should set at rest the question whether pigs can swim.

A dangerous brute is the Bengal boar. Throughout the whole of my sporting career only two of my beaters were killed, and one of these was cut to death by a boar; a leopard killed the other: not one was either killed or mauled by tigers.

But my first experiences in this line were, I regret to say, less connected with the mighty boar than with the sow, which, though it cannot rip up a horse's flanks or belly as can the boar, can gallop a little, and, instead of ripping, can bite. This chase of the female swine I saw what time I was out with the Calcutta Tent Club in their beats on either side of the Hooghly, between Calcutta and Diamond Harbour. A memorable club was this in its palmy days, and of some importance when I saw it in its decadence. It is celebrated by a large engraving from a picture by Mr William Taylor, B.C.S. (brother of the better known artist Frederick Taylor), which once was a familiar object on the walls of Indian sportsmen. In that presentment of the Club were shown several lights of the Indian turf and sporting world—Baron Hochpied de Larpent, Jim Patton, the two Brackens, and others; including that distinguished member (the central figure of the group, unless the prostrate boar be so considered) Billy Pitt, the huntsman of the Club.

I first attended a meet of the C. T. C. as a guest of William Bracken, a sportsman known principally in connection with tiger-shooting. In that pre-railway time, when the Mofussil beyond Barrackpore was only to be reached by slow and wearying travel by palanquin, or slower journeying by river in the old-time boat-house of India—the *budgerow*—the great majority of Calcutta men passed their lives without penetrating into the interior farther than a buggy would carry them; but William Bracken made an annual expedition into the tiger country along the Ganges between Bhagulpore and Maldah, and there spent a month in the pursuit of big game. That was *the* month of the twelve for him, and for the other eleven he made out his time by an occasional jaunt with the Tent Club and week-end gatherings at his country house at Budge-Budge, near which quail and snipe, and perhaps an alligator, were to be shot; and where also in their season the mango fish, dear to the epicure, was to be eaten in its prime. There was a billiard-table, too, almost as a matter of course, for every Indian house of any account possessed one; and there was occupation for the lazy or meditative ones in watching from the wide verandah of the upper floor the argosies that passed to and fro along the river—those argosies that then were to be seen carrying their white sheets from stem to stern and from deck to topgallant yards, and gliding majestically over the waters with silent strength—not the latter-day titanic craft of many funnels and dismal smoke and racket, that puff their way along with volcanic strength that is destitute of grace.

It was on the Budge-Budge gram-fields, when we were shooting quail, that I had my first gun accident. As I was loading the right barrel while the left was loaded, the latter contrived to discharge itself; some of the shot knocked off the peak of my wide-brimmed *sola topee*, and that was the sum total of the damage done on that occasion. But not long after that, while I was shooting snipe in a Howrah jheel, and when the snipe were more plentiful than I had ever seen them, the same mishap occurred; and that time it was the end of my thumb, not my hat, that was carried away. I made a desperate effort to continue shooting when the flow of blood was stayed and the mutilated digit bandaged in a pocket-handkerchief, but with only partial success. Breech-loaders, I need hardly say, were unknown in those days; and even when they had come to be common, I perversely stuck to my muzzle-loaders for two or three years. I lost a good many snipe by this ultra-conservatism; but my old chum Jacky Hills profited thereby, in that when we shot Oudh jheels together, the pedestrian advantage I enjoyed through length of limb and lighter body was neutralised by my having to stop to load.

William Bracken had experienced and survived a much more perilous incident than mine above described—an incident which was commemorated in his library by a tiger's skull, in the jaws of which a shoe was held. The shoe, with Bracken's foot in it, had been held clutched by the cruel teeth of that skull while the tiger lived. Bracken had wounded the tiger, a fighting one that charged the elephant upon which Bracken rode; the elephant fell and threw its rider; the tiger seized upon the foot that wore that shoe; the latchet of the shoe was partly severed by the tiger's fangs, and Bracken was able to pull his foot out of its dangerous position, leaving the shoe behind for the tiger's delectation, until a bullet from another howdah made an end of the tiger and the episode. Bracken's foot was sorely wounded —the effects never wholly disappeared; but this accident stayed not those annual expeditions to the Ganges Churs.

In my first Doorgah Poojah I graduated finally in pig-sticking. The Doorgah Poojah is a Hindoo holiday very strictly observed in Lower Bengal, and I observed it with the keenness of a Brahmin. This festival gave me almost a fortnight's freedom from mercantile affairs, and enabled me to go with Jack Johnston after the pigs of Berhampore and Kishnaghur. It was a sufficient privilege to be his companion. It was bliss unalloyed to share his sport.

Any man might well be proud of having served his novitiate under so perfect a master. The king of spears he was called: with him it was in very truth a case of *a cuspide corona;* and where he rode few were the first spears that went to others. What a happy fellow he was, and how much he did to make his companions happy! He was a man of fortune when associates of his own age were owing their way on pittances of Rs. 400 or Rs. 500 a-month. He had a stud of fourteen or fifteen horses, all but one of which were the best Arabs that money could buy; and every horse in his stable, except one or two racers, did he drive in his buggy or lend to his friends as if it had been a Rs. 300 hack instead of a creature worth Rs. 2000 or Rs. 3000. And while still a young man he was free to come home to England, where he has so far succeeded with his English stud that he has won his Derby.

What a revelation of sport was that fortnight spent with the jovial and hospitable indigo-planters of the Kishnaghur borderland! There was no question of hunting sows thereaway; boars were there sufficient for the purpose, if not in quantity to satiate; and every day brought to the six or eight horsemen engaged two or three chances of blooding their spears, if not always the first chance.

And that expedition led the way to another

and more ambitious one of some months later, when in very much the same country Henry Torrens, the Resident at Moorshedabad, held his great gathering of pig-stickers. I think that meet must have been then, and must still remain, unique in its way. Nearly a hundred elephants marched in line through the long kassia grass, where the pigs had their lairs; six or seven horsemen rode on either flank in pairs or threes, ready, when the pigs should break from their cover, to separate the boars from the sounders and ride them down; and on some half-a-dozen howdah elephants were sportsmen of a less enterprising kind, or enterprising sportsmen without available mounts, who helped to drive the pigs by a fusilade directed against hog-deer, black partridge, florican, leek, and hare. Twelve days did this incomparable chase endure, and ninety-and-nine were the boars whose skulls and tushes recorded the hunters' prowess. I seem to remember that, on the last day of those happy dozen, we were all eaten up by anxiety to bag the round hundred, and how, when that day was spent and night bore down upon our happy hunting-ground, we were unanimous in preferring our tally of 99, because, as we argued, people to whom we narrated the history of the great Torrens' hunt might be incredulous if we said the boars killed were a hundred, neither more nor less. Possibly we were moved to argue thus by that old-time story of the Indian colonel who, being asked why he had not given a full thousand as his day's bag of snipe instead of 999, gravely observed,—"Sir, do you think I would perjure my immortal soul for a single snipe?" However this may be, we rejoiced heartily on that last night of Torrens's hunt: we drank toasts and made speeches, of which none were worth remembering save that of our witty host, and most were worth forgetting straightway; and we sang songs, principally in honour of the noble boar, with rattling choruses in any tune and in any time, oblivious of the fact that a dirge to that animal would have been more appropriate and quite as tuneful; and, finally, we carried our host in his palanquin to the *ghât*, some two furlongs off, where his boat was moored—an agonising exploit for our unpractised shoulders—and shouted ourselves hoarse until the founder of the feast was carried down the stream out of earshot.

Apropos of the above snipe yarn, I wonder if the Indian colonel continues to the present day to play the Munchausen. Somehow, it always happened in my time that the colonel monopolised this *rôle* in public estimation, and one might have justifiably believed that the army was traduced, and the civilians let off too easily in this connection. It was of a colonel (the brilliant if erratic Teddy Oakes) that people told the tale of how, being at sea in a violent storm when hope was abandoned, and the passengers were bidden to pray, his nearest approach to orison was, "Oh, Pilot, 'tis a fearful night!" It was a colonel who, according to fable, declared that on a voyage round the Cape his ship was spoken (thousands of miles from land) by a man in a tub who would not come on board the ship, but took in a supply of biscuit and water and was left in mid-ocean. It was a colonel from whom the wily snake escaped by entering a bamboo tail first, after that colonel had twice pulled it from that refuge by the tail. And according to popular belief, a colonel told that story about the quail which nearly resulted in his prompt discomfiture. For the colonel had described a flight of quail that clouded the sky, and then, having settled, covered the parade-ground in close-packed swarm; and he told how he got out an 18-pounder cannon and loaded it almost to the muzzle with powder and No. 10 shot, and trained the gun to volley its contents into the thick of the birds, and then he asked of those who sat at mess, "How many do you think I shot?" and a subaltern of more wit than veneration answered him "a million." Whereupon that colonel changed his tactics to meet the situation, and said, "No, by G—, sir, not one!" These things were old, old chestnuts a generation since: perhaps, like many another of their kind, they have had a neogenesis.

In those Calcutta days there was often a day or half-day when I could get away into a snipe jheel, and on many occasions I was able to make bags of twenty and twenty-five couple. The Howrah jheel was the nearest, as it was the best, of those within easy reach. It was not as well known as others, and it was as much in the country as if it had been fifty miles away. The E. I. Railway, which for many years had its terminal station at Howrah, was not then, or had only recently been, constructed. The Hooghly had not then been bridged, and one made one's way from Calcutta to my jheel by dinghy across the river, and then about a mile on foot. Many a pleasant picnic of one have I had on the banks of that swamp, where the shade of luxuriant tropical vegetation made the mid-day halt restful to eye and limbs, and where a refreshing draught of cocoa-nut milk was to be had in season straight from the trees that spread their broad leaves above. The jheel was just enough for one gun; it could be compassed in an hour and a half or so; and birds that were roused in one part of it would generally, if the gunner permitted, settle in another. In later years I fancy the snarers have spoiled this and other jheels round the Bengal metropolis by netting snipe for the Calcutta market; but the Howrah jheel was a really good one in my day, and dear to me for other reasons than because it was the tomb of—part of me. Why sport should be spoiled by this netting of snipe I am at a loss to conceive: to the Calcutta Khansamah any bird of attenuated bill and legs—snippets, water-rail, &c.—passes for a snipe, just as any bird not bigger than the house-sparrow answers to his conception of ortolan. I have seen the impostor snipe—a very mocking bird—on dinner-tables outside Calcutta, and the fraudulent ortolan enters into the *menu* of most of India's provinces. For the genuine ortolan—that delicious mouthful—is, as far as my experience goes, very strictly localised. I have seen, shot, and eaten them in only one district (Kishnaghur); but I have had ground larks, sand-martins, and many other small fowl offered to me in the name of the ortolan in twenty districts and in three provinces. The sport provided by this winged delicacy is, I need hardly say, poor; it is in fact demoralising, for there can be no question of aiming at this bird or that: the shooter has to fire his charge of dust shot into the brown of the swarm that whirls over the dusty plain like unto a cloud of dust. But if one cannot get ortolan save by shooting them, then I should feel inclined to shoot.

After a year or so of town life, which was brightened by occasional spells of sport, and dimmed more frequently by wearying consideration of freights and customs dues, and grey shirtings and madapolams, and other items of commerce, I broke the bonds that bound me to a desk in Clive Street, and made for the Mofussil. I could not shake the dust of Calcutta off my feet in a literal sense, because I quitted that capital during its mud season, but I did so figuratively, and from that hour ceased to be a townsman.

I made for Kishnaghur, the happy centre of a

series of snipe jheels, that came almost up to the compounds of some of the bungalows: I travelled in a *bauleah*—a smaller edition of the *budgerow*—but I did not make direct for my destination. I had an important engagement with myself (now my only master) to keep by the way. I had to visit a snipe jheel (then famous above all among the happy initiated) where a record of fifty couple in a day had been made, and I had to break that record if I could. At that season—the month of October—this jheel was accessible by water, with some amount of running aground in the navigation of the nullah that ran past it and into the Hooghly, two or three miles distant. It was touch and go with us as the *bauleah* was hauled up this shallow stream; indeed there were innumerable touches, but, happily, there were as many goes, and ultimately my ark was brought to anchor at the very verge of the shooting-ground, just as night fell, and my floating home was lighted up for a short evening; and then dinner came, and mosquitoes and countless winged creatures that dashed themselves against the candle-shades in battalions, and upon the burning wicks in platoons, and generally make night terrible for any one but the most ardent entomologist in a new field of research. I was not a scientist that way, if in any way, nor were these flying torments novelties to me, so I sought early slumber in the darkness.

Next morning I was up betimes, to make as

long a day as possible for my record-breaking expedition. The Kanchrapara jheel was about a mile in length, and of a breadth that admitted of three or four guns shooting in line. I had it all to myself, and had to get over fifty couple of snipe out of it. It was an epoch-making occasion, and, refreshed by a long night's sleep, I felt equal to the task and in a mood to shoot my best. My first half-hour among the birds encouraged confidence and hope. Snipe were plentiful; at one time I had five couple down upon the ground, all killed before my coolies commenced picking up: when half my allotted time was done I had bagged just thirty couple, and I had then some untried portion of the jheel ahead, and all the birds that had gone back upon my course, to reckon with. At the close of the day, when I had shot to the end of the jheel and back to my boat, I had on the snipe-sticks 51½ couple: I had broken one record and set up for myself another that, in several years of steady shooting, I have never again accomplished. Other Indian shots (including colonels) may have got bigger bags—notably in the best days of that splendid snipe country that lies along the Oudh and Rohilcund Railway line, some twenty miles from Allyghur; but that is my record, and I am satisfied with it.

I devoted the following day to the jheel and the ambitious attempt to outdo my first effort. Ambition on that occasion, as is not uncommon with it, got me into trouble. I attempted to beat up some dangerous ground in the middle of the swamp—treacherous yellow bog that shook under foot, and, its crest being broken, absorbed one slowly but with disagreeable certainty. I went up to the middle in this; saved myself from sinking deeper by spreading my arms out on the unbroken surface; and was eventually dragged out, covered with mud and ignominy, by my coolie attendants. That was a grand day's shooting also, and I brought to bag forty-nine couple, including two or three birds wounded on the previous day. I thought then, and I have always since thought, that there is no shooting to compare with that of a good snipe jheel.

Many a day thereafter did I have in that Kanchrapara jheel with Montresor, then of Kishnaghur, Elphinstone Jackson, Dacoity Commissioner, stationed at Bandel near Hooghly, and C. S. Belli, Hooghly's Collector, but never with such results as to the head of game shot. Thoroughly enjoyable were those outings, however, even though our snipe gave an aggregate tale of thirty or forty couple only, and involved a variety of travel not always luxurious. Setting forth by boat up the river, we used to land at a point distant some two and a half or three miles from the jheel, and this distance had to be covered either by riding the mare known, for some recondite reason, as Shanks's, or such country *tats* as could thereaway be collected. Little choice was there among these ponies: one might prove on closer acquaintance a more vicious kicker or more persistent stumbler than another, but all were equally unkempt, ragged, and deficient in every quality that makes a park-horse: all were alike ill-caparisoned, with saddles of uncomfortably restricted seats; stirrup-leathers that, whether they were leather or rope, defied all effort to lengthen or shorten them; narrow reins that cut into one's fingers as though they had been bands of metal, and headstalls wherein string predominated. What matter? *Vogue la galère.* Those sorry steeds saved our legs for the half-day's tramp in the jheel—saved those limbs by some five or six miles of tramping, while they inflicted upon back and arms and other portions of our anatomy tortures and wounds that were unforgotten for days. What of that? We had our shooting from noon till nigh unto sunset, with an interval for lunch, and then we put ourselves upon those equine racks again and rode homewards rejoicing. And I think the one of us who got the greatest amount of enjoyment out of the whole proceeding was Belli, who, as likely as not, did not kill a bird, although he blithely fired away at dozens.

Do any of my readers know whence the snipe come and what instinct directs their migrations? They come into Great Britain and Ireland in the early winter, say in November: that is the season, also, in which they arrive in Northern India—*i.e.*, in November and the early winter; but they arrive in Australia and Tasmania in the same month, although that month commences the Australasian summer. This seeming incongruity of migratory purpose one might explain by the assumption that the time of their arrival in the places named does not depend upon the climate of those localities, but upon the necessity that drives them forth from their summer home (*i.e.*, their habitat between May and November): that they are obliged to leave that Oxygean home about November, and betake themselves to any spot whatever where their feeding-grounds are to be found. But the question is further complicated by the erratic conduct of Indian snipe. These birds arrive in Northern India, as I have said, in November, when the weather is fairly cold, or at least cool; but they come into Bengal and Southern India in September, when it is blazing hot. On two 1st of Septembers I have shot them (some two or three couple) in the Kishnaghur jheels. Do these snipe of the south start from that unknown habitat of theirs two months before the rest of their kind? and if so, why? I am told that the birds in Southern India are of a different variety from those of the north, although I could never distinguish one from the other; but that affords no explanation of the snipe's vagaries, but rather the reverse—for if all Indian snipe were of one variety, the question in hand might be disposed of (as far as India is concerned) by the bold assertion that these migrants first settled in the south and moved up northwards later on.

Their migrations are very bewildering. Thirty years ago there was snipe-shooting in Tasmania almost equal to that of India. Officers attached to the Tasmanian garrison of that time have told me of their bags of twenty-five and thirty couple. To-day snipe are found in but few places, and only in small numbers. One of my Tasmanian friends was good enough to reserve a small snipe-shooting for me one year: there were only three snipe in this preserve, and the curious thing is that every year three, or perhaps four, snipe come to that same patch of marsh. The decadence of Tasmanian snipe-shooting cannot be attributed to any physical or climatic change in the country—the birds have not been driven away from that land by drainage, as has happened with our Lincolnshire fens. There is nothing but the snipes' caprice to explain it.

This capriciousness on one occasion sold me terribly. I was shooting over a chain of jheels in Oudh, and about sunset came to the last of the series, a small one close to my camp. Although small, it often held a fair number of birds, and might generally be reckoned upon as good for at least six couple; but that evening it was alive with snipe. Even in the failing light of a land that knows no twilight I might have bagged eight or ten couple if I had shot there then, but I resisted the temptation, and fired not at all: to-morrow I promised myself a splendid bag out of that swarm. When I went there next day, brimful of hope, there was not a snipe to be seen, nor were there any number to speak of anywhere that I went after them. And this did not happen in the season when snipe gather together for their departure into space. Even the poor apology that migratory reasons compelled them to disappoint me was not forthcoming. Curiously enough, it happened shortly after I penned the above paragraph that I took up vol. xvii. of 'Longman's Magazine,' in the March number of which is a paper by C. T. Buckland, B.C.S., at one time of Hooghly. He speaks of the Kanchrapara jheel as a magnificent shooting-ground, known then to few besides the men of Hooghly, and tells how a friend of his could bag his fifty couple there. He also mentions a spot in Chittagong where he could always get a couple of snipe on the 1st September.

For some three years I made the most of such shikar as was to be had in Kishnaghur and the neighbouring districts. I had charge of zemindarees and indigo factories, and my work was mostly in the saddle, where also was a good deal of my recreation. I had a tolerable stud of five or six horses, a cast-iron constitution, and a passionate love for field-sports, compared with which my attachment to business was decidedly platonic. Wherever pig-sticking was to be had, in Kishnaghur, Berhampore, or Burdwan, I rode with the hunt. Wherever there was a snipe jheel, I paid it frequent attention. Quail and jungle-fowl were not neglected, but I got no forwarder with big game other than boars.

Indeed the only chance I had of making my *début* as a slayer of the larger feline creatures resulted in a crushing failure. A panther was marked down for me in a small thicket, and I went forth to do for it. When I reached the ground the panther was still there, and a keen-eyed native pointed it out to me. "Hitherward was its head," said this man, "thitherward its tail. Doesn't the sahib see it? There, there!" and he pointed to a spot about three yards off. But I did not see the panther—either its head or tail or anything that was its; I saw only a mass of light and shade under a dense overgrowth of greenery, dead leaves, and grass, that were yellowish where the pencils of light broke in upon the gloom and, otherwise, mysterious shadow that told nothing to my unaccustomed eye. All that I looked upon in that greenwood tangle was equally panther; I could pick out no particular patch as being any more pantherish than the rest; of head or tail I made out nothing where all was equally one or the other,—and still that native of keenest vision besought me to see the panther's head and tail and right forefoot, and many other details of its anatomy. Then there came a roar out of the thicket, and a rush which was like the volcanic upheaval of the ground at my feet, and, as it seemed, several tons of upheaved matter hit me on the chest and other parts, and I was catapulted on to the broad of my back a yard or two from where I had stood. That upheaval was the panther. The brute hadn't had the patience to wait until I saw him, or the modesty to take himself off peaceably in some other direction: he had resented my staring his way, even though I saw him not, and so had emerged out of his lair like an animal rocket, and knocked me down in his flight. As he failed to claw me, I came off scathless; but not so my attendant, who foolishly embraced the panther in view to arresting his flight: he got himself rather badly mauled, and did not come a whole man out of hospital for some weeks. That was my disastrous commencement with panthers.

It was about this time that an unfortunate beater of mine lost his life by a foolhardy act like that above described. We were beating pigs out of the long grass on the left bank of the Bhagiruti, and a boar getting up at this man's feet, or from under his feet, he jumped upon it. Why he did so it is impossible to say: it furthered no object of anybody's, for we were awaiting the pig at the edge of the higher jungle, and quite ready for it, and, in fact, we did get it. But as soon as we had speared this boar, we were made acquainted with the sad accident that had befallen the beater. The boar had ripped him across both thighs and both arms with those clean deep cuts that the boar inflicts when its tushes have not been blunted by age; and although the poor man lived to reach a hospital, he died there in spite of every attention, and the necessary amputation of one mutilated limb.

"Treacherous yellow bog."

CHAPTER III.

AMONG THE INDIGO-PLANTERS.

INDIGO MAGNATES—PLANTERS' COURTS—A NATIVE MURDER THROUGH JEALOUSY—MURDEROUS PROPENSITIES OF THE NATIVES—MURDER OF A MISTRESS—THE KISHENGUNJ ESTATE—APPEARANCE IN THE DOCK—"LATTIALS"—KESHUB CHUNDER ROY—INDIAN WRESTLING — FIGHTING BIRDS — A GWALA CHAMPION.

IN my Kishnaghur days the indigo-planter of Eastern Bengal was generally a sportsman, and often a substantial patron of sport. The industry that he pursued was more profitable then than it now is, and he lived in a baronial style that the present generation cannot attain to without ultimate recourse to the Bankruptcy Court. Within his own territory of some hundreds of square miles he was very much a king of the patriarchal type; his court was open to all who possessed the simple qualifications of fair repute and good-fellowship; his board was spread abundantly for many guests, and all the resources of his establishment placed at the disposal of those who sojourned within his gates.

Sometimes this limited monarch lived in a really palatial style—he of Mulnauth, for example. Architecturally considered, Mulnauth ranked amongst the Indian mansions that I saw second only to Government House, Calcutta, and it stood in a large nobly timbered park with which the Calcutta Palace grounds cannot be compared. Nor was the Mulnauth structure a whitened sepulchre wherein pretentious stucco sought to disguise the plebeian lath or clay: its halls were of marble, and even its bathrooms were marble paved. It was a fitting abode for a parochial lord paramount; and many another mansion like unto it, if not quite its equal, was to be found in the indigo districts of Bengal.

Indigo-planters were in Bengal something more than mere growers of plant and manufacturers of a dye; they were also territorial magnates—owners or farmers of estates from which they drew more revenue in service than in specie. Terrible things have been said about the tyranny of planter rule. In one instance a judge propounded the startling economic theory that every cake of indigo was made of, or stained with, human gore. In other instances officials have described the indigo-planter as a Legree modified to harmonise with his environment. But I think these severe critics somewhat misjudged the object of their censure, and took a too partial and one-sided view of the planter's method. They magnified the planter's exactions, while they largely ignored the countervailing advantages enjoyed by the ryots; they made mountains of the planter's demands for ryot-grown plant, and molehills of the lowered rents and other pecuniary advantages conceded to the cultivator by way of *quid pro quo.* And be it said in favour of the old-time planter, that in addition to the court he kept in the regal sense, he held one for the administration of justice that was even-handed enough, if defective in its law, and wholly innocent of the law's delay or costs. Seated on the judicial bench as an unpaid and ungazetted magistrate and judge, the planter settled the frequent differences of the peasantry with an expedition that was only equalled by the freedom of the decisions from legal quibbles and technicalities. He administered something more equitable, but no less expeditious, than Jeddart justice without Acts or Regulations, or as much even as a pocket Blackstone to guide him. He was his own Legislative Council, and his home-made law was made there and then as he dealt with the cases and causes before him. On the whole, the planter's court of justice was better suited to, and more popular with, the impecunious ryots than that where machine-made judgments were dispensed, and where the power of the purse too frequently turned the scale. In the planter's court no expense had to be incurred; no greedy *amlah* (court officials) had to be bribed either to keep the record accurately or to mutilate it, or otherwise to aid the suitor; no police took toll of prosecutor or defendant, or both, for the suppression or manipulation of evidence, or for the less congenial utterance of truth; no palm-itching *chuprassie* had to be paid for admission to the presence of the planter judge. Formula and procedure were conspicuously absent from the easily won hearing; and the suitor obtained—and obtained promptly—that equity which he desired and could understand, instead of a verdict, beautifully symmetrical as to its law, but wholly unintelligible and of no practical use to him.

In my turn I acted thuswise as a self-constituted administrator of justice—sometimes as an auxiliary or volunteer aid of the regulars of the law-dispensing army, sometimes as a usurper of the powers of the duly constituted tribunals. I think I may claim to have helped rather than hindered the district authorities. Notably I assisted in the case of a murder committed within the zemindarees of which I had charge.

This particular crime was of a character common enough in India—as common, indeed, there as it is rare in other countries. The *dramatis personæ* of this tragedy were a young and jealous husband, a faithless wife, and two men who in the calmer and more civilised atmosphere of our English Divorce Court would have figured as co-respondents, and strictly confined their subsidiary action to perjury as to their relations with the respondent; but the jealous husband of my story could not go to the Divorce Court, because there was none, and would not have gone to such a place of relief if it had existed. He preferred a more expeditious method of severing his connection with the woman who had been false to him, and cut her throat; then, with the aid of his mother, he dragged the body from the house and threw it down a well in the courtyard; and then, with the assistance of his late wife's paramours, he filled up the well with branches and rubbish and earth. That summoning of these two who had wronged him to abet him in his crime, and their calm and silent assent, would be remarkable enough in any case, but in the instance of this particular assassin the connivance with the other two was the more incongruous, because while he was a Brahmin they were Sudras of the lower castes.

If this murder had been left to the police it would probably have been another added to the many undiscovered and unavenged crimes that disfigure India's record. A handful of silver to the jemadar, a few rupees to inquisitive Thannah policemen or village chowkidars, would have secured secrecy: the woman's disappearance would have been explained away by some figment about drowning or what not. At the proper moment her remains would have been dropped into the river or otherwise disposed of, and then the whole affair would have slowly but surely passed beyond the ken of the avenging law. But, unfortunately for the Brahmin, the matter fell into my hands, and was, as to all essentials, disposed of before the regular constabulary came upon the scene. It was whispered to me by one of the Brahmin's neighbours that there was something suspicious about the disappearance of the Brahmin's wife which it might be well to investigate, and I went to the scene of murder accordingly. The Brahmin was not in his homestead or discoverable anywhere in the vicinity,—his house had been locked and deserted by all the inmates; but when an entrance had been effected, there were the blood-stained bed and walls that told of murder done. There, too, when I came to look, were the traces of a body drawn from the fatal chamber, and those traces were observable with more or less distinctness from the room into the verandah and across the courtyard to the well—and no farther. Then men accustomed to well-digging were procured, and slowly the earth and rubbish recently thrown into it were lifted out, what time the crowd grew thicker and thicker round the scene of our operations. Finally, when the body of the murdered woman was hauled up to the surface and laid out upon the ground, there was a shout of "The murderer is here!" There he was at the edge of the throng, until that cry rose up against him and drove him forth headlong a panic-stricken fugitive; thence was he pursued like a hunted animal by scores of men, to all appearance eager to lay hands upon him, but careful withal to be none too forward in the pursuing pack; so through groves and outlying gardens; so over low dividing walls of sun-dried mud and fences; so into and out of excavations of the brickmaker; so into, but not out of, a dry ditch, into which he and I tumbled together, captured and capturer, and in which I handed him over to the tardy village chowkidars.

The Brahmin was duly tried and condemned; but the Supreme Court pronounced him mad, and he was accordingly imprisoned as a criminal lunatic. Perhaps the Supreme Court had some better reason than I knew of for this decision. To me that blood-guilty wretch appeared sane enough. Certainly there was nothing in the character of the murder he committed to suggest madness; for, as I have already said, it was one of a distinctly normal type among the people of India. The Indian Newgate Calendar teems with such murders and their variants: sometimes the jealous husband, as in this instance, murders his wife and has her paramours as his accomplices; sometimes it is the jealous husband who is got rid of by the other parties; sometimes it is the paramour who is disposed of by the husband and wife, or by the husband and another paramour. Ring the changes as you will among those leading characters, the crime and its motive are pretty much as identical as they are common; and there being nothing peculiarly sacred to the Indian about human life, the stage upon which these tragedies are played is frequently occupied by some super or supers, servants or hirelings for the occasion, who assist in a murder because they are told or paid to do so. I have heard of a man being bribed to commit a murder by an orange!

If an employer of British servants were to address to a gardener, groom, or even a swineherd, a request that he would assist his master in a murder, he would be met with derision, or contumely, or assault,—certainly not with acquiescence, either tacit or expressed. The average British menial would be shocked beyond words by such a proposal, and would come to regard him who made it as a raving lunatic or criminal of the blackest dye, or as a combination of these. But the average Indian, whether in or out of service, would be nothing shocked by a suggestion of the kind. He might for prudential reasons hesitate to adopt it, but no ethical objections would weigh with him. He would not shrink with horror from the idea of taking human life; his first thought would be, What shall I gain by this? his second and last reflection would be, Shall I be found out? And if profit, however slight, and reasonable hope of security presented themselves, it is quite possible that other considerations would not stay his hand.

Possibly my opinion of the Hindoo and Mahomedan people of India is too unfavourable, but it is founded, whether correctly or incorrectly, upon long experience. Rightly or wrongly, I have come to regard the average native of the classes above named as a potential murderer wanting only occasion to become a murderer in fact. The Hindoo (not excepting even the Bengali Baboo B.A.) who, standing up to his loins in the sacred water of Gunga-mah, mumbles vocables supposed to be muntras or orisons to his mumbo-jumbo, quite possibly has murder in his mind; the Mahomedan, kneeling upon his prayer-carpet and bowing his forehead to the dust, may, for all we know, be planning the removal of some foe from this world. Parricide, matricide, fratricide, infanticide, and every other branch of homicide, are incidents of everyday Indian life for which no native blushes and only a few pay the legal penalty.

A murder case tried before me at Deoghur illustrates much of the foregoing argument. Again a Brahmin was the central figure and delinquent, whom I will call Mookerjie. This man had a *liaison* with a widow of his family and village which came to be discovered; the female offender was, after the British method, outcasted, while the male escaped from the social ban. But the woman was not of the patient Griselda order; she was not satisfied to sit down in the ashes of humility and die unmurmuring; she murmured a good deal and in many places; and being deserted by Mookerjie, boldly came to my court with a suit against him for maintenance. She won that suit in my court: Mookerjie appealed in vain, and there followed a time of much trouble before Mookerjie was made to pay into court the first instalment due under my order.

Some days after this payment had been made a village watchman reported to me the disappearance of the woman. She had set forth from her home to come to Deoghur for her subsistence allowance, and had been no more seen in or about her village. Forthwith I started an inquiry, which resulted in the discovery of the woman's body in a river, and some sort of evidence that Mookerjie and a servant of his had followed the woman along the Deoghur road. Under the English system of criminal procedure Mookerjie would have pleaded not guilty and thereafter closed his mouth, with the result that he and his accomplice would have been acquitted: under the Indian method Mookerjie made an elaborate defence, which, when he and others came to be cross-examined upon it, broke down so completely that the defence practically put the rope round his neck.

All the direct evidence to be got was the following: (1) The woman had been murdered by somebody; (2) two pairs of Ghaut-chowkidars deposed to having seen the murdered woman on a certain day cross the ferries they watched, and that Mookerjie and his servant had followed her; and (3) an idiotic peasant with the intellect of a buffalo swore that on or about that day he saw two men, whom he did not know and could not recognise, drag a strange woman, whom he could not recognise, off the road hard by into the jungle close to that river where the deceased's body was found. That peasant heeded little and recked nothing that a woman was hauled away from under his eyes to be murdered; it was nothing to him that a score of women were done to death in this or any other fashion; it was not an affair for his meddling any more than for his interest—pice and rice appealed to his rudimentary intelligence (reached only by the avenue of his stomach), not women done to death on the Queen's highway. But for the defence, the case was a feeble one.

Mookerjie was at some pains to strengthen it. He set up an *alibi*, and not satisfied with a simple lie, he thought proper to lie with a circumstance. His story was that on that day when the deceased was seen upon the Deoghur road he went to the house of a servant in another direction; that there he was bitten by a kerait snake, which fell upon him from the top of the screen that served as a door; that he struggled home, assisted for the last furlong or so by two men who chanced to be going that way; and that, having reached his home, he sent for a snake-doctor, who promptly came and cured him. He cited those two wayfarers who supported his tottering steps, and the snake doctor, as his witnesses, and they gave him away as far as he had not effected this for himself.

The two wayfarers who played, according to Mookerjie, the part of Samaritans, deposed that they saw him first some 200 or 300 yards from his village, and that before he saw them he was making for his home jauntily enough. (Here I may notice that, as regarded the *alibi* set up, there was no reason why Mookerjie should not have been where these witnesses saw him, although he had committed the murder; distance and time did not preclude that by any means.) These witnesses further deposed that when Mookerjie saw them at his heels he began to totter, then stayed his steps and asked them to help him home, as he had been bitten by a kerait. The snake-doctor (who as a witness before me was less of an impostor than might have been expected) deposed that he had attended Mookerjie that day for snake-bite, but that there had been no bite, whether of a kerait or other snake. Nor was it necessary to ask him what I knew already—viz., whether the bite of a kerait was not as absolutely fatal as that of a cobra.

The defence having broken down, Mookerjie's servant deemed it prudent to take that independent line which promised best for safety: he confessed, and being accepted as Queen's evidence, effectually sealed the doom of his master. I do not remember what that servant received by way of payment for his share in this murder, or whether he was paid anything: it is quite possible that he played his part as an amateur, or that he regarded murder as one of the duties covered by his wage of 3 rupees a-month.

Doubtless these days in the indigo districts of Bengal were lawless ones. But it would be cruelly unjust to the planter to pronounce him responsible for this state of things. Generally he was the victim of circumstances; often enough he was a victim who suffered from what was bad in a system: at the most and worst he fought for his own against those whose one business-creed was "might is right," and whose only commandment was, "Do not be found out."

I succeeded in the charge of the Kishengunj estates a man who had been practically driven out of the position by the tyranny of neighbouring zemindars. A raja on one side of him had forcibly assumed the right of grazing on the Kishengunj lands, and when my predecessor sought to drive this raja's cattle off the land where they trespassed, the myrmidon in charge challenged him to fight the matter out upon the spot. Right stood him in no stead when supported only by peaceable argument, and he retired from the field, leaving the raja's cows still grazing there.

But worse was to befall him at the hands of a zemindar who was his unneighbourly neighbour on another side. This zemindar had him forcibly arrested under a summary Revenue Regulation

(5 or 7) of that time, and kept in durance vile shut up in a dirty hut for two or three days. He was kidnapped with some ingenuity. As he rode along the river-bank some natives presented a petition to him, and while he looked at this they seized him, dragged him off his horse, and tumbled him down the river-bank into a boat they had in waiting for him. Then they landed him and lodged him in that prison-hovel, and the European Deputy Magistrate of the subdivision visited the prisoner — but only holding communication with him from outside — and went away, leaving him still in that unusually vile durance to be released by civil process and the necessary red-tapism so precious to the self-respecting official.

That story reads very much like one of those told of the good old times when men were crimped for her Majesty's navy: it would be an impossible yarn of the present day in India; but it is absolutely correct as a description of what might, and did, happen in India at the time of which I write.

Kishengunj had been managed aforetime by an Anglo-Indian who was a good deal a typical character of his time. He was a strong man physically and as to his will—a "*zubberdust*" (high-handed, masterful) man, the people said, and those people trembled at his nod and paid scrupulous respect to all rights of property whereof he claimed ownership; native swashbucklers ran hither and thither at his bidding; native mothers hushed their fractious babes by the mention of his awful name. And this giant—this Titan among pigmies—led the roaring, rollicking life peculiar to his era and so wofully destructive of the British liver. Day and night the wine-cup and the beer-flagon were passing round his hospitable board, and all the long night through bacchanalian revelry went forward, until the weaker vessels sank below the table and the stronger went staggering to their couches. He, the host, strongest of all, cared not for such effeminate luxuries as bed and blankets; for him a morning shave was ample equivalent for a night's slumber, or if he snatched from the fleeting hours some fragment of time for something more restful than the barber's operations, any convenient strip of turf or puddle served him as well as, or better than, a canopied four-poster. He it was who, as report said, used to take the candle-shades from the wall-sconces and quaff his beer from them in heroic measure. He was a man who should have died in the prime of life as the gallant leader of a forlorn-hope; but it has to be admitted that his mettlesome career had a dismal termination that in no way encouraged imitation of his heroic methods, for while yet comparatively a young man he became a confirmed rheumatic and broken-down invalid.

And, as a matter of fact, that which happened to my predecessor, or something very like it, might very well have happened to me at or about that spot from which he was hurled down the river-bank. It chanced that I was there to direct that certain trespassing cattle should be driven off to the pound, and the driving had only just commenced when down upon us descended some three-score of *lattials* (clubmen) bent upon the rescue of those beeves. Two or three attacked me—they were in front; behind me was the river-bank some twenty feet in height, and almost precipitous. I saw it was wiser to risk a broken head by going forward than a broken neck by being driven backward; I rode at those three assailants, hitting right and left with a heavy hunting-crop, of which I gave them the advantage of the handle-end. That charge turned the tide of battle: two of my foes were disabled by broken crowns, the third retreating unhurt; and my attendants rallying to me, the attacking force were about to withdraw when the police arrived. The appearance of the guardians of the law hurried the movements of all who were able to quit the scene: nor did it occur to the too cautious constables to interfere with the freedom of those rioters who were able-bodied,—they preferred to deal with the two broken-crowned ones, who were now pulling themselves together; and to simplify proceedings, or to impose blackmail upon the sahib, they took charge of these as the injured innocents who should bear witness against me in a charge of aggravated and unprovoked assault. Their action was such as effected a complete *bouleversement* of the facts of, and parties to, the case. I who had been wrongfully attacked became the defendant, and the rascals who had assailed me were made the innocent plaintiffs.

This performance of the police was by no means inconsistent with their ordinary attitude as myrmidons of justice, or the national regard for truth. The Bengali as a liar is a scientist who thoroughly deserves all that Lord Macaulay said of him in this regard: he is an artist who throws his whole soul into the business, like that actor who, having to play the *rôle* of Othello, blackened himself all over; he is not satisfied with a veneer of perjury only, but prefers to make out a case which is false in every particular rather than be hampered by a modicum of truth.

I knew so much when the police, as above stated, proposed to frame against me a charge that was ridiculously false in its spirit; I knew also that a hundred rupees or so would have purchased the suppression of the indictment, while for five hundred I could have bought, as a substitute therefor, a substantiated charge of murder or arson or any other heinous offence against my opponents. But thrice armed in the justice of my cause, I preferred to stand the brunt of the case as the police proposed to present it.

So I made my first and only appearance in the dock, summoned to appear there before a European Deputy-Magistrate to answer the charge of aggravated assault. Unfortunately this Rhadamanthus was of the uncovenanted service, in which promotion in those days came but slowly to the most successful, and not at all to him who failed and had no interest to push him. My Rhadamanthus had no interest behind him or any brilliant record, and he was perturbed by a great fear of being denounced by the natives as one who favoured his brother Britons. Accordingly his demeanour towards me was that of the stern and unrelenting judge: he made light of my plea that what I had done had been done in self-defence; he made heavier far than the facts required the blows I had dealt upon the scoundrels who bore witness against me; and with apparent exultation he pronounced the verdict of the court that I was fined 500 rupees.

But I was made nothing poorer by that decision, inasmuch as it was reversed on appeal to the District Judge. Justice in a round-about way came to me as to those broken-pated witnesses, and came to them in somewhat melodramatic fashion; for as they were discharged from the witness-box they were arrested on a far more serious charge than that just disposed of. They had been recognised as notorious dacoits whom the police had been long pretending to look for; and the result of their detention and subsequent trial was that the pair of them were sentenced to seven or fourteen years' penal servitude. Oddly enough, no one ever thanked me for the service I rendered to the State by indirectly bringing these scoundrels to justice.

And scoundrels more or less after the pattern of

these two—men at arms whose business was fighting and whose recreation was dacoity—were to be found by the score in the retinues of the native landowners throughout those districts. Justice prevailed there so little for the weak—the arm of the law was so feeble a protector of individual rights—that every man who desired to defend his own had to do so with a strong hand that was a law unto itself. And when the ordinary establishment of fighting men was insufficient for some engagement of unusual importance, hirelings were engaged at a rupee a-day—*lattials* or quarter-staff men, who were mostly Gwalas (the cowherd caste); *surfi* or *surki* wallahs, who carried half-a-dozen darts that they threw at the foe as they advanced, and a shield and a longer dart that were retained for defensive purposes only; and *phinghi* wallahs, who used the simple weapon with which David slew Goliath, the sling. From the east and mostly from Jessore came the dartmen, from the west the slingers, and from every quarter the *lattials*; and on occasion they flocked together by hundreds. Free-lances like unto Dugald Dalgetty, they gave their services to any cause that paid them, and only as long as they were paid; and short of serving two employers at one time, they were free to enlist under any banner and at different times to fight on different sides.

Although these gatherings of potential head and law breakers tended to turbulence always, and occasionally to a deplorable casualty, it cannot be said that the battles waged by these archaically armed people were of a very serious nature. There was a good deal of gasconading before the battle joined—if ever that junction came about: there was much shouting of "Kali mah ki jai," much brandishing of staves and waving of bucklers, but the shock of battle was a poor affair by comparison with the terrors threatened. Doubtless those warriors argued that the rupee that was sufficient remuneration for shouting themselves hoarse was wholly inadequate as a recompense for a mortal wound. They were hired for the day, not bought right out; and, arguing thus, they confined their feats of arms to a demonstration,—then counted heads, and having given the victory to the larger battalions, returned to report how they had, in spite of heroic effort, been overwhelmed by numbers. Then perhaps that defeated employer retained these heroes for another day or more, called in further contingents from all the points of the compass, and with augmented strength wrested the crown of victory from the now outnumbered foe.

If the employer of these fighting men did not always see any advantage to him arising out of these bloodless encounters, he was apt to see many disadvantages produced by the slaying of one of the belligerents. Among these was the inconvenience caused by a dead *lattial* being deposited in his compound, or even in his verandah, with a demand for some large ransom for its removal. I have heard from good authority of such a case as this, and was led to believe that it was a common practice of the hired fighting men, when they could, to carry off the body of a man killed in one of these affrays and levy black-mail upon it as I have described.

They were lawless times those fifties in the Kishengunj country, and of the inhabitants, Keshub Chunder Roy was perhaps as little law-abiding as any. As his name indicates, he was of Rajpoot descent, and he was yet largely Rajpoot in nature, notwithstanding that he was Bengali by birth and breeding. Not for him were the effeminate ways of the Bengali, who loathes all exercise more fatiguing than that he occasionally takes in a palanquin, and who would go to some extremes in the way of exertion rather than imperil his physical comfort by engaging in a fight. Under ordinary circumstances the well-to-do native of Bengal would submit to much inconvenience rather than walk half a mile, but he would run for miles rather than have his head broken in an affray. Keshub Chunder Roy was a virile man: his figure was a marked one as he rode about the country, on a big country-bred of pace very unlike the amble of the baboo's pony; and this figure was often seen at the head of his fighting men in action.

And Keshub Chunder, as far as I could make out, lived in a chronic state of war either at home or abroad, and more frequently at home than anywhere else. For the house of the Roys was a very divided one, two of the brothers being of one faction and two of the other; and as the brothers shared the family mansion, the four wings of which enclosed a large quadrangle common to all, the opportunities of fraternal strife were constantly at hand. In fact this internecine war was rarely, if ever, stayed by a permanent peace: it sometimes simmered, as it were, when a few of the retainers of the two factions exchanged blows of more or less harmless character; at other times it boiled, and then all the available myrmidons were engaged in the courtyard or outside, and the brothers from their apartments fired guns at each other—I suppose by way of demonstration, for never during my time was any brother hit by fratricidal shot or bullet. I fancy a few of the retainers were killed in these domestic conflicts; but the world heard little of these casualties, and the police being auricularly treated with rupees heard nothing.

It was fortunate for the people of the country around that the Roys were thus kept full-handed as to riot by their home affairs. But for this their bands and Keshub Chunder would have harassed, and in some cases plundered, the peaceful folk of the neighbourhood whenever a mischievous effervescence prompted a raid. Keshub Chunder, judged by his capacity in the way of turbulence, might have been an Afghan or a medieval Rhine baron.

But however fully occupied the Roys were at any time in a faction fight, there was one contingency that rarely, or I may say never, failed to bring about a temporary suspension of hostilities, —that was the seizure of their trespassing cattle; and as their herds were frequently occupied in grazing down the ryots' crops, there was only too often occasion for driving them to the local pound. But the ryots were helpless in this matter: it needed a stronger hand than theirs to seize redress after that fashion; and so it came about that, for the protection of such cultivators as were my tenants, I had now and again to sweep off the Roys' cattle and impound them.

It was in the pursuance of this duty that I discovered how materially a cow can be made to aid a human swimmer. Those trespassing kine had to be swum across the Bhagiruthi: sometimes across that river, when in flood, it was a mile or so in width; and when the river was in spate, cattle and drivers were carried some three miles down stream before the opposite bank was reached. But the cattle, sometimes a hundred or more, took to the rapidly flowing water as naturally as ducks, and the men who drove, holding on now by the tail of one cow and anon by another cow's tail, did the three or four mile swim with little or no fatigue. The men whom I accompanied on these excursions were mostly Gwalas, and the Kishengunj Gwala, besides being almost invariably a *lattial* and very frequently a dacoit, was as much at home in the water as the hippopotamus or the human frog, or any other amphibious creature.

Those Gwalas were by no means effeminate, as are the Bengalis generally, and they were sportsmen in a way. Some of them were accomplished quarter-staff players, and could have shaped fairly well, I fancy, in a bout with Little John or Friar Tuck; some were also wrestlers of the first class, who would have shaped fairly well against their rivals of Cornwall or the North Country; and those who were expert in these arts were as greedily enlisted in the service of rajas and other magnates of large revenues as were the giants of Europe for the Gargantuan corps of Frederick William of Prussia.

And those employers also engaged the services of up-country *pulwáns*, men of the Sepoy class drawn mostly from Oudh and the North-West Provinces, who did little or nothing with the quarter-staff of the Gwala, but much in wrestling. The services of these men consisted only, in fact, of wrestling and constant training for the arena; and their most arduous duty was the struggle with a dietary scale of awful character and dimensions. Vast quantities of milk, a bilious sweet concocted of curd and sugar, and other uninviting food, had to be consumed daily, so that the *pulwán* should put on flesh; and all day long, when not engaged in demoralising his interior economy, he had to exercise himself violently with Indian clubs and other calisthenics, so that some portion of the constantly superadded flesh should be solidified into muscle. I have seen these *pulwáns*—men celebrated through more than one province—enter the wrestling-ring in a condition that seemed to suggest expediency of tapping for dropsy rather than promise of athletic feats, and those corpulent gladiators have, amidst the cheers of an admiring crowd, amply sustained their reputation.

Indian wrestling differs *toto cœlo* from that of England; there is more of art and less of mere brute force in it. When I was a learner of this science there were 360 *penches* or dodges to be acquired, and to-day there may possibly be more. Even then the practised English wrestler who knew nothing of those many *penches* would, I fancy, have had the worst of an encounter with one of those trained *pulwáns:* as likely as not he would have been put down on his back before he had come to grips with his antagonist, or thought the tussle had commenced.

As a sport pursued by the natives of India generally, wrestling occupies a pre-eminent position. Second in the public estimation comes another display of the amphitheatre and survival of the gladiatorial time—the contest between two picked men armed with quarter-staff, or sword or shield. Then, *longo intervallo*, comes kite-flying, the sport whereof consists in cutting through the string of one kite with the string of another, the victory going to him whose string holds out and kite remains. This game is, I think, more in vogue in Northern India than elsewhere. In the towns thereaway scores of kite-duels are to be sometimes witnessed waging at once, and the uninitiated globe-trotter might assume that these aerial toys were being flown by the youth of the place whose inexpert hands permitted much unpremeditated fouling; but that impression would be wholly incorrect, those kites being flown by sportive men, and fouling being an essential feature of the game.

Then for the nobles and men of large establishments and means there is cock-fighting, which is not confined to duels between game-birds of the gallinaceous order only, in that quail and bulbuls and other birds are pitted against each other. The quail is notorious for its quarrelsomeness: being confined in cage or quailery, it has to be kept in the dark if it is to be kept alive. Let the light be sufficient to show the male bird that there is another of its sex and kind within reach, and there will be trouble; the gage of battle will be thrown down and accepted, and those feathered pugilists will straightway emulate the *à l'outrance* procedure of the Kilkenny cats. I believe the Chinaman also in his own country indulges in this sport, and carries his fighting birds where Ah Sin carried kings and aces—up his sleeve.

But it is sad to think of the bulbul as a brawler reduced to the level of that game-bird whose only form of song is a crow, and out of whom not even a laureate (if we had one) could make any poetical capital whatever beyond the bare statement that it is the herald of the morn, but not to be trusted in that capacity, in that it is sometimes unpunctual, and often too previous in its heralding. The bulbul is the very antithesis of the game-fowl in this respect. To Eastern poets, and notably to Hafiz, it stands in the position occupied by the nightingale in regard to poets of the West. The Gulistan, or place of roses, might almost as well be named Bulbulistan, or place of bulbuls, seeing that the rose and the bulbul are equally prominent in that poem, and very frequently represented as holding long rhythmic conversations with each other, after the manner of Tityrus and Melibœus. Lastly, he who studies Persian in the Indian schools is taught to translate bulbul into nightingale; and Thackeray, who had some little Indian teaching, associated the rose and the nightingale in that ballad, "The Rose upon my Balcony," which Becky sang at Gaunt House.

And yet the bulbul of India, whatever the bird of Persia or Arabia may be, is no songster: its warbling is no more dulcet than that of the house-sparrow. Can it be that the nightingale is a greatly overrated bird, as Shakespeare tells us in the lines—

> "The nightingale, if she should sing by day
> When every goose is cackling, would be thought
> No better a musician than the wren"?

However that may be, no

> "Melancholy Philomel,
> Thus perched all night alone in Indian groves,
> Tunes her soft voice to sad complaints of love,
> Making her life one great harmonious woe."

No creature more harmonious than the jackal, the pariah dog, and the bull-frog wakes the echoes of the Indian night; no bird save the cooing ring-dove breathes forth a note of music during the Indian day; and so the bulbul doubtless finds its proper level in the ranks of the fighting birds.

I know of no other sports than those I have mentioned as part or parcel of the Indian native's life. The average native does not hunt, or row, or play cricket, or follow any pursuit that calls for physical exertion: he does not dance, and would consider it degrading to be seen dancing, albeit some latter-day maharajahs and princes have gone the length of lounging through a quadrille at the Viceregal balls. He enjoys, or at any rate he suffers, all these things vicariously: professional dancers or nautch-girls, boatmen, quarter-staff-men, wrestlers, and broadsword-players do for him all that he requires in such active pursuits as concern him, and it is no more possible to think of an Indian Caligula or Commodus entering the arena to fight with trained gladiators than it is to imagine an Indian woman of position for any or no reason emulating the terpsichorean feats of the daughter of Herodias.

Let not the British public be misled in this

regard by the success of the Parsee cricketers, a success that has recently culminated in their victory over Lord Hawke's team. There is evidently good stuff in those Parsee wielders of ball and willow, as is plainly manifested by the fact that only they and one other eleven (Englishmen) were successful against the Yorkshire captain's team. But, admitting this excellence on the part of the Parsees, my argument about Indians stands unaffected, inasmuch as the Parsees are no more Indians than any other foreigner, be he Jew or Gentile, whose birthplace and domicile are in Hindostan. I know that the honourable member now sitting in the British House of Commons for Central Finsbury has been styled the sole representative of the Indian people in that Assembly, but I cannot help thinking that this peculiar position has been claimed for him on insufficient grounds. Racially, as a Persian, he is as widely differentiated from the Indians as is the Briton; and as a Fire-worshipper, his religion is not one whit more in accord with the creeds of India than is the Christian faith. It seems to follow, then, that any member of the House of Commons who has made a career in India such as that of Sir Richard Temple or Sir George Chesney, has as eligible a claim to be regarded as an Indian representative as Mr Naoroji. But even if my contention upon this political point be wrong, and if Mr Naoroji may justly claim to represent Indians in the House of Commons, it remains clear enough to my mind that the Indians cannot claim to be considered cricketers because the Parsees may. It would be more reasonable on the part of Hindostan's many millions to claim to be a race of billiard-markers because a considerable number of Eurasians are such—more reasonable, indeed, because the Eurasian is in part native to the soil of India.

Of the few sports practised by Indians, wrestling is certainly the most popular. Immense crowds gather around the arena in which performers of eminence are to try a fall, and while the wrestlers are silent and seem to be exceedingly placid, the audience may be seen on occasion wild with excitement. The arena at Gwari Kishnaghur (a great wrestling centre when I knew it) was of considerable dimensions, and was enclosed by palisades of unusual height and strength; but in spite of this strong barrier many policemen were required to restrain the excited spectators from entering the ring either to aid some favourite combatant or to hustle some unpopular one.

In spite of the science and classical suggestiveness of Indian wrestling, it must at first strike the Western observer as being slow. Too much of the Fabian policy; too patient waiting and watching for an adversary's blunder; too little of plain and direct attack; too much absolute inaction,—thus would the athlete of Cornwall or Cumberland criticise his fellow-practitioner of Hindostan. But the initiated sees and appreciates the skill that is being exercised even when the two opponents are to all appearance motionless as the bronze statues that they so closely resemble; and he knows that the chances are in favour of many trials of that skill, rather than of strength, and many changes of fortune before the contest is ended by one of the combatants being laid out on his back so that both shoulders at once touch the ground. There is no calling of time: from the moment that the two opponents enter the ring until that fair and square back-throw the strife must proceed without pause, unless one of them turn craven and yield, or an unruly mob break into the ring and interfere—both very improbable contingencies.

Very often there is considerable delay in getting to that grip which in English wrestling is speedily determined if, as is the case in some counties, it be not arranged by agreement at the start. The Indian wrestler has to be wary in his approaches to embrace his opponent, for he knows of *penches*—deftly dealt jerks of his thumb and elbow, &c., by which he may be thrown before he holds his adversary at all—and therefore he indulges in much fencing at a respectable distance what time he breaks the silence of the moment by slapping his biceps and his thighs with hollowed palms. Nude save for a scanty cloth around his loins, as the athletes of Sparta, he is, when not too obese, a graceful animal as he moves lithely and cautiously round his foe, and indeed all through the encounter when he is in motion.

At last the two get hold of each other, and a

struggle commences. Now it appears that one is about to be thrown, his balance seems to be going, and the audience look to see him deposited upon his back; but it is not to be yet awhile. Albeit he cannot keep his foothold facing his foe, he can do something else, and he does it: he turns a somersault, using his enemy as a fulcrum; his legs go over the other's shoulders, and he comes down firm-footed on the ground behind the other's back, and possibly with an advantage that imperils the stability of his opponent. Now one of them finding himself hard pressed and upon the point of being thrown upon his back, anticipates this move by throwing himself down with his back uppermost. "This side up, with care," is his motto now as, face downwards, he hugs the ground while his opponent sits athwart his loins and applies all his art to the prostrate foe in view of placing his shoulders where now his chest is. So they remain for many minutes, while a breathless crowd look on and wonder which of these two, if either, shall come victorious out of what seems an *impasse* for both: and now there is a kaleidoscopic change, due to some incautious move of him who was uppermost, and he who was below and half vanquished has risen from the earth invigorated like another Antæus, and has the other stretched beneath him —perhaps even with shoulders that touch the ground, and so end the combat.

In my Kishengunj establishment I had a wrestler and quarter-staff-player, celebrated as a champion in both departments. He was a Gwala, and, as a *rara avis* among the Gwalas thereaway, had never been engaged in a dacoitee or made himself a nuisance to his neighbours by depasturing his cows in their crops. He was a popular man in spite of his un-Gwala-like virtues, and when opposed in the arena by any local athlete was held to be invincible.

This hero's record was broken once by a local and very insignificant rival—a poor little village chowkidar. Great was the surprise of my Gwala and his friends when this mean watchman threw down the gage of battle: nothing doubting of the champion's prowess, all ridiculed the daring of the chowkidar; but the challenge was accepted as a matter of course, and the unequal contest was arranged. So did Goliath go forth with over-weening confidence to meet the stripling David.

But the champion and his friends had not reckoned with the possible effects of superstition. That chowkidar had something of a reputation as, or some of the disrepute of, a wizard: he was an uncanny person; he was ugly enough for a very Shaman, and he turned his unprepossessing appearance and character to full account. Entering the ring, he prepared for the encounter by mysterious invocations that overawed the Gwala. While my athlete looked on and waited, this amateur sorcerer went slowly to the four points of the compass and solemnly cast dust into the eyes of his opponent, who, as these rites proceeded, grew more and more demoralised : then, when the moment was seen to be ripe by the basilisk eyes of the chowkidar, the contest was commenced, and in two minutes the Hector of the country-side was on his back, fairly and easily beaten.

Anger then displaced superstition in the champion's breast: he demanded another trial forthwith. There was no more invocation or dust-throwing; the two were agrip again within the minute, and barely so when the sorcerer was heavily and decisively thrown. Then I had to rush in and rescue the chowkidar from the grasp of the victor: all the sorcery had been knocked out of him already, and but for my interference his life would have gone out after it.

CHAPTER IV.

THE SANTHAL REBELLION.

THE DAMUN-I-KOH—ST GEORGE AND THE YOUNG TIGERS—THE OUTBREAK—RECONNOITRING THE REBELS—A VOLUNTEER EXPEDITION—A CATTLE-RAID—ESCAPE FROM DROWNING—JUNGLE-FEVER—SIR GEORGE YULE—TIGER-SHOOTING IN BEHAR.

AFTER about three years of this Kishnaghur life I went north, and well into the jungle of the Damun-i-koh (foot of the hill), lying along the Rajmahal hills, which at many points spread their spurs out almost to the banks of the Ganges. Jungle was there in every direction of my station, on the hills timber from foot to crest, and on the alluvial plains below dense and tall grass admirably suited for tiger-cover. Tigers and panthers and bears were in the neighbourhood, and seen or heard by men from time to time: but it was only after two years spent in that country that I realised my burning desire to kill a tiger. I very nearly encountered one some time before this, while out after swamp partridge with two companions, but, fortunately perhaps for me, the encounter did not come off. The swamp partridge were driven for us out of heavy grass cover by a line of beaters. In one of our drives I took my stand in a clear patch in the middle of a strip of this grass, one of my colleagues standing on either hand outside. The beaters neared us, the partridges rose and flew our way, and when I had emptied both barrels and dropped a brace of birds, a roar broke from the cover close at hand, and there was a wild stampede of beaters, then silence. There was no mistaking that roar, which came from the grass in front of me not twenty yards away from where I stood. I had never heard a tiger give tongue before outside a zoo, and this was another tongue than that of the caged beast; but I knew what voice it was, and told myself that my chance had come at last. The tiger did not break, but turned back from the cover's edge, and I proposed to my fellow-shooters that we should pursue it straight away through the grass. We had no elephant at hand; we had no missile larger than No. 4 shot; but I argued that if we went three abreast, and poured six charges, more or less, into the tiger, we should do for him. A few years later I should not have made this suggestion, but at that time I was wholly inexperienced, and, moreover, was spoiling for a tiger-shoot. However, my companions were unanimously of the other way of thinking. They would not bear me company in such an idiotic enterprise, and when this point was settled it was hopeless—if indeed it was not hopeless from the first moment—to follow the tiger with any idea of seeing it. I commenced a return beat of the cover with a rallied line of beaters, but soon abandoned my tiger-chase, and reverted to the partridges.

For two years I possessed my soul in such patience as was attainable, making an occasional excursion across the Ganges into the Purneah country, where tigers were to be had by favoured shikaris, but where I had to be satisfied with one rhinoceros-hunt, in which I had not a chance of letting off my rifle, and the successful pursuit of some wild buffaloes. In and about those hills in whose shadows I lived there were tigers and panthers at my very door, but, save as above related, I never heard them, and none did I ever see.

Others in my immediate vicinity were more fortunate, and one of them had an experience that is, I imagine, unparalleled. Poor St George! He was an Irishman, characterised by the recklessness of his race in fullest measure. He would ride any horse and anywhere. He would face any danger without a moment's consideration of the consequences, or even of the better method of meeting the risk he faced. He had several hair-breadth escapes during the short time that I knew him, and not long after we parted he rode hap-hazard to his death. That last adventure of his short life doubtless struck him as of a very ordinary character, by comparison with many more reckless things that he had accomplished without very serious accident. He and another came to a flooded valley, across which the waters, some feet in depth, swept like a mill-sluice; the road was submerged for half a mile, and on either side of it were cuttings—some of considerable depth—into which it was quite possible to ride. St George's companion pointed out the danger of the passage, and urged that they should both return to the bungalow they had left. St George would not listen: he had started to go to his home on the other side of that valley, and no argument could move him to change his purpose. He rode on alone, rode on into the flood, albeit his horse showed evident signs of terror; and before he had got half-way across, his horse reared and fell back upon him into one of the roadside excavations, and killed him in the fall. So was stilled as brave and generous a heart as ever beat.

And to this gallant soul the news was brought that a couple of tigers (young ones fully or nearly fully grown) had tumbled into a blind and shallow well close by. St George went off to the place at once, and there, sure enough, in the dry well, were the brace of tigers. What would he do with them? Anybody else would have done one of two things—(1) would have shot them out of hand, or (2) would have made the proper arrangements for netting them, in view to handing them over to the Zoo, or disposing of them to some Indian Jamrach. There was a *tertium quid* for St George which, I think, he alone could have hit upon. He managed somehow or other to drag those tigers out of the pit which held them. He made no sort of arrangement for giving them a suitable reception on their arrival above-ground; of course he never stopped to think that the tigers would cease to be harmless creatures when released from their earthen prison. His whole programme consisted in releasing them, and what was to happen later was an extra to be arranged when the time arrived. Fortunately, the tigers, when they were hauled up, were moved to make use of their newly given freedom by going off, and they did so without pausing to thank or maul their liberator. I do not suppose that gratitude influenced them in their considerate treatment; and it is quite possible that they were too utterly bewildered by St George's eccentricity to be equal, on the spur of the moment, to any other course than immediate flight to less abnormal society. Poor St George could never give any convincing explanation of his conduct on that occasion. Why he hauled those tigers from their pits remains a mystery to me. Why he did not shoot or shoot at them when they were close to him above-ground I can explain to myself. I do so by remembering that he had neither skill nor keenness as a shot; that very possibly he was too slow with his gun to have a shot; and it is not improbable that he lost all interest in the affair when the programme proper—*i.e.*, the release of the tigers—had been completed. This may read like one of those Indian colonel's stories that I have quoted, but I have every reason to believe that the facts were very much as I have described them.

It was St George's good fortune, too, to have a panther offered to him for slaughter in his garden. The panther came into his compound at night, probably in search of sheep or goat, and was marked down by some lynx-eyed servant in a bush. In that instance St George was equal to the occasion, and deliberate of action. He went forth with one of Osler's double reading-lamps or some such sporting contrivance, flashed this upon the recumbent panther, and dealt the creature its death-blow with a charge of No. 6 shot, fired at a distance of 3 or 4 feet only.

I might have been a more successful shikari during my first two years in the Damun-i-koh but for two distractions that made very serious inroads upon my time—to wit, jungle-fever, and the Santhal rebellion. The former came upon me as a necessary consequence of my environment, and my frequent and lengthy expeditions into swamp and forest. The greater part of that tract of country was a hotbed of disease—a dismal and malarious territory after the manner of Martin Chuzzlewit's Eden, with the additional scourge of an Indian sun. To Europeans it proved a veritable plague-spot, and the mortality among the British railway employees upon that part of the East India Railway which lay in this ill-favoured land was terrible. It was quite in order that I should take the fever, and I took it. It proved an enduring and exacting possession: it lasted off and on for some two years, and occupied much of my time and of the time of doctors; and the only advantage that the most optimistic reasoning can extract from it is that it thoroughly seasoned me against the fell malaria of the Nepal Terai which, fatal to many, proved innocuous to me during the fifteen years that I shot over it.

But, as far as I was concerned, the Santhal rebellion was distinctly unexpected, and, when it arrived, unintelligible. These people had for years been harassed by the Bengali usurers. They had sought redress in vain from the Government officers who ruled over, and knew nothing of, them. They had fairly warned the authorities that, if redress were not to be had otherwise, they would seek it *vi et armis*. And when every form of appeal failed them, they were as good as their word, and took the field against they knew not what, and with no better arms than bow and arrows and the light Santhali battle-axe.

If this outbreak came as a complete surprise (as it did) to the sapient officials who had received timely warning of it, with much more reason did it come as a surprise to me who had received no warning, and who, moreover, knew nothing whatever about the rebellious tribe. My case was very much that of all the Europeans with whom I was then associated. It was not our business to study the native races or differentiate them. The Santhals of the villages under and beyond the hills, the Paharis or Naiyas, who lived on the hills only, and the Hindoos or Mahomedans of the river-side hamlets, were all one to us under the wide-spreading term of "native." And when it was reported to us that the Santhals were looting and murdering in the country close at hand, the news came upon us not only as a surprise, but as something wholly unintelligible. We might just as well have been told that a Jabberwock was around.

As soon as I heard of this wild affair I rode out to reconnoitre, and within three miles of my camp came in sight of a few of the rebels in retreat, laden with plunder. They were scattered over a plain, and making for different points, so that I had to devote my attention to one of them, whom I captured, without serious opposition on his part, and led back to the camp. As we pursued our way, the dig-diggi of the Santhal drum sounded from the jungles along the hill-ranges, a music new to me; but beyond serving as a melancholy accompaniment to my return journey, it concerned me not. My prisoner went with me quietly, and after our arrival in camp remained quiet even to excess. Innumerable questions (which he may not have understood) elicited no response from this uncommunicative being. He told us nothing about the rebels, good, bad, or indifferent, and very possibly knew no more than he told; for, I believe, he was ultimately discovered, by people who knew a Santhal from a Pahari or Hindoo, to be a low-caste Hindoo, who, after the fashion of some European Socialists, had turned the local disturbance to account by plundering for his own advantage.

But I knew from my own observation that there was such lawlessness abroad in the country as called for the intervention of the strong arm of order. I posted off, therefore, to Colgong (distant some seventeen miles), where there was a detachment of the Bhagulpore Hill Rangers. St George joined me on the way, and he and I both urged upon the commandant of that detachment to take the field forthwith against the rebels. But we urged in vain. That commandant was evidently of opinion that a day or two more or less of rebellion and widespread outrage signified nothing; that one time was as good as another for meeting such an emergency, or that the later time was preferable, even though meanwhile the rebellion gained head and the rebels confidence. Also, he required the authority of the civil power and the reading of the Riot Act, and several other things that were not available; and, ultimately, we had to leave him.

Then we took counsel together and resolved to sally forth next morning with such a volunteer force as we could collect, and without the authorised civil arm, the Riot Act, and many other desirable adjuncts, including appropriate arms and ammunition. Accordingly, we raised our army, consisting of seven Europeans armed chiefly with revolvers, and 150 natives (Hindoo and Mahomedan *burkundazes* and *chuprassies*) armed with tulwars, and, in a few instances, with firearms about as effective as the arquebuss. And we sallied forth, all of us apparently brimming over with martial ardour, and as far as St George and I were concerned, confident that we would march triumphantly right through the disturbed land, driving the rebels—or all that was left of them—before us.

Our native band encouraged this hope greatly by their bellicose demeanour: shouting their terrible war-cry, "Jai, jai, Kali mah ki jai!" the Hindoos brandished their swords, shouting *væ victis*. After their own fashion, the Mahomedans flourished their arms; and all marched on, eager, as it seemed, to reach the field of battle. They cooled perceptibly, those coloured auxiliaries, when, passing through a village that had just been sacked, we came upon the grim evidence that murder had here been done; and when we came close to a jungle from which the dig-diggi resounded, and would have led them onward to the fight, they, to a man, disbanded themselves and went off post-haste homeward.

Four of us Europeans went on in the direction of the Santhal drums, while two for strategic purposes rode so much on the flank of the enemy that they never encountered him; and one, for more obvious strategical reasons, remained behind at the edge of the jungle, and there was picked off by a lurking Santhal, who put an arrow into him. We who engaged the Santhals had a lively ten minutes with them, and then half our number, at least, were *hors de combat.* One had been knocked off his horse and wounded in the wrist, and him I took out of the press, only to find St George with an arrow through his foot, his foot so transfixed that it could not be pulled out of the stirrup, and his saddle shifted so far round that he was sitting on his horse's bare back. All that could be done for him then was to lift him and get his saddle back into position, and that was done; and then there was no course open to us but to retreat in as good order as circumstances permitted.

To this day I have not been able to understand why those Santhals let us off so easily: a day or two after our affair they met the tardy Hill Rangers (disciplined sepoys with proper arms and ammunition), and killed several of them, together with two Europeans. But although we halted to repair damages almost within bow-shot of them, and then retired at a snail's pace, they let us go without molestation of any sort. I came to know afterwards from themselves that they were 2000 strong that day. I suppose the novelty of our attack, and the damages they had to repair, explains their inaction,—they were paralysed.

St George had a rough time of it for the next twenty-four hours: no one at our camp could extricate the arrow from his foot, no one within forty odd miles could do this, and he had to ride that distance on an elephant with this arrow in him. Nor was a bed of roses prepared for me then, although beds of sorts were my constant portion for many days thereafter. For a Santhal hit my *sola topee* a blow that broke off so much of it as protected my head from the sun: fever and delirium were my lot ere that sun went down; and at night, when my camp was broken up and its members dispersed, I was carried off across the Ganges to Purneah, where the kindly and most hospitable medico of the station nursed me back into comparative health.

This was the dismal conclusion of what I had at the outset regarded as a splendid substitute for the tiger-shooting which came not to my hand. Later on I accompanied the 7th N.I. in an expedition directed against the rebels in the heart of Santhalia; but during the weeks that I served with them we saw only fugitives, and were much more occupied in the humble work of the commissariat department than in glorious war. It is true that we stormed some villages after the most approved system of military science: our forces descended upon these strongholds from various points, the several detachments so timing their advance as to arrive simultaneously on three sides of the place attacked; but invariably, when we reached the point of attack, there was nothing to fight with except a few fowls, wherewith we promptly did battle. These fowls and some blue rocks constituted all the shikar I had during that jaunt through Santhal jungles, and all the food-supply of our mess save the rice we got out of the deserted villages.

Although that expedition could hardly be styled war, and certainly was not magnificent, there were sufficient novelty and excitement about the proceeding to make it enjoyable enough for those concerned. It cannot be said that we had a sufficiency of anything else, unless it were rain or mud. Our commons were as common as they were short; rice, fowl, and pigeon—pigeon, fowl, and rice, made up our three courses and dessert. Boil, broil, or serve them as we might, these three articles (undisguised by condiments, because condiments were lacking) contributed our unchanging *menu*. M. Gabius Apicius would have hanged himself at sight of any one of our meals; Lucullus would have fallen upon his sword rather than give such banquets as we sat down to; and yet I am inclined to the opinion that this simple feeding was more enjoyable than the heavy feasts of the too hospitable London guilds, that commence with calipash and calipee and end with dyspepsia. And if our feeding was destitute of *ragout* of nightingales' tongues and other dainties dear to the Roman epicure, our potations were proportionately moderate. No ripe Falernian was quaffed; no brimming beaker, save of water, graced the board; one glass of sherry and one of brandy per diem constituted the ration of alcoholic liquor for each unit, and by that narrow margin were we saved from universal blue-ribbonism.

Our camp equipment was similarly restricted. We had two tents, a mess-table, a charpoy apiece, and never a chair. The charpoys, ranged round the table, served for our sitting accommodation at meals, suggesting further classical associations and accubation rather than comfort; and as our camp was generally pitched in mud, we made our way around the tent by stepping from bed to bed. But this rough housing was luxurious indeed by comparison with one night's experience that broke the monotony of our lives; that night came down upon us, together with a steady drizzle, when our camp had missed us somehow. Puddles to right of us, puddles to left of us, puddles in front of us, although they did not volley and thunder, made things exceedingly unpleasant. We were tentless and benighted in a swamp out of which it was impracticable to make our way; for miles the country around us was, as far as we could judge, equally water-logged. We made the best of matters as we found them, substituted an extra pipe for the rice, fowl, and pigeon meal of other and fuller days, and made our lodging upon the cold ground with due resignation. That was my first night in a water-bed of this sort (but not the last), and to those who see in damp sheets the certain cause of pneumonia and death it may appear remarkable that we were none of us any the worse for that watery lodging.

Nor were these our only aqueous difficulties; now and again a hill-stream in full spate occurred upon our line of march, and in the absence of ferries, boats, or any other facilities whatever, had to be negotiated by wading or swimming, or left to subside before crossing was attempted. On one of our expeditions an adventure of this sort went perilously near to bringing my career to an end. Our force had set out from camp in the early morning to attack the Santhal enemy, reported to be gathered in considerable number some miles away, and within a mile or so of our tents we came upon one of those hill-streams, then ankle-deep only and fordable without let or hindrance. There was no reason for our anticipating that we should find it otherwise upon our return: the day was fine, and promised to remain so; there was no sign in the heavens of impending rain in our neighbourhood that should fill the rivers with rushing floods; and we went on our way, heeding nothing that possible barrier which, when we crossed the river, we were placing between our army and our camp.

Our expedition was as fruitless as usual. We marched some miles; we came to the spot where the Santhals should have been; Santhals were there none, or any sign of them save the village where they had assembled, which we left alone, and one or two hundred head of cattle that we drove away; and to this day I have never been able to comprehend the motive that guided us in that cattle-raid, or what possible good was to result from our becoming drovers thuswise. But I accepted it then as a part of the authorised programme—as some strategical movement that my lay mind could not fathom—and joined in the driving of those beeves with all the enthusiasm of a Smithfield expert. And the sun shone upon us as we wended homewards; and our hearts were light (as was our mid-day meal of biscuit), and we hailed with rejoicing our first glimpse of the banks of that hill-stream, which was as the first milestone from our camp; and we reached the verge of what we had left a babbling brook, and behold! a torrent rushed between those banks turbid and deep, coursing along at express speed, and carrying on its bosom up-rooted trees that, revolving as they went, thrashed the swollen waters into foam. Here was an *impasse* indeed!

What was to be done? Council of war held

straightway could only determine that we wanted to get across and could not,—it being decided that not even the elephants we had with us could ford the river in its then condition. The council of war, now unable to solve the question of crossing, found that our retention of those raided cattle was no longer a strategical necessity, and let them go their ways; and settled nothing else except that it was desirable to get back to dinner and our tents—as to which there was perfect unanimity.

Then it occurred to Vigors and myself that we might swim our horses across, ride to the camp, and bring up the reserve there to the aid of our stranded force. I have no idea what assistance they were to give, or could have given; but any action seemed better than absolute inaction, and Vigors and I proceeded to carry out our purpose. Why Vigors joined in this attempt I cannot imagine: he was no Leander; only a few days before this I had had to help him across a smaller and less turbulent stream than this. But he may have depended upon his horse; he may have known that animal to be a strong swimmer (horses, according to my experience, being very differently gifted in this respect), and may have gathered confidence from his steed or from my companionship in the waters.

We found a narrow track that descended to the river, and went our way into the flood in single file, I leading. What happened to Vigors from the moment of my leaving the shore I knew not, my attention being fully occupied by my own difficulties. It was only when the adventure was ingloriously terminated that I came to learn how he had been forced back ere the plunge was taken by the obvious impracticability of the passage. While he hesitated and turned, all my senses were devoted to my own proceedings. The descent down a precipitous, rugged, and rain-sodden path was one that called for caution and a ready bridle-hand. *Haud passibus æquis*, my horse slipped and slithered and stumbled down and riverwards, now sliding a yard or two and catching foothold just in time, anon losing hold with its hind-feet and squatting on its haunches, and finally going anyhow into the torrent.

Being in those troubled waters, it became immediately apparent that my horse was not equal to the occasion. Do what I would I could not keep its head up-stream, and in a couple of minutes it was treading water and going whithersoever the current directed. If I had done the more prudent thing, I should have left my steed to fend for itself while I made my way across alone: I chose the less prudent course, left the saddle, swam to the horse's head, and tried to guide the panic-stricken creature. I was driven to abandonment of that attempt by a blow on my right shoulder delivered by one of the pawing hoofs with which the horse aimlessly beat air and water; then, disabled as to one limb, I sought the nearest bank, which was that from which I had started.

Dragged down by heavy water-logged riding-boots, crippled as to one arm, and hurried along by rushing water as of a mill-sluice, I was not very confident that I should reach the land again otherwise than in the form of a demned damp disagreeable body, as Mr Mantalini would have described me. Landing-place I could see none that I might hope to reach,—only precipitous bank, with here and there a tree whose branches almost touched the water. In one such bough I seemed to see a hand held out to save me; that, and that only, I thought, offered a rescuing chance, and I put out all the strength that was in me to seize it as I was carried along, when—I just missed it!

At that particular moment, if I had conducted myself after the standard manner, I should have hurriedly reviewed all the incidents of my career from my teething upwards. That hasty biographical sketch is, I believe, generally considered to be required of him to whom sudden death seems imminent. But on two or three occasions when Death and I have been, without warning, brought face to face, I have failed to conform to that practice, and have given all my mind to the practical question of finding a way out of a tight place rather than to the preparation of an obituary notice that could only, like Toots's letters, be delivered to myself.

When I missed the branch I thought that Finis had to be written by any biographer who dealt with my career. Hope was there none of stemming the flood to regain the water over which it hung; hope was there none in the form of bough or landing-place that I could reach ahead; hope was there none left in me of any kind, but in its stead a calm philosophical despair of a bovine order that was not vivid enough to be classified as thought; and then I was in an eddy, just when I contemplated going down to join the Lorelei of the stream, and the swirl of water brought me back to that branch, and I seized it and was safe.

For after taking breath and resting a few minutes, I was able to draw myself out of the water and shout for aid; and deliverance came in the form of two havildar's sashes, by which I was hauled up on to *terra firma*, where was Vigors, much to my relief, undrowned—where also were all our army and everything belonging to them except my horse, which having done its best to drown me, did what I sought to make it do—*i.e.*, crossed the river and went home to camp. The rest of us only succeeded in this when, the flood having abated somewhat, we were able to cross upon elephants, towing our horses behind.

Do any of my *bons camarades* of that time linger yet upon this planet, and give an occasional thought to those days when we hunted Santhals in the Damun-i-koh? Tom Vigors, generous and fiery

Celt that he was, has, I know, joined the majority. Are any of the good 7th N.I.—Parlby, Lockhart, Travers, or the rest—still in the land of the living, and, as retired generals, adorning the Rag or 14 St James's? If Parlby be to the fore, let me thank him once again for the raiment wherewithal he clothed me (a man made clotheless save as to one suit by the devastating Santhal) when I went from the Damun to Calcutta.

Not as much as a twinge of rheumatism or bout of catarrh came to me as the consequence of that moist outing; although I was only just convalescent after a relapse of jungle-fever—the most dangerous foe of him who seeks the tiger in its Terai or Morung lair. The man who once contracts this fever may, unless he take a sea voyage, expect it to cling to him for years with more or less virulence, and with occasional attacks that shall bring him to death's door, and end by carrying him beyond its grim portals. For over two years I was the thrall of this masterful disease; during that period I never commenced a day with any certainty that ague would not be shaking me to pieces in the afternoon and fever raging in me before night. In those weary years I had three attacks of the more severe form, each of which brought me to the verge of the grave; and I only shook the enemy off after I had placed the Bay of Bengal between me and it. Down in the spice-laden palm-groves of Ceylon I severed the bonds that had enchained me, and thenceforth ague came to me once only—and then it found me in Dorsetshire. What the radical change did for me in whole, a slighter change did on one occasion when I was lying, ague and fever stricken, in my jungle encampment. Things were very bad for me then. I was taking nothing in the form of nourishment, because I could retain nothing that I took; my only refreshment was lime-juice fresh from the fruit; and I was taking in more bane in the form of malarious air than antidote could cope with. It seemed, in fact, as if I should not much longer require air, poisonous or salubrious—as if my hours were numbered.

At this critical juncture there arrived upon the scene the good Samaritan in the form of Brown Wood, one time a distinguished cricketer of Bengal, and aforetime a pupil of that cricketing Ajax, Wollenstrott (or Felix) of Blackheath. Wood had me promptly removed in a palanquin from my tent to his boat on the Ganges some two miles distant: the removal occurred about noon, and that evening I was eating prawn-curry ravenously and with a power of retention that seemed equal to the secure stowage of a sirloin or two. Change is the best remedial measure in cases of malarious fever: quinine taken beforehand as a preventive is effective so far; but, the disease having laid hold of its subject, quinine, although, if presented in very stiff doses, it may check an attack for the time, will not cure as will change of air. This medical advice I offer to Indian shikaris free of charge.

But many an apparent evil is a blessing in disguise. The Santhal rebellion brought Sir George Yule (then plain George Yule) out of the seclusion of Eastern Bengal to Bhagulpore; and the jungle-fever which played havoc with me, and seemed my bitter foe, led to my introduction to that fine sportsman and brilliant administrator. Under him I served my novitiate in tiger-shooting and the duties of civil government; through him I obtained congenial employment, and splendid opportunities in the field of sport; and in him I found the best and truest friend man ever had.

George Udney Yule—if ever the name of man deserved to be written in letters of gold it is that which, with loving respect, I have just penned: I am one of many whose admiration of Yule is only exceeded by love for him—would that I could seize this opportunity of writing a monograph that would worthily describe him and his brilliant services and his large-hearted beneficence. I have sought in every direction for materials for such a sketch; but the singular modesty and reticence of the man baffle the biographer. No one knows a tithe of his good works; and the harshest critic, even with an intimate knowledge of his life and acts, could make no more adverse comment than that he hated dinner-parties.

George Yule was the eldest of three brothers, and the only one who made his career that of a civilian. Of the others, Sir Henry Yule entered the Royal Engineers, and distinguished himself as a statesman and author; and Colonel C. Yule rode gallantly to his death at Delhi in 1857 at the head of the 9th Lancers. But although George was known in his family as the peculiarly quiet and peaceable one of the trio, the martial spirit burned strongly within him. When opportunity presented itself in the Bhagulpore division, he led a force against the mutineers of '57. He offered to lead a band of volunteers against Kooer Singh of Arrah, and was bitterly disappointed when his services were declined. With all that quietness of manner that characterised him, he was as much a soldier at heart as Bayard, and often spoiling for a fight as badly as if Limerick instead of Inveresk had been his birthplace.

That mild exterior, as Sir F. Halliday has observed, covered the *ingenium perfervidum Scotorum* that was ready to blaze forth when occasion required its display. I saw one instance of this that had some amusing features in it. We were a *partie carrée* at Yule's table—the host, two Purneah magnates, and myself—and they of Purneah and I were in hot argument as to the character of a certain contractor who had purchased an estate and set up a comfortable establishment out of a fortune largely made by the pilfering of his coolies' wages. I was contending warmly that this man was a thief; the Purneahites (two to one) were arguing with equal warmth that he was a good fellow, and must be an honest man because he entertained so liberally. So the argument went on for some time—my solo against their duet—

while Yule sat silent. Then came the moment when Yule's patience gave way, and springing up from the table, he said, "I cannot sit and hear that fellow called an honest man." Immediate collapse of the Purneahites followed, and the contractor was by them forthwith abandoned as one to be safely recommended for inspection by Diogenes.

This scorn for everything of a knavish character has another illustration that came to me on excellent authority. Yule's purse was open to any and every one who needed aid; his pensioners were many and of every class and creed; and, free-handed with gifts, he was easily wooed and won by the borrower. He had lent a large sum, even for him who thought little of giving Rs. 2000 for a wedding present, and had for security a bare I O U. The borrower made some difficulty—what difficulty I do not remember if I ever knew it, but enough to show that he was dishonestly inclined. Yule put the I O U on the fire.

Nor was this lofty resentment of wrong-doing confined to the humble tricksters of private life. Yule was no time-server or respecter of personages who would tamely see injustice done by those in authority over him. When the Government of Bengal, setting aside the perpetual settlement of Lord Cornwallis, resumed the fisheries of the Bengal rivers, Yule alone, I believe, of all the Bengal Commissioners, entered any protest, and his was so strongly worded that, as he told me, he expected to be dismissed from the service for it. But his calm and honest judgment was fortified by the decision of the Supreme Court: the resumption of the fisheries was abandoned, and Yule remained to finish his work of regenerating Santhalia, and rise to higher, if less congenial, positions in Oudh and Hyderabad and the Viceregal Council. It is highly creditable to Sir Frederick Halliday, the Lieutenant-Governor to whom Yule addressed his protest, that he subsequently wrote thus: "Not a few such men the Indian Civil Service has produced. . . . None of them did better for India than George Yule, and no one has better deserved the affectionate remembrance of its people."

This intolerance of anything savouring of injustice has, I have reason to think, marred his reputation at the India Office. He is held by those in high places to have been influenced overmuch by Sir Salar Jung. But they do not know Yule who imagine that he could be made the puppet of Machiavel himself, or persuaded to surrender his judgment to anybody. I have worked under several official chiefs: none of them has been the intimate friend to me that Yule was, and none has been so hard to win from his views to mine.

Yule, for reasons that would, I am sure, commend themselves to unbiassed minds, held that injustice had been done to the Nizam of Hyderabad in regard to the Berars—those districts which the Nizam assigned in 1853, and reassigned in 1860, as security for the maintenance of the Hyderabad contingent, with a condition that any surplus revenue after payment for this contingent should be transferred to the Nizam. Yule resented what he styled the attorney-like device of calling these Berars ceded districts, and the failure of the Government of India to hand over the stipulated surplus, although the cost of the Hyderabad contingent had been reduced from forty lacs to twenty-four lacs per annum. I do not propose to argue this matter out here: I will only add that Colonel Davidson, another Hyderabad resident, took the same view, and that Yule does not seem to me to have been appreciated by Downing Street as he deserved to be.

Always outspoken when occasion demanded full and free utterance, Yule was by no means lavish of speech. Always amiable and cheerful, the brightness that was in him rarely came out in the "wut" of his country; but humour emanated from him now and again, and he has said some good things. For example, when a rumour reached Simla that the Viceroy (Sir John Lawrence) was about to be raised to the peerage as Lord Liffey, he exclaimed, "Then I hope he may soon fall into his title." The quiet fun that worked in him was evinced on one occasion at my expense. I had just been appointed Commissioner of Excise, and he sent to me a bottle of fluid, closely resembling in appearance the native spirit, with a request that I would test it. I found that it was only a fraction above water strength, and water it proved to be.

Yule did not care for the policy of "masterly inactivity" or the author thereof. There was too much that was chivalrous in his nature to fit in with inaction, however masterly. Where good work was to be done his policy was a forward one, as when, in 1867, he wrote to the 'Friend of India' suggesting that a subscription should be raised for the equipment of a volunteer expedition from India for the relief of the Abyssinian captives, and promised a contribution of £1000 towards the fund; as when, also, in 1885, he denounced in a London paper England's refusal of Australia's proffered aid in Egypt.

Nor did Yule regard with favour Mr Gladstone or his unmasterly activity. Of this statesman he said, "A man must have a positive talent for incapacity to be able to make so many blunders." On the other hand, he admired Lord Beaconsfield, and was one of those who assisted Sir George Birdwood to inaugurate the celebration of Primrose Day.

His chief home pleasures in his retirement were flowers, ferns, and books; his recipe for a happy summer day was "a visit to the Temple azaleas, followed by an hour among Tinsley's reliefs." Whether as a District Magistrate in the wilds of Eastern Bengal, or as Chief Commissioner of Oudh, or as a member of the Viceroy's Council, or as a pensioner living in retirement among his ferns and flowers at home, Yule was always the same unpretending and sweet-natured man. He was true to the core; love and honesty shone forth from his eyes, and nobility of purpose in every action of his life. No man has been better loved than he, and none has been more deeply mourned.

If Jack Johnston was king of spears, George Yule was emperor. He had killed his hecatombs of boars. He had shot tigers on foot, from horse and from elephant, and killed from first to last, I have no doubt, more than any man living or dead; and up to the time of the Santhal rebellion he had been quite contented to finish his Indian career in a remote district where promotion would come to him with lagging gait, and fame (save that of the shikari) not at all. Notwithstanding his great gifts, there never was a man more truly modest and retiring than he. It was not that he sought to hide his light under a bushel—in fact, he was blissfully unconscious that he had a light to hide or show. But even while isolated in that outlandish district, his fame for other things than sport had come to be known at headquarters; and when Santhalia was ablaze from end to end, and the strongest hand and ablest head were wanted to restore order, the Lieutenant-Governor of Bengal at once chose Yule as the one man fitted for the task.

How Yule succeeded in this great work—how, with infinite mercy to the poor misguided Santhals, he built up for their country an admirable form of civil government—need not here be recorded. From that time he was appreciated at something like his real value to the State; promotion and honours came to him in abundance. But no elevation or distinction could alter the man, and Yule remained to the end the same simple-minded, true-hearted creature that he was as a Bengal magistrate. Truthfulness, courage, and a rare generosity were his chief characteristics. Of him as of another George (Washington) it can be said, "He never told a lie."

It was by the barest chance that Yule had survived to be the reformer and ruler of the Santhal districts. It is impossible to conceive a narrower escape from death than his in an encounter he had with a tiger. He was standing outside the jungle from which a tiger was being driven by beaters: the tiger emerged, not at the point where Yule expected, but within a few feet of the spot where he stood. There was a rush. Yule had time only to bring his rifle up to his hip and fire as the tiger sprang upon him: he was borne down upon the ground by the tiger's weight, and by blows of the brute's paws that smashed in his *sola topee* and cruelly tore his shoulder and chest. It seemed for Yule that the end had come, but the tiger was dead when it reached the ground—killed instantaneously by that one chance shot.

When, as a fever-stricken wreck, I went to his house at Bhagulpore, as to an asylum open to all who needed aid or solicitude, Yule was still the keen and active sportsman, even though administrative duties and responsibilities absorbed much of his time and attention. He had a stud of a dozen first-class walers—mostly tried pig-stickers—and ten magnificent elephants, staunch as any, which, when he left Oudh in 1864 to fill the position of Resident at Hyderabad, were sold at prices averaging, I think, Rs. 10,000 each.

Very soon after this I had a few days' sport with Yule and others in the grass country on the right bank of the Ganges, and shot my first tiger. I am constrained to admit that, when this beast broke in front of the elephant I rode, and gave me an easy shot, my success was tinged with disappointment. Exciting enough was the hunt when the tiger was afoot in front of our small line of elephants, and still unseen; but when it dragged itself into an open patch out of a swamp, a sneaking fugitive, voiceless and drowned-cat-like, and yielded up its life without a show of fight, or even a roar of protest, it struck me as being a poor creature by comparison with the noble beast of my day-dreams. Indeed I think I took more satisfaction during that expedition out of a tiger —a dry and noble-looking animal, whose appearance sadly belied its sneaking proclivities—that we mysteriously lost in a small stretch of cover surrounded by open country and melon patches. That tiger broke fairly in front of one of our party, who, for some inscrutable reason, did not fire at it; then was lost in the long grass, and lost to us for ever. For though we beat the cover backwards and forwards over and over again—though the tiger must have been seen if it had taken to the open — we never saw it again, or saw even the peculiar waving of the grass that indicates a tiger's progress. Twice only in my long experience and intimate association with him did I see Yule show the slightest sign of temper, and this was one of those occasions.

But one would do injustice to the species as a whole if one judged of all tigers by those two. A magnificent animal is the large male tiger when, with head erect and noble mien, he walks the glade or forest where he is king; or when, undaunted by the serried ranks of foes, he charges down upon a line of elephants. Grand, too, is the tigress fighting for her cubs. Unfortunately, all tigers are not animated by this bolder spirit, and not a few persist in the attempt to fly until they are rolled over as tamely as if they were rabbits. I have shot some half-dozen tigers without seeing a hair of them until they were stretched out dead or dying on the ground—shot them as they went through the reeds or grass that covered them and yet betrayed. And it is something strange that, after a little experience, one comes to judge with absolute accuracy whether the grass or reeds wave for a tiger, or for deer or pig.

CHAPTER V.

THE SANTHAL COUNTRY IN THE MUTINY.

WITH THE PURNEAH EXPEDITION—HEADING THE MUTINEERS—THE BATTLE OF THE BUND—RETREAT OF THE REBELS—THE SANTHALS—TIPOA THE HEADMAN—SANTHAL SUPERSTITIONS—VILLAGE GOVERNMENT—THE SANTHAL REGIMENT—DACOITEE—THE REVOLT IN DEOGHUR—THE 5TH IRREGULAR CAVALRY—MUTINY OF THE INFANTRY—GREGOR GRANT—BREAKING THE GAOL—TRYING THE PRISONERS—A WOULD-BE SATI—DISTRICT WORK.

IN 1857 the Indian Mutiny occurred, and this was the final cause of my introduction to wholesale big-game shooting. The district officer of Deoghur (in the Santhal Pergunnahs) was one of the many European victims of that terrible outbreak, and I was appointed his successor.

But before I went to my civil duties, and the tigers, panthers, bears, &c., that awaited me in the Deoghur country, I accompanied Yule's military expedition into the

Purneah district, and away up to the jungles lying at the foot of the Himalayas. The mutineers were moving about there, and were the main object in hand, but shikar was also a possible feature. We made first for an outlying station of Purneah, on the bank of a river celebrated for its mahseer fishing, and close to a large expanse of good pig-sticking country, where we were to wait until scouts brought in news as to the movements of a mutinous irregular cavalry regiment that was believed to be somewhere in the neighbourhood. Reaching this in the evening after a long march, we rested for the night and started early the next morning after the pigs. By lunch-time we had killed three, but not without casualties. A young boar jinked under Yule's horse and cut that animal: he came at me, got my spear well home in him, but still pressed on, so that I had to fend him off with the sole of my stirrup iron; and then, sorely wounded as he was, he cut the horse of another rider. But this was nothing to the trouble a very big boar was to give us in the afternoon. That brute charged out of his lair straight upon the pony (no bigger than the pig) of F. B. Simson, missed cutting the pony, went off for a quarter-mile canter, and then pulled up to fight. And he fought three of us, including the emperor of spears himself, for over an hour, cutting, though not severely, all three horses once or oftener during the engagement. The brute had an absolutely impenetrable hide; and the spears we delivered at him, riding round and round the beast, were but as pin-pricks that only urged him on to further fight. That boar beat us,—we could not kill him; we could not even get our spears to stick in him: he had no proper sense of sport, and we relinquished him to the less artistic form of death by powder and ball.

Just as the sun was declining upon that plain of many pigs, the scouts came in with news that promptly stopped our sport. That irregular cavalry regiment was marching in exactly the opposite direction to that which we had assumed for it; they were doubling upon us, and making for Purneah—the town that we had left the day before in pursuit of them. There was only one thing to be done to save Purneah from loot and worse—*i.e.*, to make a forced march by night to head the mutineers. So, after an early and hurried dinner, we set out to do the forty miles between us and Purneah with what speed we could. Yule and his six volunteers (a very irregular cavalry) rode their horses; fifty men of the 5th Fusiliers and a hundred of the Naval Brigade rode elephants; and through the night watches we worried on. What happened to others in those weary hours I cannot say. I slept a broken sleep, with countless awakenings that always mocked me with the delusion that the roadside trees were rest-houses where refreshments might be had; and always that same fond delusion as to the comforting B.-and-S. recurred, although, had I been equal to thought, I should have remembered that not a single rest-house was there in my path.

We reached Purneah none too soon; for while we were bracing ourselves up with tea and coffee, the news arrived that the mutineers were close to the farther quarter of the town. We all went out afoot to save the weary horses, and reached the threatened point just as the advanced-guard of the enemy was coming upon it. Then I had my first experience of action with regular troops, and it was impressive. F. B. Simson and I, as men acquainted with the ways and language of the people, led our party through the narrow streets into a lane beyond, and as we turned a corner two of the mutinous sowars came upon us, fired their carbines, and retreated: our foremost infantry, who had seen nothing of those sowars, opened fire into space, and into the body of a harmless villager who happened to be in the line of fire; and then our rear-guard dragged a light gun into position and fired into a blank wall. After this demonstration we advanced through the lanes into the open, and there across the open plain, a mile from us, the enemy were ranged in the shelter of a mango-grove.

We got no nearer to the mutineers that day, for they rode off and defied pursuit. But that evening, while we sat at dinner, news was brought to us that the enemy had camped on a plain some twelve miles from Purneah; and in the dead of night, when preference might have been given to bed and pillows, our small army set out for that Ascalon. This second night march brought us to the field of battle just when the first streaks of dawn made darkness visible, and there before us lay the foeman's camp and burning fires. We had surprised them, and were able to take up our position before they rose to the occasion. Our fifty regulars mounted an embankment whose peaceful purpose was to withstand the floods; behind that *bund* were ranged the men of the Naval Brigade; and we of the volunteer dragoons, with our noble captain, mixed with the Fusiliers.

Then commenced the battle of the Bund—a battle interesting to me because it was my first experience of regular warfare. Our force (with the exception of Captain Burbury commanding the sailors, and two comrades who had missed their way in the dusk) had barely effected this disposition when the enemy bestirred himself. Loud cries of "Allah illa Allah" and the equivalent of "boot and saddle" rent the dew-laden air as the sowars scrambled upon their horses: more shouting of *deen* and Allah and unpublishable Billingsgate hurled at the Feringhi, and these horsemen came thundering along the plain upon us. In line formation the Fusiliers poured a volley into the country facing them (one Enfield bullet out of fifty finding an appropriate billet in a sowar's leg), and then formed square to receive cavalry—and one of the 250 was received! He, anathematising the Feringhi with his last breath, charged home, was shot by one of the volunteers as he rose in his stirrups to sabre Yule, and fell dead at our feet, deeply regretted by Simmy, who could not be persuaded that it was otherwise than regrettable that such a good-plucked one should have been cut short in his career. The 249 more discreetly passed right and left of us, but, even so, paid the toll of death—three of them being dropped by the Brown Besses of the sailors.

Then the enemy, broken into twos and threes, rode round us and offered themselves as running targets for our rifle practice, and then I received an object-lesson explanatory of the very small proportion of hits to misses in the military shooting of that period. The Fusiliers had in their volley fired into a massed regiment at a distance of 100 yards or so, and obtained the creditable record of 2 per cent of hits; but they added never another hit to the list of misses achieved, and one of them, possibly to save his record, stopped his rifle performance by loading with his cartridge-bullet downwards. We amateurs who were shikaris made better use of opportunity and ammunition, and every now and again a saddle was emptied and another human form added to those that lay upon the field.

Then, and suddenly as if a cloud had dropped upon us, we belligerents were enveloped in a dense fog, fit rival of the London particular, save that it had not the rich colour and nutritious properties of the London article, which, if it be death to many, may be said to be food and drink to all. This fog saved the Burbury trio, who, coming upon the scene in the midst of the action, had formed a square of three to resist cavalry or anything else that might present itself. As Paris was spirited by Aphrodite out of his dangerous situation with Menelaus, so was Burbury out of his predicament.

Under cover of the fog some of the sowars, dismounted, crept in close upon us and directed a carbine-fusilade at the spot where they thought we stood. They knew we were above the level of the plain, but they over-estimated the height, and their bullets showered harmlessly over our heads. Ping! ping! ping! went the song of Bellona for a quarter of an hour, and then silence undisturbed by ring of bullet or rattle of firearm. Then, after some other fifteen minutes, an array of spear-heads, visible above the earth-embracing fog, approached us along the edge of the embankment. Nothing was to be seen by us but those spear-heads and the waving pennons that rose out of the murk and cautiously approached our position: nothing could the men who held those spears see of us; but if they came on, a few moments must have brought them and us into close quarters. They did not come on: I fancy they had not designed giving us battle, but, intending to retreat, had come our way by mistake. Very little made them change their course, and I was the unfortunate origin of that little cause. The temptation offered by those spear-heads was too much for me: I borrowed an Enfield from one of the Fusiliers, aimed at one of the shafts, lowered the rifle in a downward line until I fancied I had reached the holder of the spear, and fired : down fell that spear (preserved, I believe, as a trophy of that day's engagement by the 5th Fusiliers), and off went the mutineers, carrying their wounded with them, save him who was shot in the first volley, to be no more seen by us. Their retreat was, indeed, the best part of their performance of that day, and, if not altogether comparable with that of the Ten Thousand, deserves mention if only because of the distance they covered straight on end after a skirmish engaged in without breaking fast, some hard riding during the preceding forty-eight hours, and the disadvantage that many of the fugitives laboured under in that a score or so had to ride double, carrying their wounded comrades. They rode without any halt worth mentioning until, having reached the Nepaul Terai, they were clear of British territory, and had left the field of the Bund action over sixty miles behind them.

Our small force also went junglewards, and met an occasional adventure with a minimum of shikar, but here my account of this expedition closes.

Before the Santhal rebellion of 1855 I had but a shadowy idea who or what were the people who have given their name to the tract of country now known as Santhalia. These people of the plains of the Damun-i-koh were to my untutored and undiscriminating mind identical with the Naijas or Paharis who lived only on the ranges of the Rajmehal hills. But I came to know both races, and my introduction to both was of an inauspicious character. I made the acquaintance of the Santhals by hunting down and arresting those of them in my neighbourhood who had been concerned in the murder of Europeans during the recent rebellion, or had taken a prominent part in that *émeute.* The Paharis I first came to know when, similarly, I hunted down and arrested a notorious gang of dacoits. But while my association with the Santhals ripened, in spite of its unpromising commencement, into something like friendship, it never improved with the Paharis, for whom I entertained a just contempt without the incitement thereto of any familiarity.

In my pursuit of those rebel Santhals I was largely aided by some of their race, and notably by my right-hand man Tipoa. These allies, who must, I fear, be styled informers, put me on the track of fourteen rebel leaders, whom I seized from time to time and forwarded to Bhagulpore for trial. And I had another ally in the form of a jemadar of police, a scoundrel who quite unwittingly aided me to do what he utterly failed to do himself. For, being greedy after the rewards offered by the Government for the arrest of those rebels, and maddened by my success in catching two or three, he proceeded to extremities that Jonathan Wild himself would have condemned: he went to a village in which were the homes of a couple of the fugitive rebels and cruelly tortured the women of their household to extract information as to the men's whereabouts. It was as brutal a piece of business as a Hindostani policeman could accomplish, and that is saying a good deal. It was promptly reported to me by the Santhals, who if they saw in me an enemy, recognised that I was not an enemy wholly destitute of justice and humanity; and I forwarded their representations and the criminal subject of them to the Commissioner—with the happy consequence that the jemadar got fourteen years' hard labour instead of the blood-money that he had schemed and tortured for. After that my way was smoothed for me: some of those I wanted came into my camp and voluntarily surrendered themselves, the rest were easily apprehended, and Tipoa and his colleagues received a reward (Rs. 500) for the acquisition of which that jemadar would have tortured every woman in the land.

Brought into intimate relations with the Santhals thuswise, I took some of them into my service as domestics. This was an entirely new departure, I believe; for never before, within my knowledge, had a Santhal entered the household of a European in the capacity of a servant. Hitherto these aborigines had been peculiarly exclusive, and had come as little as possible into contact with the people of any other race. What business they had had with Europeans had been strictly confined to revenue matters and exceedingly rare appearances in the Courts. Their business relations with other natives went no further than the absolute necessities of trade required; and while they knew as little of other people as those others knew of them, they had been taught by bitter experience to suspect and hate the Bengali *bunneas* by whom they had been wronged, and, in their ignorance, classified all aliens in the same category as that fitly occupied by the Bengali extortioners.

A simple and very interesting people were the Santhals, and I can only hope that they have retained their characteristics of that time undefiled. Aborigines of the land, they had very possibly lived amidst the forests of Santhalia what time Alexander and Porus joined issue in Northern India, and had been then little more unsophisticated, little more of barbarians, than they were in the middle of the nineteenth century. Barbarians they were to a considerable extent when I knew them, but they were barbarians in whom there was much to admire. Civilisation had done little for them in all the centuries that had followed the Aryan invasion. They had not attained to a written language, their arms and dress and methods of cultivation were as primitive as those of the early Biblical period, and, in spite of their environment, they had retained a confirmed habit of truth-speaking that was altogether out of place in Bengal.

Truth and honesty were the most striking

features in the Santhal character. During my four and a half years' experience as a magistrate in Santhalia no Santhal was ever brought before me on any charge save that of witch-murder. It certainly was not due to any general abstention from crime of other sorts that the Santhal refrained; for the Bengalis and Paharis practised on the most liberal scale every iniquity known to the Penal or Criminal Procedure Codes. The Paharis, also barbarians and aborigines like the Santhals, were just as untruthful and criminal as the more civilised Bengali, and in the matter of larceny and gang-robbery gave me more trouble than any other race. How it had come about that these hillmen were so inferior in morality to their neighbours of the plains is inexplicable. In another particular the two people differed: the Paharis used poisoned arrows that killed whatever creature they punctured, the Santhals used unpoisoned arrows only.

Even in the matter of witch-murder (as to which, by the way, the Santhals were only two centuries behind the people of Great Britain), there was no concealment or evasion. The witch was executed in accordance with Santhal law or rule, and it was the misfortune, not the fault, of the executioner if British jurisprudence had been so unconservative as to abolish this method of dealing with a woman who cast evil eyes about her and brought blight upon the crops, murrain in the herd, and pestilence in the homestead of law-abiding citizens. So, doubtless, argued the unenlightened Santhal in his nebulous mind, while, wanting perspicacity to see that this thing was murder according to latter-day British law, he was not ashamed of the deed done. One case of this sort came up to me for trial, and the delinquent unhesitatingly confessed,—nay, almost effusively admitted what I regarded as his guilt.

The Santhal had some sort of pagan belief and ritual, if of an unenlightened order. He was possessed with a vague idea that the trees were peopled by spirits of the Dryad order, and a flaccid reverence for a Supreme Being, known to him as Chanda Boonga, which he confounded more or less with the sun. There were no Santhal priests (the Santhal Church might have satisfied the Welsh in this respect), and every man was, as a rule, his own primate, rector, curate, churchwarden, and beadle combined. But on occasion, when there was a village gathering, a rite of unusual solemnity occurred, and a cock, after due ceremonial, was sacrificed to Chanda Boonga and eaten by the company. The incantations or invocations of this simple demonism were of a casual description, the main point in the sacrificial preliminaries being the holding of the fowl under one arm—and I think the sacrificial priest had to stand on one leg while he held the bird. In the matter of religion, again, the Santhal differed from the hillman. The Santhal had a dim sense of a Superior and Superhuman Influence; the Pahari had no faith or any approximation thereto. His whole religion and moral code were rounded off by the three commandments—(1) Commit theft or murder, or any other enormity, whenever it suits you to do so; (2) Lie whenever lying is convenient; and (3) Do not be found out. I have no doubt that the missionaries in Santhalia have brought many Santhals within the fold of the Christian Church—they had very promising material to work upon in the case of the Santhals; but I cannot imagine the Paharis being converted to anything, and for their perversion there was certainly no room.

Another point in which these two aboriginal races differed was that of sexual morality: the Santhals were immaculate in this respect; the Paharis had no morality of this sort, or of any other that I was able to discover.

Village government was understood and largely practised by the Santhals, each hamlet having a form of Home Rule that, if only because it precluded resort to the courts for settlement of local disputes, was wholly beneficent in its operation. Doubtless this was something more than the mere gas and water Home Rule advocated by certain Gladstonians at the last general election; other than this it necessarily was, in that gas did not exist for the Santhals, and water was only known as nature laid it on by springs and streams. In a central spot of each Santhal village was the modest Parliament House in which the elders assembled for the discussion of public affairs and adjudication of local squabbles: there were settled matters of weight such as the date and plan of operations of the next great hunting-party, and the time and nature of other tribal or village functions; there, I fear, the local witch was tried. In the open space around this hall the tribal dances were performed; men and women joined in these functions, the former in an inner, the latter in an outer ring, and with much posturing and weird shouting moved to the savage measure of the Santhal drum and reed. They were night dances mostly, and torches played a conspicuous part in them. Without exception, as far as I can remember, the Santhal village communities were homogeneous, no native of any other race being found in them, any more than any Santhal was to be discovered in the villages peopled by aliens. That was a feature that harmonised entirely with the racial exclusiveness. The Santhals kept themselves to themselves in their clusters of well-cared-for homesteads, as they did in their shikar gatherings and all their ways and words. They interfered with nobody outside their own class; they resented the interference of foreigners with themselves: a wholly agricultural people, their commerce with the world beyond the Santhal pale was confined to the settlement of their rent (as to which they never devised any remedial measure of the Land League or Plan of Campaign description), and the barter of some of the produce of their fields for such simple necessaries as they could not themselves raise. I add, with regret, that in the category of these necessaries intoxicating liquor was to be frequently found, and notwithstanding his many virtues, the average Santhal had a marked predilection for drink, and no higher view of local option than the privilege of getting intoxicated as frequently as possible.

But even as far as I have got in my analysis of the Santhal's character the balance largely preponderates on the side of virtue, and if it were necessary, his courage could be invoked to kick the beam. A born and plucky sportsman, he would have been content to live at peace with all men if the *bunnea's* oppressive hand had not driven him into rebellion; but being forced into the open resistance of the powers that be, he carried himself valorously enough: armed only with bow and arrow or the light Santhal axe, he encountered trained sepoys armed with muskets and bayonets and led by British officers—and, what is more, on two occasions, by dint of pluck and numbers, worsted their better equipped foes.

Even if my description of them has failed to make the Santhals appear interesting, there is something to be added that must infallibly have that result. The Santhals, like the Paharis, Coles, and Bheels, and other aboriginal tribes dotted about the plains of Hindostan, are the veritable sons of the soil. They are the descendants of those Indians who were driven from their possessions into the wilds and forests by the Aryan invaders, whose successors now pose as Hindoos. They were prior to this irruption a more civilised people than their conquerors from the cradle of the human race, as now they are, as far as the Santhals are concerned, more estimable in many ways: archæological research has proved so much of the past; and in the present who shall deny that these aboriginal people, lapsed away from civilisation though they be, are not the true Indians whose just heritage will be that brightest jewel of the British Crown whenever the India for the Indian lunatics shall have their way? The spectacle of India with Tipoa Santhal for its King or Prime Minister would be highly entertaining to those whose sense of humour eclipses all other emotions; but the Bengali, and especially the *bunnea*, would certainly fail to see the fun of it. And what would De Souza say to this new dispensation? For it is the way of De Souza, who is one part Portuguese and nineteen parts hybrid Indian, to talk of England as Home, and therefore to regard himself as one of the British garrison. Neither he nor any of his forebears has ever visited Europe; neither he nor any of his descendants is ever likely to cross the "black water." For many generations his family have known no other home than Cossitollah, and yet England is home to him by word of mouth. I had such a De Souza in my establishment, and he never spoke of England in any other terms. He did his best to live up to this claim to British nationality, as far as forms of speech were concerned: thus he always spoke of the hills of the Rajmahal range as the Highlands, just as if they had been the Caledonian mountains.

Tipoa, not elevated to the exalted position of Sultan or Vizier of Hindostan, having been my right hand in the arrest of fourteen rebels of his race, was of immense assistance to me in raising a Santhal regiment. It was at the special request of the Lieutenant-Governor of Bengal (Sir F. Halliday) that I set about recruiting for this important addition to the native army, and I was specially thanked by his Excellency when I had enlisted the limited number required, between 250 and 300. But Tipoa, who was a very efficient recruiting-sergeant, obtained no thanks save mine, no pecuniary reward whatever, and no other recognition of his services beyond that of being regarded by the corps in the light of a regimental flag; for from the outset, whenever my regiment was paraded, Tipoa's presence was an essential feature of the function,—not that he was required to, or could, do anything beyond being there in the flesh. He could not drill them any more than I could; he could not have been relied upon to address the men in convincing terms on any subject whatever; he was necessary only as something to look at, and in this respect he was so entirely indispensable that even when drunk he was brought upon the parade-ground and laid out there to be seen, not as a warning beacon but as a rallying-point. He was just as effective when in this condition as when he was sober.

I should say that my experience as commandant of this regiment during the first month or two was as unique as the regiment itself. My men in the early part of their military career were clothed only in the national dress—a scrap of cloth round the loins, which was the Santhal's concession to sartorial exigencies and the first advance beyond the fig-leaf stage of costume. Falstaff would not have marched with my men through the smallest hamlet, let alone Coventry; and wild as was the dress of my men, it was not more hopelessly unmartial than their drill and bearing. The goose-step was for them—even for the centurions of these legionaries—as abstruse a matter as the differential calculus: I had no information to impart to them upon this and other rudiments of their profession, and as to Tipoa, the honorary second in command of that time, he was not required to do or know anything more than a flag-staff.

But, wholly undrilled, and, in that sense, undisciplined as they were, they behaved admirably during those early days when mostly they were on the line of march. They were willing, orderly, and obedient, and they relinquished the drinking business to Tipoa, who would have been more aptly named Tipsy at that time, and who in this matter of tippling seemed inspired by an unholy desire to compensate by his solitary efforts for the abstinence of the 300. Perhaps it was by way of further compensation that the 300 took to physic while in my charge; at any rate they speedily emptied my well-stored medicine-chest, the last physic parade that I held having found me with only two drugs left—rhubarb and magnesia—which I doled out alternately.

I did much more for my regiment medicinally than in any other way; when cough seized upon some of them, I gargled rank and file through the whole force. I had plenty of honey and vinegar in store, and these supplied the material for this astringent application in quantity. The regiment when gargling in full blast ought to have been very terrible to any enemy not absolutely stone-deaf.

But my medical attentions culminated in vaccination. I vaccinated the 300, duly paraded to receive more or less of a lancet and a less uncertain quantity of lymph. It was my first appearance as a vaccinator, and I could not adapt my operations to the pachydermatous variations in my patients: now a hide presented itself that resisted the lancet as if it had been that of a rhinoceros, and that I barely punctured; then came a more delicate epidermis, such as the pigskin used for saddles, and into that the lancet entered to the depth of half an inch. But truly were those men patients in the fullest sense. Vaccination of the roughest, gargling, and physicking all came to them, if not as unmixed and unveiled boons, as blessings in disguise that it was meet to receive gratefully and with faith: after all, faith is everything in medicine. Faith and bread-pills combined may be freely backed against the whole College of Physicians and entire Pharmacopœia where faith is not. And my Santhals flourished under my 'prentice hand, and were transferred, sound and contented, to trained officers and a duly qualified surgeon. Poor patient savages! I was loth to part with them when they were marched away from Deoghur to their quarters in Hazaribagh.

Delightful as Deoghur was in many respects when I first went to it, nothing very favourable can be said of the character of its people other than Santhals. Many of those others had hitherto been law-abiding only so far as they had been coerced in that direction, their natural proclivities inclining strongly towards a more convenient lawlessness, and the mutiny of Deoghur enabled them for a time to follow their inclination. The murder of the Assistant Commissioner removed the restraint of a local magisterial authority, and the destruction of the station buildings emphasised the suspension of British authority and administration of justice. With the magistrate and other symbols of order, departed such lymphatic respect for the laws as had hitherto been extracted from the evil-minded of the people. Moreover, as if there had not been already more than enough of rascaldom in the enjoyment of undeserved freedom, the mutinous sepoys opened the doors of the Deoghur jail and let loose upon the world a stream of scoundrelism that would have effectually polluted an immaculate population.

Dacoitee, highway robbery, and other heinous offences against persons and property had become dangerously fashionable, and, developing in vogue, had come to be patronised by rajahs and other leaders of native society. Gang-robbery had come to such a pass that robbers, yet new to their profession, abandoned caution as they had the semblance of honesty. So incautious were they that in my first month at Deoghur I rode down a band of them, catching them *flagrante delicto* and vainly trying to escape with their plunder. This success and the *kudos* that came of it resulted, I fear, in my becoming something of a thorn in the official flesh of my chief, Sir George Yule; for, disregarding the instructions of Talleyrand, I became zealous, and by way of striking at the heads that directed plunder and pillage as well as at the hands that executed those offences, I clapt some half-dozen rajahs into jail for six months, and gave quite an aristocratic tone to that place of retirement. This my Commissioner pronounced a high-handed business, but came to approve of in appeal. But when zeal for the purity of my court led me to the summary punishment by stripes of two perjurers who should in due course have been committed to the sessions for trial, Yule could not signify approval in any way, any more than he could undo those stripes that had been administered immediately after my fiat. It was a terrible business. As a magistrate I had finally dealt with a case that a sessions judge should have disposed of, and I had sentenced the perjurers to a penalty that not even a sessions judge could have imposed. My offending was to Yule such as parricide was to the ancient Greeks — so enormous that it was inconceivable, and therefore unpunishable. Yule declined to put his wigging of me upon the record; he invited me to come to him and receive it by word of mouth. I went, and the awful judgment descended upon me in the brief form, "Well, you are a pretty fellow!"

It was some compensation for this blighting verdict that after that summary affair witnesses in my court were careful not to lie too outrageously.

The Mutiny, which was responsible for much of the demoralisation of the Deoghurites, deserves something more than mere passing notice. As there was much that was wholly inexplicable about the revolt of the sepoy regiments generally, so, too, was it with the two N.I. companies at Deoghur and the headquarters of the 5th Irregular Cavalry at the adjoining village of Rhooni. The history of the sedition of India's pampered native army was throughout a long chronicle of surprises and contradictions: almost always it was the unexpected that happened, or the expected that happened at a time when it was least looked for. One regiment, not marked by any special attachment to the European officers, having mutinied, marched those officers down to the Ganges, put them comfortably on board covered boats, and sent them off unharmed with an advance of a month's pay out of the pillaged regimental pay-chest: another regiment, not regarded as specially inimical to the white officers, mutinied *en masse* and shot their officers down as they left the mess. Here a regiment broke out thus unanimously without any preliminary sign of disaffection; there a regiment threatened and murmured, and remained, or mutinied and went off in detachments. The whole history of that great upheaval is, in fact, a narrative of contrarieties, and the Deoghur episode forms an appropriate page of it.

It began with the 5th Irregular Cavalry stationed at Rhooni, two and a half miles from the Deoghur station, and the beginning was quietly murderous. Major Macdonald, the commandant, Sir Norman Leslie, the second in command, and the doctor were sitting outside the mess after dinner quietly enjoying their tobacco and the cool air of night, when they were attacked from behind by swordsmen, who cut down Sir Norman Leslie with a mortal blow across the neck, scalped Major Macdonald, and wounded the doctor in the arm. Poor Leslie fell dead in his lounging-chair; the other two, wounded as they were, sprang to their feet, seized each a dining-room chair, and hitting at their assailants blindly in the dark, made for the mess bungalow. There the tragedy of the situation was relieved by a touch of grim comedy; for Macdonald and the doctor, stumbling into contact in a dark room, were about to batter each other with their chairs, when the voice of one stopped the conflict, and both gave way to a burst of laughter instead of the angry shout of battle.

But lights being brought by the startled servants, it was soon seen that the hour was not one for mirth. Macdonald and the doctor were only slightly wounded, but there in front of the mess-house Leslie was stretched dead. The question was, Who had done this foul thing? upon whom should vengeance fall? Macdonald was a man likely in such a case as this to prove unrelenting in the pursuit and punishment of the murderers—a very Nemesis to whom the manes of his butchered comrade should not appeal in vain. But whom should he pursue? He could not believe that his own troopers had been guilty of this atrocity: he and the native officers took counsel together, and decided that some wandering party of another regiment must have made this night attack as they passed through Rhooni.

So, lulled in the happy belief that their own men were innocent, the officers looked elsewhere for the guilty ones, and, but for the vigilance and splendid loyalty of the *wardi-major*, so might they have continued to look, and look in vain always; for the murderers were there within their gates—the troopers of their own too greatly trusted regiment.

It came to the ears of the *wardi-major* (the senior native officer) that one of the 5th troopers had gone to the native regimental doctor early in the morning after Leslie's murder to have his hand dressed. The trooper presented this hand and a plausible cock-and-bull story as to how it bore something suspiciously like a sword-cut upon it, and the *wardi-major* having heard of this incident, made it the starting-point of a new line of inquiry that was immediately successful in eliciting the truth. The crime of the night was, before the next day closed, traced to three of the 5th troopers. On the second day those men were tried by a court-martial, of which the native officers were members, and Macdonald president: the unanimous decision of that court was for all three prisoners guilty, and the sentence death by hanging on the following morning.

If this finding of the court-martial was a severe tax upon the loyalty of the native officers, still more heavily was that quality taxed by their presence at the execution that followed; but they flinched not, albeit some among them were yet to become mutineers. Not yet had their faith succumbed. The whole regiment paraded on an open space surrounded by the groves of Rhooni; the two companies of N.I. from Deoghur were also drawn up on the ground to witness the death of the three traitors to the British raj; and all these—sepoys and sowars alike—stood mutely by while those executions occurred, and patiently bore with an example that was for the majority of them only of temporary effect.

And these native soldiers who saw their brethren in arms, and the comrades of some of them, die a disgraceful death, were subjected to some temptation to mutiny there and then; for one of the condemned men, when the three were led to the gallows, commenced to harangue the assembled natives with such appeals to their religion, their passions, and their self-interests as might well, if uninterrupted, have resulted in a general rise and the rescue of the murderers. But an interruption came in time. Macdonald was as prompt as courageous: he saw the danger of unbridled talk of this sort, and he put a stop to it by a threat to blow out the brains of the speaker if he uttered another word. I cannot explain why that sowar preferred being hanged from the branch of a tree to being shot—but so it was: perhaps he, like other natives on the ground, was overawed by Macdonald's undaunted front. Be that as it may, he went to his death by the rope in silence, Macdonald's pistol covering him until the chance of speech had gone from him for ever. Then the parade broke up, and the sowars and sepoys went to their quarters peaceably, and to all appearance loyal to the core.

Soon after that the headquarters of the 5th Irregular Cavalry left Rhooni to join the wing of the regiment at Bhagulpore. Week after week, month after month, went by, and still the 5th remained in their lines, to all appearances contented and true to their salt. It really seemed as if this was one of the very few regiments that were to escape from the widespread contagion of mutiny; and then, *à propos* of nothing, without rhyme or reason, or a warning note, more than half the regiment rode off one night for Delhi,—the great point of attraction in the Mutiny maelstrom,—whitherward the revolted native troops, horse and foot, Mahomedans and Hindoos, poured from the various cantonments of India to swell the forces of the last of the Moguls.

So went the majority of the 5th, while the minority and the gallant *wardi-major* remained true to the flag to the bitter end; and with the majority went two young sowars whose father and two brothers were left with the loyal section of the regiment.

One could hardly have a better illustration than this of the inconsequence, the violation of probability, that characterised the Indian Mutiny. Here were a father and his four sons serving in a regiment with which it was a distinction to be connected, and suddenly two of these sons broke with the nearest ties of blood and honour, and were off, heaven knows where or to what end. But that does not represent the whole incongruity or improbability of this affair, as I proceed to show.

On the morning following immediately upon the desertion of those two sons, the father went to Major Macdonald and fell at his feet with piteous plaint. Two of his sons had been misled by the *haramzadas* of the regiment and carried off, he said; "he was heart-sore at their desertion of flag and father, and would be lost—a broken man—if they were not restored. There was hope, however, that this cruel fate would not befall; he had yet two sons, and one of these might overtake his mutinous comrades, and rescue his brothers from their hands." Then came the entreaty that a third son might be sent upon this mission.

The third son departed, the time went on, and reluctantly the father had to accept the terrible consequence of that effort to recover his two lost ones—he had now to realise that a third was gone from him. But another and last chance remained to him in that fourth son, and, with the commandant's assent, that Benjamin of the flock went forth. And he returned; but he came back alone. His brothers had refused to listen to his entreaties: casting honour to the winds, and ignoring all duty to their father, they had ridden away unyielding and forsworn.

Inconsequence was a marked feature of the mutiny of the two companies of infantry at Deoghur. There were with these sepoys two British officers—a captain who, for some considerable time, had devoted himself to his men, and a subaltern who had consistently ignored the existence of the sepoys otherwise than duty compelled him to give his attention to them. The captain had for months spent his pay in treats to the rank and file, and his time in arranging wrestling-matches and other *tumashas* for them. The subaltern had consistently abstained from any share in these frivolities, and kept himself to himself so disdainfully that his men, exhausting their whole fund of charity in his behalf, decided that he was a harmless lunatic.

A succession of *tumashas* and gifts from the open-handed captain may have stayed the mutiny: it did not prevent that mutiny bursting forth when the hour was ripe for it. The outbreak commenced in the early morning on the parade-ground. The prologue of the tragedy was performed by one man, who lunged at the captain with his bayonet. But for the captain's intervention that act of overt disaffection would have been promptly punished by the senior native officer, who offered to run his sword through the mutineer. Who shall say whether prompt retaliation such as that the subadar proposed to administer would or would not have arrested the mutiny, which was so far confined to the action of one offender? At the worst, it would not have effected less in the way of checking a general *émeute* than the course adopted by the captain, who, still seeking to placate the implacable, dismissed the parade and retired. That was the signal for open revolt by all whose sympathies were with the forces of disorder; and before the British officers (accompanied by the subadar, two loyal sepoys, and a *bheesti*) could reach the Assistant Commissioner's bungalow, a furlong distant from the parade-ground, shots were fired and the mutiny was a terrible reality, not now to be hindered or mitigated by largess or wrestling—not now to be dealt with otherwise than with lead and steel, if only there were enough of these.

By the time the six persons above mentioned reached the bungalow they were obviously retreating before an enemy, and the bungalow was their refuge and the fort they had to hold against 150 bloodthirsty sepoys. Here they were joined by the Assistant Commissioner, who unfortunately returned to his home in the belief that English authority would prevail. He and a friend who was staying with him (Mr Grigor Grant) had started from the bungalow as soon as the first shots were fired: they had gone about a furlong in the direction of the Byjinauth jungle, where safety was to be had, when the Assistant Commissioner paused. Duty was stronger in him than care for personal safety: he was the one civil authority of the district, and he convinced himself that the situation was not so utterly hopeless that the performance of duty must necessarily involve sacrifice of life; so he went to his death with that quiet and unsung heroism which marked the close of many an Englishman's career in 1857.

He argued with Grant that the two might safely return, that the mutiny was the work of but a few; but as he spoke these reassuring words there came a volley from the lines and the pattering of many bullets upon the hard ground about them. That volley decided Grant's action: he continued his retreat, gained cover in some ravines close at hand, and by these made his way unmolested and unsought to a hut, whose peasant proprietor gave him asylum, fed him, and escorted him by night on his way to Bhagulpore. Grant did not forget the man who had done so much to save him. That peasant received from Grant a gift that made a *jagirdar*, or landowner, of him.

So were there seven in that beleaguered bungalow, and surrounding them sevenscore sepoys, who, keeping up a steady fire through the venetianed doors and windows, closed in unceasingly in narrowing circle. Resistance might have kept them at bay, or indeed have driven them off,—at least resistance would have encouraged the better disposed of the sepoys to stand aloof from, or possibly to actively oppose, the revolt; at the worst it could not have been a more disastrous policy than quiescence. Unfortunately, there was no resistance. The captain in command of that small garrison sought to the last to move the foe (now wild with passion and elated by partial triumph) by all the arts of propitiation; he would not permit of a shot being fired upon the advancing enemy, even when they came with lighted brands to fire the thatch of the bungalow and drive out the unfortunates it sheltered.

The subadar and two sepoys were shot down in the bungalow, but the three Englishmen had escaped from death or wound by bullet, when it became a question whether they would perish in the flames which gathered force and volume every minute, or run the gantlet outside. When this critical moment arrived some of the sergeants and corporals (the havildars and naiks) of the regiment came close to the door of a bathroom, into which the three sahibs had been driven by fire, and made overtures to save one of those three. It might have been expected of these men, regarding them as reasoning creatures, that the subaltern who had disdained and ridiculed them would have been the last to receive mercy at their hands. Incongruity being an almost necessary factor of Indian Mutiny procedure, he was the first, and, unhappily, the only one chosen. Him, and him only, would they spare: him, when he had gone forth to them from under the burning roof, the four or five protectors surrounded and shielded with their bodies from the more evil-minded sepoys who threatened bayonet-thrust or musket-shot, or might not be trusted lest they should do worse than threaten. So those better disposed of the mutineers guarded him out of the press and on to the now deserted lines, where they put him into a dhoolie, drew the curtains round him, and had him carried off Bhagulporewards; they escorted him throughout, and, where it was necessary for his safety, replying to curious inquirers with the figment that the dhoolie contained a native woman—the wife or sister of him who spoke. And while these few were thus mercifully engaged, the many effected a purpose in which there was no hint of ruth. The two white men who now remained in the burning bungalow were doomed; chance of escape there was none that they could reckon upon. There remained to them only the choice between death by the fire of their asylum and death at the cruel hands of the sepoys outside. They chose that which was the less absolutely certain—death in the open. They burst forth from the bathroom, made a dash for the ravines, and were killed before they had covered half the distance to such slight cover as those ravines provided.

Having thus effaced British authority as represented by Englishmen, and having also completed their work of destruction of the Deoghur station buildings, the two companies (save only those who had gone on escort duty with the subaltern) marched Delhiwards. The most evil-minded and the least evil-minded united in this movement, and not a man of them remained.

As I have already said, these sepoys opened the doors of the Deoghur jail and let loose so much of rascaldom as then happened to be cooped up within the walls of that prison. Among those who were thus released, and without doubt the worst of them, was a Pahari lying under sentence of death for several murders and dacoitees, and more than one case of arson.

This man and another had been the leaders of a gang of Pahari dacoits some twenty to twenty-five in number, including six or seven women, who were only mitigated scoundrels by comparison with their male associates in crime. There had been no concealment about the operations of this gang: the law and its few and feeble guardians had been frankly defied, and the people generally paralysed by sudden and ruthless attacks that they could no more resist than can the lamb when the eagle swoops down upon it.

Now here, now there, these dacoits descended from their hill fastnesses upon the peaceful hamlets of the plains. A shower of arrows — possibly poisoned arrows—heralded their approach, and fire applied to the roof expedited the opening of doors barred against them. Murder and arson were not necessarily employed, but there was no hesitation about the employment of these extreme measures upon very slight occasion. These plunderers would brook neither opposition nor delay, and if a peaceful villager had to be slain or a village burned in the course of business, so much the worse for the obtuse peasants.

When I arrived at Deoghur, this gang, under the dual leadership of Dilbur (the escaped from jail) and Mundila, were plying their nefarious trade more energetically than ever. They had just before my advent signalised their objection to any interference of the authorities by cutting the throat of a spy sent to look them up in the Phuljoori hill, and were now raiding the country-side from their retreat in Teeur. The capture of these scoundrels was a necessity of the situation that had to be met by unrelaxing energy: other matters were of secondary importance, and could well be postponed until Dilbur & Co. were effaced somehow; so I pitched my camp close under the Teeur heights, placed a cordon of volunteer police round the hill, and laid a siege which I knew must be more or less protracted.

It was idle to expect that any good would result from an attack of the dacoits on the hill conducted by ill-armed or unarmed peasants; such an attack, delivered by half a company of disciplined native infantry, had failed signally. I reckoned upon capturing them in the plain, to which commissariat necessities must drive the dacoits, inasmuch as the hill of Teeur produced nothing edible of a vegetable nature, and very little animal food that the Paharis could get hold of; and in the course of four weeks I and my auxiliaries had captured the whole gang save and except the joint-leader Mundila, who died on the hill. The smoke ascending from Mundila's funeral-pyre was the only indication of a fire on Teeur during those four weeks.

Then I had to undertake the heaviest criminal case, as far as the number of prisoners was concerned, of my magisterial career. Dilbur and thirteen other men, with half-a-dozen women, stood in the dock, a round score of unmitigated scoundrels. Their faces should have been sufficient to hang them; guilt-hardened, brazen, and animal stood declared as obviously in those twenty countenances as it is wont to do in the adumbrations of notabilities (statesmen, divines, &c.) with which certain penny and halfpenny journals illustrate (but not adorn) their pages.

Of course they pleaded not guilty. True to nothing else, they were true to their reputations for consistent falsehood. Even Dilbur, already tried and sentenced to the death penalty, persisted, as far as his intellectual gifts permitted, in describing himself as the Naija equivalent of a Christian martyr and latter-day saint. But the cases against the prisoners were too strong: they were all convicted. Dilbur was hanged and the remainder sentenced to various terms of imprisonment. So ended dacoity as far as the Paharis were concerned.

Dilbur accepted the situation with that complete equanimity which characterises alike the Indian native aboriginals and the Aryans. I endeavoured to be impressive (being then a novice) when I pronounced his sentence to capital punishment. I am afraid that I was something theatrical in my delivery of the awe-inspiring sentences suitable to the occasion. I played very touchingly upon the tremolo stop; but, as I ought to have foreseen, none of my auditory was moved by my address, and least of all Dilbur, for whose especial advantage I had exerted myself.

This reminds me of the very free and appropriate rendering given by an interpreter to a similar delivery by an Anglo-Indian judge who spoke in English to the condemned culprit. The judge endeavoured to be impressive, and at all events succeeded, like myself, in being voluminous. For ten minutes or more our Rhadamanthus spoke eloquently about the terrors of the prisoner's pitiable state and the pressing need for that hurried reform which, in the case of British criminals, is supposed to convert a life-long offender into a spotless member of the elect in five minutes. But the interpreter knew his man better, and the discourse of many minutes was put into four words, "Iao sala, pharsi hogo!"—"Go, brute, you will be hanged!"

Dilbur, like Indians generally, was no more moved by the execution than by the sentence. Lest he should break jail again, he was put into irons of unusual weight, but he carried those bonds up the steps of a rudely constructed scaffold without assistance. Being under the gallows he helped the hangman to arrange the rope round his neck; and the only remark he made before the bolt was shot was in the form of a request that I would provide for his wife during the remainder of her life. I suppose that some glimmering of reason had penetrated that animal carcass at that critical moment, and that this inspired the idea in Dilbur's mind that his execution was a meritorious performance on his part which might fairly be rewarded by a pension to his relict.

The *churruck—i.e.*, the swinging of men from lofty poles during the Churruck Pooja—was interdicted by the Government of India while I was at Deoghur; but the edict did not receive that immediate attention or implicit obedience that one could have wished. In one place I intervened when the *churruck* was, so to speak, in full swing, and stopped the proceedings; but I could not be everywhere at once, and in some localities in my district the *churruck* proceeded in the first year of the interdict without let or hindrance. I supposed that it could hardly be expected that implicit obedience should be given at once to an order which deprived the people of a time-honoured practice and festival—even now one reads of the *churruck* being perpetuated in some parts of India; and it is quite possible that the more baneful rite of suttee, in spite of a much older prohibition, is still occasionally performed.

It was my duty in those Deoghur days to prevent a young widow from immolating herself upon her deceased husband's pyre. Information of her intention to suttee herself reached me, and I rode hard to the scene of intended burning—only arriving just in time. Terribly in earnest was the woman and terribly obstinate. It is to the average man such an unusual experience to meet a woman who is determined to have her own way, and is also regardless of logical reasoning, that, having encountered such a woman in this Hindoo widow, I almost felt at times that it would have been infinitely more comfortable to me if I had found her in ashes instead of in tears and a passion. I am not sure that the whole village community of which she was a member did not share this opinion. The baulked martyr showed infinite capacity for becoming the loud-mouthed virago, and when I restored her to her native hamlet under surveillance, I have little doubt that the principal motive that induced her to continue living was the consciousness that her neighbours would have greatly preferred to have mourned the loss of her.

What elements of romance were possible to the situation of that rescue! I think Jules Verne has turned them to account in one of his books ('Round the World in Eighty Days'), and it is with all possible regret that I am not privileged to make copy out of them here. It would have been agreeable to me to write of myself as another bold Lochinvar, and of her as a drooping and unwilling beauty dragged to the funeral-pile by inhuman priests of Moloch; snatched from the burning, and borne away from her cruel fate upon my swift Arabian (and the agony-inflicting crupper of my saddle); and, when we had sought rest and shelter in a grove, beaming upon me with gratitude and love out of a newly-awakened heart and unfathomable brown eyes (of the ox, or fawn, or any other ruminant) draped with cheek-sweeping lashes, &c., &c. That sort of thing would have been especially pleasant to dilate upon, if it had had any foundation in experience. As a fact, the woman I rescued from a self-imposed destruction was an ill-tempered tangle-headed vixen, with no more sentiment in her than is to be found in a tadpole, and as much ill-nature and power of vituperation as goes with a drunken fishwife.

During the week of this present writing a good deal has been said and written about recent *churruck* performances in Southern India, and not a little exaggeration perpetrated in regard to the character of that ceremonial. Now I saw a good deal of it in Lower Bengal when it was allowed to be practised without restriction, and although I think it well to put a stop to it as a brutal spectacle not likely to edify or improve those who witness it, I believe the immediate performers or victims suffered no serious physical pain and no permanent injury, and, moreover, suffered nothing except by their own free will.

Possibly these victims, when for a day or two before the *churruck* they paraded through village and hamlet with iron skewers through their tongues or ears, and when on the day of the festival they were swung from the *churruck* pole—possibly all through the piece these victims were drugged to a certain extent. But they were never sufficiently stupefied by bhang or gauja to be unconscious of the facts that they were the heroes of the occasion, and that their heroism was paid for; and, after all, when it came to the half-hour of their supreme trial, when they were swung by hooks thrust through the sinews over their shoulder-blades, they were not held aloft by the frail skin and tendons only, but more by strong bandages of cloth swathed round their chests that would have supported them even had there been no iron hook with a loop of human flesh attached to it. But, even so, it is a ceremonial that may well be dispensed with—another incitement to insensibility as to physical suffering and human life withdrawn from the observation of people who need no teaching of that sort.

Although, as Assistant Commissioner of Deoghur, I came to discover what work really was; although I had to toil in court and study some ten to twelve hours a-day, and bear, as a sort of initiative Atlas, the whole Deoghur world upon my shoulders,—I enjoyed myself fairly well during the four and a half years that I held that post. Indeed, in some respects the District Officer is of all Indian officialdom the most fortunately placed. If he possess reasonable energy and force of character, he is throughout his own jurisdiction something much more powerful than the Rhine baron of the feudal days—something only slightly less potent than a Plantagenet or Tudor king. It is true that the people know of a *lat sahib* (the

Viceroy and Governor-General) by hearsay; but that being supreme among men is up in Simla, or down in Calcutta, and as completely removed from the life-sphere of the Indian ryot as if he were a resident of the planet Mars. The commissioner or judge who presides over a superior court at the district or divisional headquarters is, when an appeal is forward, of some importance to litigants; but for general purposes neither of these high officials comes into such close and frequent contact with the people as the District Officer; neither has such influence over and knowledge of the people as he.

Perhaps the most trying duty that falls to the District Officer is that interminable one of report-writing. Official routine requires of every Indian departmental head at least an annual report: it demands of the unfortunate District Officer various contributions of that sort, and, in addition, occasional reports upon every conceivable subject under the Eastern sun. It requires of the writer much wholly wasted logic and ingenuity to prove something that baffles demonstration—*e.g.*, that a 5 per cent increase of burglary is explained by a 20 per cent falling off in attendance at the Zillah school, or some such out-of-the-way feat of ratiocination. Sometimes it calls for unaccustomed or non-existent scientific knowledge, as, for example, when the officers of Gangetic districts were called upon to report on the Gangetic dolphin. But for these reports the District Officer's life might be a sufficiently happy one. The baneful effect of them upon the officer's intellect and energy is strangely shown by the fact that, although they encourage an outrageous style of imaginative writing, they have educated very few of the writers of them into novelists; the reports have absorbed all the powers of fiction possessed by those who penned them.

Another thorn in the flesh of the District Officer of my day was the Hunterian method of spelling—I am too old-fashioned to call it orthography. When Sir William (then Mr W. W. Hunter) descended upon the land as a reforming lexicographer—when he smote the official report-writer hip and thigh with novel consonants, vowels of strange values, and accents that were as new as they were uncertain—then the annual and other reports became much more of a weariness than they had been theretofore. But the new method spread in spite of a healthy conservative opposition to such new-fangled ideas—perhaps its novelty and uncertainty recommended it to many to whom any change whatever in the dull routine of official life was acceptable. The restless, the revolutionists, and the iconoclasts accepted it with enthusiasm, and would have out-Huntered Hunter by profane transformation of time-honoured names, precious to the Indian historian, into unrecognisable shapes. Cawnpore they would have converted into Khanpur; Lucknow into Lakhnau; and so with many others. But to this the great body of public opinion was so strongly opposed that the new form of spelling had to be confined to places of minor importance; whence has arisen the curious flaw in the Hunterian system, that it must depend a good deal upon the consequence of a city or town whether one shall spell its name intelligibly or as Hunterism directs.

During my career as District Officer I had ample experience of a fact which is of very general application, and very creditable to British rule in India—to wit, that the natives infinitely prefer to have their cases heard and decided by an Englishman rather than by one or more of their own people. Circumstances forced this knowledge upon me with considerable emphasis. I had throughout my four and a half years at Deoghur very heavy files,—civil, revenue, and criminal,—and many of the cases before me were such as should have been more appropriately heard and decided by arbitrators of the litigants' race and caste. Complicated inheritance suits, which involved nice points of native custom and debatable questions as to whether the Mitakshara or some local law applied; suits involving intricate accounts running over many years, and others, would have been more readily comprehended by natives familiar with the matter in hand than by any alien. But my suggestion that any of these should be referred to arbitrators was almost invariably met with the assertion that the suitors preferred that I should decide their case; and more than once those suitors have clearly intimated to me their view that the principal feature of arbitration was the bribing of the arbitrators.

Is there not here a cogent—nay, an unanswerable—argument against the cry of India for the Indians? Apart from all considerations of social differences that make the government of India by any one of its several peoples impracticable, how shall we get over the difficulty that comes of this preference of the natives for British rulers rather than rulers of their own race and sect? The native mistrusts his own brotherhood almost to a man (and more to a woman), and loves them just as much as may be convenient. He loves the Englishman no better, or even less; but, as a rule, he believes in him and looks to him as the only possible fount of justice. He doubtless regards the Briton's views about truth as ridiculously strait-laced and unpractical, but he respects him in a way because of that strange veneration for an inconvenient virtue; and because of that and the Briton's larger sense of justice (as an unsaleable commodity), prefers the alien rule to that of any of his fellow-countrymen.

More than this the natives do not want of us; they certainly do not want to mix with us intimately in social life. In the court, or cutcherry, or office, or at the durbar, they forgather with Europeans and transact business or go through barbaric ceremonial with them; but there is no intercommunion between the two races in any matter concerning the family and inner life of either, and the native is, I think, exclusively to blame for this state of things.

What encouragement does the native give that should cause the Briton to open his heart to him? None! When the Rajah or Reis calls upon a sahib, he does so as a disagreeable duty. He talks about the weather (and that is the only English feature of the occasion), the crops, the electric telegraph, or maybe the balloon; then he fidgets uneasily, so that the sahib has to release him with the necessary *rooksut* (high polite for the Yankee "get"). Then he shakes hands with his host; and then, as likely as not, he goes straightway to a retainer outside the door, who holds in hand a basin of water, wherein the Reis or Rajah may wash off the pollution of that handshake with the Christian. Is that sort of thing calculated to make us rush into the arms of our Aryan brothers the Hindoos? Can there be any intimacy with men of whom to ask how their wives are is a dire offence against good manners—to whom one may not address one word about their female relatives, even down to their cousins and aunts? Can one adopt as one's own especial Pylades a man who regards one's wife in the light of a hireling nautch-girl because he is permitted to see her waltzing round a ballroom—who admires her (if at all he admires) in a peculiarly reprehensible way, and who wonders, as a certainty, why this dancing is not done by paid *coryphées* from the bazaar?

CHAPTER VI.

THE DEOGHUR TIGERS.

THE SHRINE OF BYJINAUTH—MAN-EATING TIGERS—A NIGHT IN A *MACHAN*—THE *FIRST* BYJINAUTH TIGER—THE SPRING-BOW—A HYENA—A CAVE INCIDENT—BUFFALO FOR BEAR—PANTHERS—WOLF-SHOOTING—TRACKING A WOUNDED TIGER—A BRACE OF TIGERS.

AT Deoghur I found myself not only in the midst of big game, but, happily, clear of the malarious country. Jungle was there throughout the district, interspersed with cultivated tracts and towns and villages. Sometimes the cultivated lands were but mall clearings in the forest depths, sometimes the forest was a mere fringe of the settlements; but everywhere and always the jungle was more or less at hand—tree jungle with a dense undergrowth, wherein the tiger and the panther found congenial homes, and the bear a pleasant hunting-ground.

For the most part the country was undulating throughout, and had, as a frequent dominant feature, a hill that rose sheer out of the plain—a stony outcrop, unconnected with any range, that varied from the dwarf mountain of 1200 feet in height, such as Teeur or Phooljoori, to the unnamed rock-pile of 50 feet. The rivers were hill-streams that, in dry weather, trickled through their gravelly beds, and after rain rushed seaward as torrents. I have ridden across one of these rivers in the morning when the water only covered my horse's fetlocks, and, returning in the afternoon, have had to swim it—then ten feet of rapid, bearing upon its angry bosom uprooted trees and other wreckage of its course. These rivers provided for the district a splendid drainage-system, and the only scheme of sanitation known or required.

The station of Deoghur (which consisted of the bungalows of myself and my assistant, the Government cutcherry, and the ruins of the barracks where two mutinous companies of a native infantry regiment had been quartered) stood upon a height which commanded the native town and the renowned Hindoo temple of Byjinauth. This temple, served by 360 Brahmin priests or pundas, ranked in the Hindoo mind with that of Juggurnauth at Pooree, and pilgrims in hundreds of thousands poured into the town at certain seasons to lay their votive offerings at the idol's feet, to fill the purses of the pundas, and to disseminate amongst the town's folks such smallpox or cholera as might be going then. Byjinauth's fane was a constant thorn in my official flesh, and provided me with a considerable amount of work. There was a standing difficulty about the chief pundaship that was always at hand to occupy my diplomatic skill—a difficulty that arose, if I rightly remember, out of this *de facto* high priest having failed to observe the rule of celibacy required by his office. He was a man of strong family instincts, and would not give up his wife and children; he was also a man of marked acquisitiveness, and would not forgo the emoluments of the chief pundaship,—and no diplomacy of mine could adjust this difficulty. When I left Deoghur, after nearly five years, that obstinate flamen was still battling with a less domestic priest who sought to oust him from the musnud. Then the other 359 pundas were always at loggerheads with each other or with any available outsider,—frequently about their *chelas* or disciples, but about anything or anybody when the chela failed as motive for a row. And, finally, the wretched pilgrims gave constant trouble, in that they were plundered by the priests and other robbers no less professional, who found their opportunity of thieving in the crowded town, just as if

Deoghur had been Trafalgar Square on a demonstration day.

The work provided for me by these people and others of the district was sufficiently to my taste, and I slaved in the Deoghur cutcherry and in camp when I went on tour as magistrate, collector, judge, &c., eight, ten, and twelve hours a-day, and every day, with one reservation—that whenever news was brought of a tiger, panther, or bear anywhere within twenty miles, my court was to be closed *instanter*. That rule was appreciated by the people I had to deal with: many of them had a liking for sport, and would turn out in hundreds to beat the jungle for me without fee or reward; many of them, and notably the Santhals and Paharis, did some amount of shikar on their own account; and all of them either had been or might be sufferers by the cruel work of the animals I went forth to slay.

For during the time of my predecessor (who did not shoot) these creatures had increased to a very serious extent. Now and again, but at rare intervals, a native shikari would kill a tiger or panther for the sake of the reward (10 rupees); but these occasional exploits did not by any means balance the natural increase of those animals from year to year, much less reduce the number existing. An organised attack was necessary, and I organised accordingly.

And it was an evil feature in the tigers and panthers of that district that they were very generally, if not universally, man-eaters. I have heard it argued that tigers only become man-eaters when, in their old age, their teeth have been worn down and their strength and activity impaired; but this apology could not be made for the Deoghur tigers. Young and old alike, their prey was, on occasion, man or woman: they killed the wretched wood-cutters, or the old women who picked up sticks in the jungle; they carried off the wayfarer from the highroad; they broke into the grass huts of the sleeping peasant and carried off the husband from his wife's side; and panthers emulated the tigers in these evil doings. Every year brought its long death-roll of men, women, and children killed after this fashion, and one tiger alone, of which more hereafter, was credited with, or discredited by, a hundred victims.

Necessarily, as an exigency of their situation, the Deoghur tigers and panthers had to indent for their commissariat upon the resources of civilisation: they had killed off all the deer, they had left very few pigs and neelghaies, and their food-supply had to be drawn from the herd or home of man,—all that is remarkable in the matter was their preference for the human being when there was an alternative in the form of a cow almost always at the tiger's disposal. In one instance within my knowledge, a tiger, neglectful of the beeves close by, killed and ate a bear; but, as a rule, the Deoghur tiger preferred a ryot or cowherd, or other specimen of humanity, to any other mammalian.

And of these man-eating tigers there were, when I went to Deoghur, four close at hand. The town that lay at my feet, three furlongs from my bungalow, was on three sides enclosed by a belt of jungle, which held at that time four tigers whose confirmed habit it was to devour the Deoghurites. A long period of immunity had encouraged such confidence in these brutes that they made occasional night-raids into the town itself, and dragged their unfortunate victims out of the houses. They even stalked abroad by day, as I saw for myself very shortly after my arrival, when one of them sauntered through my compound some time before sunset, as if bent on making an afternoon call on the new Hakim. But they had reason for this calm assurance, in that they were under the protection of Byjinauth, who would not suffer them to be slain. So the pundas informed me, and they should have been the best authorities as to the scope and direction of that deity's protective influence. They should have been, moreover, prejudiced against the tigers, if prejudiced at all, inasmuch as those animals discriminated not between pundas and other folk in their selection of victims. And it was contrary to their apparent interest to represent, as they did, that any attempt of mine to shoot these blackmailers must be futile. The pundas were very rarely agreed upon any subject under heaven, but they were unanimous upon this point.

It only struck me as ridiculous that they should talk in this way to one who thirsted for the blood of many tigers: a score of Byjinauths, backed up by ten thousand pundas, could not have quenched my tigercidal thirst or stayed me in the attempt to slake it. The jungle was not such as could be beaten by elephants with any promise of success, and I therefore did not court defeat in my first endeavour by using the few elephants that, as it chanced, Yule had then with him at Deoghur. I tried a *machan* with a tied-up buffalo below.

That *machan* was a small *charpoy* (Indian bedstead) fastened securely to the branches of a tree, and surrounded by a screen of boughs. I started for this perch soon after sundown, so as to have as much as possible of the moonlight for my operations; tied up the poor buffalo in an open patch close to a tiger avenue, where it and the tiger that attacked it could be seen, and then clambered off the elephant I had ridden, into my nest some sixteen feet from the ground. My shikari joined me, and we settled down for a close and silent watch.

Soon the last glimmer of day was spent: the moon, casting spectral shadows in the glade, tinselled the leaves with glittering silver, and brought out the sandy forest-track in pallid clearness amidst the shades. And as night closed upon us more and more the silence grew. At first the sounds of human life, the beat of drum, the bark of dogs, reached us from the town, while our buffalo chewed the cud audibly and the tree-crickets made music of their own; but as the night advanced these sounds decreased, then, save a rare insect voice, died away, and left a silence that one might have felt,—an active not a mere passive silence—silence that was not so much the negation of sound as a painful actuality. And the moon passed in her solemn course, and sank, and darkness fell upon the land, while still the tied-up buffalo, spared of the tigers, slept.

> "Night, sable goddess, from her ebon throne,
> In rayless majesty, now stretches forth
> Her leaden sceptre o'er a slumbering world;
> Silence how dark!"

Before this time I had come to wish more than once that I had been smoking the comfortable pipe (denied me here) with Yule and Robinson in their Deoghur camp, instead of roosting like an unfledged unpiping bird on a forest-tree. But it was idle to think of this when the moon had sunk to rest: it was also idle to continue watching when I could see nothing—not even the white sand of the road below me—and so I accommodated myself to the very restricted area of the *charpoy*, and went to sleep.

I was awakened before dawn by a significant pressure upon my knee—a pressure that called me to wakefulness more emphatically and effectively than human voice or trumpet-call. It was a *réveille* not to be disregarded, and I sat up wide-awake to look into darkness, and feel the silence once more—and then the hush was broken, as I would have chosen, by a roar which was sweeter to me at that moment than Patti's mellifluous notes or the soft music of the spheres (which, by the way, I have never heard). That roar came from the distance, but pervaded, as it seemed, the whole earth and the black starlit vault above; and another came, this time from a different and somewhat nearer point, and so, at intervals, those roars betrayed the tiger's zigzag course towards my buffalo. The brute was quartering the ground with instinctive skill that would have been creditable in the most perfectly broken pointer, and his leisurely strategy was highly impressive.

And as the tiger worked his way towards my tree, I looked for the chance of the dawn preceding his arrival. That, too, was close at hand, as the position of the morning star distinctly told me; but would it come in time? Never did the breaking of an Indian day (generally an abrupt proceeding) seem so tardy; and the tiger was steadily and stealthily coming on. And then, when I made the tiger out to be less than fifty yards off, silence reigned again—a silence of deadly omen to the slumbering buffalo, happily unconscious of its impending fate. For a couple of minutes the deadly stillness lasted. Then came the noise of the tiger's rush upon its prey, that was killed as it slept, and then only the sounds of the tiger's movements and sucking of the victim's blood. And still the day had not dawned, and the tiger was hidden from me by impenetrable gloom. For some few minutes the situation remained as I have described, and then (probably because it had come to know of my presence) the tiger dragged the dead buffalo from my tree into the jungle-road, where, at last, I saw it dimly outlined against the sand. This was a tactical blunder that cost the tiger its life. In the glade below my tree it would have remained for some time longer veiled from my sight by the shade cast upon the spot by overhanging trees; and from that spot it might have retreated into the jungle from which it emerged, carrying its prey with it, without my seeing it. But on the forest-road there was no shade to hide; on the contrary, there was white sand, which caught every gleam of the early light, and served as a background to the tiger's silhouette.

As the tiger was evidently making for the jungle across the road, I seized my chance and fired. The thud of the bullet and one sharp roar of pain from the tiger told me I had not missed; but the disappearance of the tiger told me I had not killed, nor, when it had passed off the road, could I see it to fire a second shot.

So ended my first *machan* shooting. As soon as I had given the wounded tiger time to settle down somewhere clear of my path, and to forget any nasty views of revenge, my shikari and I descended from our tree, and walked home. After *chota hazri* we were ready with half-a-dozen elephants to follow that tiger up; and we found it, after beating in close line backwards and forwards in vain, about a hundred yards from the point where it had been wounded. It was moribund, and not of a mind to fight when we did find it. The *coup de grâce* was given, and the tiger padded. The first of the sacred tigers of Byjinauth!

We were in some sort a triumphant procession as we went homewards through the town of Deoghur. The townspeople flocked out in street and road to look upon their stricken foe, and cry, "*Waugh, waugh!*" Even the pundas—the priests of the tiger-protecting deity—came out and joined in the popular acclaim, and were not ashamed. Wonderful are the Hindoos for accepting the inevitable! Tell one of these that he must take castor-oil, and he will drain the oleaginous cup to the dregs, and smack his lips. Tell him that his leg must be amputated, and he will present the limb for dismemberment, and smile as he sees it severed. Tell him that he is to be hanged, and, with no touch of emotion whatever, he will reply "*Jo hookm*" ("Whatever is ordered"), just as if he had been told that he must have his corns cut. Our tiger was the inevitable to those pundas, and had to be accepted accordingly; and all the statements made in regard to Byjinauth's position as tutelary saint of the Deoghur tigers were, for those pundas, as if they had never been.

Flushed with this success, I sought every opportunity of killing the three tigers yet remaining.

I tried the *machan* system again, but without effect. I went out after them whenever they were reported to be abroad in the scrub and lighter jungle that lay outside the heavier cover, and in the course of three months No. 2 was killed from elephants almost in the open, and in a disgustingly peaceable fashion; and, to make a long story short, within twelve months all four of the Byjinauth tigers had been destroyed—No. 3 falling to me in the scrub and light grass jungle much after the manner of No. 2, the fourth and last falling more ignobly still, to the poisoned arrow shot from the spring-bow of a native shikari; and thenceforward, during my stay at Deoghur, the Byjinauth jungle (which I had come to regard as my own particular preserve) knew tigers no more, and the wood-cutter and the cowherd were free to traverse it in safety.

The spring-bow by which the fourth Byjinauth tiger was killed deserves some mention. It was the only form of trap employed in that district, and was, I think, peculiar to the Santhal country. It was, moreover, the only method by which the Deoghur tigers were attacked with any degree of success, for the shikaris who tried shooting from *machans* very rarely brought their tiger down, and the Santhals in their great hunting parties left these more dangerous creatures religiously alone. It used to be said, I know, that the Santhal, having put up a tiger or bear, would encompass it by a ring of bowmen, whose arrows would generally kill the formidable game, or, when the arrows failed, whose battle-axes would serve their purpose. But, although the Ghoorkas will deliberately attack a tiger, surround it in a circle, and cut it to death with their *kookris* only, the Santhals, as far as my experience justifies an opinion, will certainly not court an encounter of this kind, but rather do all they can to avoid it. I have been out with them on their shikar expeditions frequently, and on several occasions I have seen them get out of the way of a tiger or bear, even when they had to break their line to do it. But they were death on tiger in another sense—*i.e.*, in the matter of eating it when dead. Tiger stood at the head of their game list, occupying a position analogous to that of the woodcock in the British poulterer's list, and could not be too high for them: the Santhal gourmet said the tiger's meat was so strong; and very frequently there was good reason for that strength. I have had more than once to place a guard upon a buried tiger, to prevent my Santhal friends from exhuming and eating it.

But I have wandered away from the spring-bow, which I will now revert to and describe. This instrument (of the cross-bow order) is charged with a poisoned arrow that is levelled the proper height for the tiger or panther for which it is intended: the machine is so set in the path by which its victim habitually walks that the tiger or leopard, as the case may be, itself discharges the arrow, and so actually commits suicide. It does this by striking against a string connected with the trigger, and this string is carried round pegs at such a height that the tiger or panther must breast it in passing. This string is the *mar suth* (or death-thread), and when it is pushed by the tiger or panther so as to release the arrow, the arrow aims at about the animal's shoulder. There is also another string connected with the trigger, the *dhurmo suth* (or thread of virtue), which is carried round an outer series of sticks at such a height that while man or cattle will hit it in passing, the tiger will walk under it: when the trigger is pulled by this string the arrow is discharged at a point ahead of the creature that moved the string.

I bagged no more tigers as near to my home as were those of Byjinauth, although once I thought for a few blissful minutes that I had got one even closer—that is to say, in a heap of large rocks (I cannot describe it as a hill) that stood just outside my compound. Thither was I summoned one day to kill a tiger that had been seen in a small cave—the only cave that mound possessed. I went off forthwith, was led to a point above the cave, and had pointed out to me the tiger's stripes lying about ten feet below me, and visible enough through a wide fissure between the rocks that constituted the roof of the rock-formed domicile. Never, as I thought, was tiger given into the hand of man as was this one into mine. Knowing that, if I had a shot at all, it would be a close one, I had brought a smooth-bore, No. 12, and I felt that the two barrels of this ought to settle the affair. I fired the right barrel. The striped thing was convulsed in its death-throes, then motionless. I threw stones upon it, and it made no sign; then, when there was clearly no life left in the creature, I went with my attendants to the mouth of the cave, and drew my quarry forth into the light of day. It was painfully light to draw, and my heart misgave me: it came out into the sunlight, and proved to be a hyena.

I suppose that "sells" of this sort are on occasion necessary incidents of sporting life, where so much depends upon chance and hastily-formed conclusions. If this be not so as a general rule, it has been my honour to afford a generous exception. Nor was this hyena incident the worst of its kind. I did get a hyena then at all events, and hyenas found a place at the very bottom of my list of creatures to be killed. I can remember two days when under very similar conditions of promise I got nothing, and the ill-starred moment in which I got, instead of a beast of the chase, a domestic animal that I had to pay for.

One of those blank misfortunes was shared in by Jacky Hills and others. We were out after tiger in the Nepal Terai, and one of our shikaris directed our attention to what he pronounced to be a tiger. This sporting guide, whose business it was to be lynx-eyed and of sight unfailing and infallible, saw the tiger in a cave hollowed out of the precipitous bank of a ravine. The cave was of dimensions so narrow that we might well have questioned how and why a tiger had packed himself into such a lodging; but it was not ours "to reason why." The shikari saw it, saw its head resting upon its paws, saw the white spots on the ears, saw all possible details, and of course we saw it too. And we fired shot after shot across the ravine into the tiger we saw, and then resolved unanimously that we had killed it, and finally, on closer examination of its carcass, discovered that there was none, whether of tiger or any other creature. I rather think Sir William Ffolkes, who had shot with me one season in the Terai, was present as a performer on that occasion. History very much repeated itself in this incident, for again, and for the third time, it happened to me to shoot an imaginary tiger in a cave.

But disappointment and wasted ammunition were all that I had to deplore on those occasions. More calamitous was the disaster that befell me once when I was after bears. The beaters were driving a promising patch of jungle, and when they were yet some 150 yards from me, a black object broke in front of the line. "*Dekho, sahib! baloo*" ("Look, sahib! bear"), said my shikari. I entirely agreed with him. I saw the black animal distinctly enough, fired, and dropped it.

I even more emphatically agreed with the shikari when he said it was a good shot; albeit that is the invariable criticism of the Indian keeper, according to whom, as a rule, every creature shot at by the master is mortally wounded, even though it go off to all appearances unhurt. But I knew that I had hit and dropped that black object, and was not a little surprised when the beaters emerged without having come across a defunct bear. I sent them back to beat the last 150 yards of the cover up to me, with explicit instructions to look out for the bear, and they made a detour, formed line, and beat back to me as instructed—still with the same result—the cover drawn blank, and no bear living or dead seen by any beater. Then, when I was about to make my way straight for the spot where my bear had fallen, our proceedings were interrupted by the advent of an excited peasant, who, with much uncultured and noisy rhetoric, demanded the price of his murdered buffalo. Here was a situation! No gun other than mine had been fired: I had fired once only, and had dropped a black animal, and the only black and dropped animal to be discovered was the buffalo of this peasant. And it unfortunately happened that this particular buffalo was a peerless creature of its kind, a paragon, a pearl beyond price, or, at least, beyond any such price as might be determined by the law of averages. So said its owner, crying aloud to me in my dual capacity of magistrate and cherisher of the poor, and the woe-stricken man had to be silenced and sent away with rupees. He was thoroughly satisfied with the result of my too fatal shot; so were the beaters who ate the buffalo; so was not I, who had only the adulation of my shikari—the accessory before the fact of that buffalocide — to compensate or console me.

If I got no more tigers so close to my Deoghur home as those of Byjinauth, I obtained three panthers still closer. One of these I shot in my garden, where it had sought cover in a small patch of Indian corn. Once before had my bungalow been besieged. Then my predecessor, as district official, two native infantry officers, and three loyal men of the native infantry held out in it against two companies of mutineers until they were driven forth by fire. Now it was close shut against that panther in the interests of a couple of children, happily unconscious of the whole proceeding, and two trembling ayahs.

The engagement with this self-invited guest did not last long, but was lively enough while it lasted. There was not cover enough to admit of the panther's ordinary tactics. Although I very nearly got a shot at it before it broke, it did not cling to the shelter of the Indian corn for any time; but after some five minutes of hullabaloo, sprang out and in the same bound reached the back of one of my party, who promptly made a cut at it with his tulwar, and, missing the panther, cut his own leg. Then the panther jumped off its unwilling mount and made for the hedged bank that enclosed the garden, and close to that boundary I killed it. The panther did not hurt the man it attacked half as much as he hurt himself.

The other two panthers of this trio I shot on different occasions, divided by some few days, in the same patch of sugar-cane, and under similar circumstances. Both of these were convicted man-eaters, and one of them had carried off into the same sugar-cane the body of a young girl it had killed the night before I shot it.

My Santhal sepoys acted as beaters for me with both of these: both panthers broke the line occasionally, and left their marks upon three or four beaters whom they clawed as they broke, and both were shot as they crouched in the cover. Of them, as of several others, this was the recreant fate—at first some show of fight, and then, instead of standing at bay, the attempt to hide. I came to know that when there was a marked pause in the beating I might expect a summons to some spot where the panther cowered. As often as not this anticipation was realised: a beater would issue from the cover and beckon to me, and when I joined him, would lead me to the panther's hiding-place, and point to the animal lying almost at our feet. I, after a time, would distinguish enough of the animal's outline to determine the direction of my aim, and then one shot almost invariably ended the business. That one shot was always fired from a smooth-bore. Such was the end of those two man-eaters and of many another panther of Deoghur district.

But my success with panthers was as nothing compared with that of a man of Eastern Bengal who, while I was at Deoghur, shot over a dog some surprising number (between thirty and forty) in one year. He had trained his dog to hunt and point panthers, or the dog had developed a natural aptitude that way, and with this result. Unfortunately that dog pointed once too often—perhaps pointed in a manner that no self-respecting panther could tolerate; but, however that may be, the dog concluded a good season's shikar by getting itself killed.

The Eastern Bengal country was then, and perhaps is now, a splendid one for big game. It was thereaway that Yule rode and speared panthers by the score. I managed to do this with a couple in the Deoghur district, but the natural features of the country did not lend themselves to this class of sport: the too frequent and too heavy cover presented obstacles that balked one at every turn; riding through some of the jungle was difficult, through some impossible, and the panther that was followed by a horseman through the dense undergrowth was almost immediately lost to view, and lost irretrievably for that time.

But occasionally a panther in the pursuit of

its nefarious objects would be driven to the shelter of some plot of maize or sugar-cane in the midst of a cultivated plain; and I rode down and speared a couple that had ventured thus into an area of comparative civilisation. Those twain were not in all respects worthy of rank beside the Bengal boar: they gave me a harder run, but there was no fight in them. The spear-thrust that would have goaded a fighting boar to battle cowed them: what mind was left to them was given up to thoughts of flight, and when too sorely hurt to fly, no life was left in them for other measures.

Pigs were there none to ride after in that district, but wolves as well as panthers gave me an occasional opportunity of having a gallop. There were wolves in several localities of the Deoghur district, and one pack of six or seven frequented a broken bit of open country that undulated below my bungalow on the opposite side to that which faced Byjinauth's temple and the town. These suburban wolves had become a standing or prowling menace to the village flocks, and, emboldened by their long immunity, had once, at least, attacked a belated peasant. Twice or three times I rode after them, carbine in hand, but always in vain. I sighted them and pursued them up and down, and in and out of ravines; galloped as hard as those too frequent ravines permitted; galloped as long as wolf or hope remained with me; but I never got a shot. Always the finale was the same—the wolves had vanished. The dejection that comes of failure accompanied me, as my *atra cura*, on my homeward ride. I was beaten morally, and, as its heaving flanks betrayed, the horse I rode was physically beaten.

It has been often noticed how fast a wolf travels by means of a lounging louping trot that is by no means suggestive of speed. While one gallops after it as hard as a good horse can go, the wolf pursued, never apparently hurrying, lollops along at a pace that equals that of the following steed. I have heard it said that no horseman ever rode a wolf down; but to this statement I must demur, inasmuch as I have done this thing. Perhaps my wolf was sick. Be that as it may, I did when out pig-sticking in the Ganges country over against Colgong follow a wolf, and that wolf turned sharply when I closed with it, and the horse I rode (a rare good one) kicked it over with his fore-feet, and made the matter of spearing my wolf simplicity itself. One of my companions of that day found explanation of this performance in the fact that I had ridden another man's horse with my own spurs.

It was not long, however, before I was enabled to inflict condign punishment upon two of those Deoghur wolves—my next-door neighbours. The report was made to me that some of the pack had been marked down in a patch of sugar-cane, and I set out to beat them up. The work was soon done. I took up my position in a good strategical point about the centre of the frontage of the sugar-cane field. The beaters almost immediately after their start towards this point drove one wolf out close to me. That I sent back into the cane with a charge of shot in it. Then after a short interval another emerged, and that also I sent back bearing a charge of shot; and, finally, the beaters came forth dragging out two dead wolves. A third wolf broke at one end of the cover and got away, in spite of several Santhal arrows sent to stop it. But the slaying of the two served as a sufficient hint to the remainder of the pack, and never more, during my time, did any of them infest that neighbourhood. Those two wolves made up, with the tigers, panthers, and hyena above mentioned, the sum-total of wild animals that fell to my gun within a half-mile radius of my home.

There was one especial charm about the shooting of my Deoghur time, in that it mostly occurred as a surprise. If I missed the joys of anticipation, I had not to experience the worry of preparation made long beforehand. Ordinarily, the news of a kill by tiger or panther, or of the marking down of some bear, or what not, came post-haste—if necessary by relays of village watchmen, whose chief I was—and found me in camp or station prepared to take immediate action: then, if the distance required it, I rode off to the spot where my services were demanded as fast as my horse could travel. The worst feature of this impromptu sport was that I had to depend entirely upon the resources of the place where my game was for beaters, and for every other form of assistance. But if there were any people within reach, they were glad enough to turn out and beat for me; even the superior Hindoos—Brahmins, Khetris, and Rajpoots—who elsewhere in India would deem it derogatory to their caste and honour to do this coolie's work, turned out for this service willingly enough in Deoghur.

Beaters, however, were not always immediately available at that particular moment when they were wanted. Operations against the object of the chase had to be commenced promptly or not at all, and this precluded the hunting up of beaters from afar. In some jungles, too, and under some conditions, a beat by shouting, drum-thumping, horn-blowing men was almost certain to be ineffective. And so it came about, for one reason or another, that on several occasions I shot tigers from *machans*. This somewhat questionable form of shikar was always more practicable (for me), and often more effective than any other. I could procure the materials for this structure when I could not get beaters; I had no elephants, and could not have raised in all Santhalia enough for threshing out some of the Deoghur jungles; and I was almost always alone, and had therefore to depend solely upon my own hand and eye for success when the quarry presented itself. It was, moreover, necessary to that success that the quarry should expose itself to my fire, and not break cover out of my sight and take itself off into space unseen.

Nor were all the tigers that I shot out of *machans* finally disposed of without some such excitement as the shikari loves. Tame as was the first shot, treacherously fired out of ambush, there was sometimes sufficient animation before the last bullet was fired and the tiger laid at rest. I will give a typical example.

One day when I reached my camp at the edge of a large jungle, *khubber* awaited me of a kill close by. I went out to inspect, and found the kill—a cow of which little or nothing had been eaten: decided that the tiger which had killed would return at nightfall to eat, if not disturbed meanwhile; and had a *machan* constructed in a tree that overlooked the small patch of open in which the carcass lay. I could not have got that day half the number of beaters necessary to drive the tiger out of its lair, and had it been driven out I should in all probability not have seen it. Just before sunset I took up my position in the tree; the sun went down, the short Indian twilight waned, and before darkness had encompassed my eyrie, the moon rose, full of face, and when it had risen above the earth-haze, bright in its fulness. Very considerate was the tiger with which I sought an interview; it did not come on the scene during the evil quarter of an hour when the cow's carcass was obscured by the shade cast by the rising moon from overhanging greenery; it did not keep the stage waiting when Cynthia ceased to frown most darkly upon the murdered beef; it came silently as a shadow stealing along the ground, and like an evil phantom moved about its prey. The cow was clearly discernible, the tiger only sketchily so, and hardly to be seen at all, save when it stood out, a darker object, against the cow's white hide. My only chance lay in choosing the moment when the tiger was thus outlined, when the silent victim should betray its murderer by posthumous evidence. I could not wait, nor would the tiger, until the moon cast its full light upon the scene, if indeed the moon would have penetrated to it at any time through the foliage that overarched and embowered it. If 'twere to be done, 'twere well—nay, 'twas indispensable—that 'twere done quickly. So, when I thought that I made out, approximately, the shoulder of the tiger, I aimed at that appropriate limb and fired.

A hit—a palpable hit. The thud of the bullet might have proceeded from the defunct cow, but not the sharp angry roar that almost synchronised with it: and if the tiger had not been hit, it would not have charged the foot of my tree as it did, in an evident paroxysm of pain and passion. My position was a peculiar one. I had no idea that the tiger would join me on my *machan* and fight it out on that first-floor lodging, for, in spite of occasional narratives about tree-climbing tigers, I did not then, and do not now, believe that tigers are tree-climbers as bears and panthers are; but for some moments it was obviously just below me, in the only passage of my temporary lodgment, and I could not finish it off with a second shot because, in the deep shade cast by my tree, I could see nothing of it. There it was, and yet a good deal unfinished, as I knew from its movements and an occasional low growl; but when it ceased to move and growl, there was a necessary and uncomfortable doubt in my mind whether it was not still there, patiently waiting to give me a warm reception when I climbed down to its level. I did not hurry my proceedings, but gave the tiger ample time to die, if death was to be the immediate consequence of my bullet, and more than enough time to convince any proper-minded tiger that I was not at home to it. I listened long and keenly—not a sound came from below (and I think I could have heard the tiger wink had it done so), and so I descended to the ground, prepared, gun in hand, for any emergency, and with my shikari got back to camp for the night.

Next morning I went out with a few beaters to follow the thing—*i.e.*, the tiger—out to its end, bitter or otherwise. There under my *machan* were blood-stained tracks, showing where the tiger had moved to and fro, and how hard it had been hit. In one spot close to my tree was a small pool of blood: then, away through the jungle, more blood-stains for a hundred yards, and at that point a larger pool of blood, that, to my mind, betokened a dying creature whose life had here oozed out, leaving just so much strength as would permit it to crawl into some adjacent thicket, and make an end of all in that dim solitude.

But I was all wrong: instead of leaving that pool with faltering steps, and decently dying close at hand, the wounded tiger seemed to have taken a new lease of life there—just as if phlebotomy in an exaggerated form had been the special treatment needed for its cure. From that point the tiger ceased to leave its trail of blood, but, indiscreetly, substituted a trail of clawed and bitten saplings. It had evidently started, after its copious blood-letting, in the worst of tempers, and the evidence of its rage and power struck me as something extraordinary, even though I knew what immense strength the tiger possesses. Good-sized saplings were smashed by this beast in its course—not at long intervals, but so frequently that one followed it by these on a breast-high scent. Apparently it had vented its rage upon every object it encountered where clawing and biting could be practised: in every tree and sapling it had, I suppose, imagined yet another man such as that one of the *machan;* and, its instinct obscured by frenzy, it had not sought safety by a traceless flight into cover, where I should probably have never seen it, but had ostentatiously left in its path a challenge to me to track it down.

The jungle through which the tiger took its way was by no means heavy, and the undergrowth was light and patchy. For about a mile I followed in its track, always with eyes wide open, to detect it crouching in some brake ahead or on either hand; and then I saw it lying within ten yards of me, in the shade of a bush that in a great measure concealed it. I saw it, and it saw me; and as I levelled my smooth-bore at it, it rose and roared and tried to charge. But mine was not to be the fate of those torn and broken saplings; one bullet, full in the tiger's chest as it came head up towards me, dropped it, and the cow and the dryads were avenged. Mostly, my *machan*-shot tigers were killed there and then, and died within a few yards of my bower—sometimes within sight of it. Those afforded little sport in the shooting, and none after the one or two shots required had brought the forest king to earth, unless it can be deemed of the nature of sport to descend from a tree in some uncertainty as to whether an exceedingly angry and sufficiently lively tiger is or is not at the foot of it. In some instances the tiger went away mortally wounded, and was found dead the next day, if it could be tracked; or later on, when, perhaps, the vultures led to its discovery. On other occasions I followed and found the tiger still alive, and animated by a greater or less degree of pugnacity, which was usually in excess of its physical power, but with results no more exciting than those I have just described. Never did one of those tigers or any other place me at the disadvantage of being charged before I had seen my enemy. It was reserved for a bear and my first panther to do that: no tiger ever made good its charge upon me or any one of my beaters.

But I always had the feeling that in shooting tigers from a *machan* I was an unworthy foe—a mere assassin—and, at the best, that the performance, however largely beneficent, was distinctly inglorious. The peasants whose cows or wives or sons were killed by tigers were other-minded. They were not disposed to criticise methods so long as the tiger was destroyed. They even approved of murder by strychnine, and would have canonised the Marchioness de Brinvilliers herself had she practised some part of her toxicological art upon those beasts. They saw no merit, no good point whatever, in a tiger, which I, rightly or wrongly, regarded as the veritable king of beasts, and far more worthy of this style and title than the over-vaunted lion. Those benighted peasants were eaten up by prejudice as well as by tigers. I suppose it was much the same with the relatives of those maidens who were requisitioned for the larders of dragons. Those biassed people would have thought St George quite in the right had he employed dynamite, and destroyed thereby the whole dragon race.

It was otherwise, however, with the tigers that I shot from the ground, even though here I took such advantage as I could of the enemy. There was the inevitable advantage that came to me as the one forewarned. I knew the tiger was coming (or might come), and that it might be expected to emerge from the jungle at or about a certain spot.

The tiger did not know that I was awaiting it, and would have all its attention directed to the shouting, drumming, and braying that was driving it forth. Then I usually had in front of me a low screen of boughs that hid me to some extent, and acted as a piece of furniture against which I could place my spare gun and rifle ready to my hand, should more than two shots be necessary; and, having the pick of the ground, I could take up a position that would, in all probability, give me a further and important advantage, in that it would expose the tiger to a flank attack, to a deadly shot in or behind the shoulder, which could be repeated before the tiger turned upon his aggressor, if it did turn.

I thought quite enough of myself when, thus, I had shot two or three singly: it was the proudest moment of my life, as post-prandial oratory hath it, when I bagged a brace right and left. They came out of the jungle close together—a tiger and his consort; and I had hardly realised the fact that this king of beasts had walked into the open, when the queen was there, two or three yards behind her sovereign lord. Slowly they came forth, with backward glance, that told of some bewilderment, and, on the female's part, it may be conceived, some curiosity. No fear quickened the pulse or stride of the twain; no suspicion of my presence crossed their minds. Calmly those splendid beauties of the forest sauntered on, giving me full broadside shots at a distance of some twenty-five yards.

Crack! crack! right and left the bullets from my smooth-bore went home, and the two tigers dropped—the female never to rise again. The tiger, terribly hard hit, rose and made a feeble demonstration in my direction, but another shot settled it; and there were the couple bagged, and the curtain dropped upon this splendid drama of the forest. It was to be my lot, later on, to kill three, and on one occasion four, at one time; but those subsequent performances found me more *blasé* than I was now, and were the results of much more elaborate preparation than the impromptu sport I have just described. Those triplets and quartet were, moreover, shot from elephants, and, with one exception, by two or three of us. These two, like most of the animals that made up my Deoghur bag, were the spoil of my gun alone.

CHAPTER VII.

THE JAMTARRA MAN-EATER.

THE TIGER OF A HUNDRED VICTIMS—"BAGH! BAGH!"—DEATH OF THE MAN-EATER — DIFFERENCE WITH A MAHOUT — CHEETAHS — BEAR-SHOOTING — THREE BEARS — WILD ELEPHANTS — THE "FEKSIARI."

I THINK I have said enough of those Deoghur tigers generally; but there remains one whose infamous career and execution call for description—the Jamtarra man-eater. It was said of this beast that it had killed a hundred men and women; and although there was doubtless exaggeration as to the number of its human victims, there can be no question that its notoriety stood upon a solid foundation. Over and over again reports were brought to me of some one killed and carried off from the particular locality (close to a large village), believed to be the preserve of this one tiger; and very often the man so killed was attacked upon the highroad, where it immediately abutted upon the jungle. One report of the kind, and about the last, was to the effect that a sepoy, making a night-march with his company, had been carried off from the highway at that point by a tiger which, under the shadow of night, had got clear away from more than a hundred guns. The officers of the regiment, when they arrived at my station two days after this, confirmed the report, and spoke with very natural regret of their inability, in the darkness, to follow the tiger, either to rescue or avenge the sepoy.

Unfortunately, Jamtarra was too far from my headquarters to admit of my acting upon the reports of that tiger's doings. Even if the beast had, contrary to its stereotyped habit, killed a cow or bullock or buffalo, the carcass whereof would have been left on the ground, I could not have reached the scene until after the tiger had relinquished what remained of the carcass. But its victims were human beings, whose remains were promptly removed by relatives. Only once did I persuade the family of a man killed within easy reach of me to leave the corpse on the ground for one night. Speaking generally of these bereaved people, a cynic might say that this tender regard for the remnants of their relations was a new development by no means foreshadowed by their previous behaviour.

On two occasions when I was in the Jamtarra neighbourhood, I tried to get the tiger beaten out of the jungle it frequented; but these were chance efforts almost necessarily foredoomed to failure. There had been no kill; there was nothing to tell what part of that wide expanse of jungle the tiger was in, or if it was in any part. But Nemesis, if somewhat lagging, was represented in my person, and the hour was not far off when I should kill that tiger red-handed (or red-pawed) upon the corpse of its last human victim, and kill it, too, with little or no trouble in the way of beating or riding or otherwise.

I was on tour in my district with Yule and Robinson when our march brought us to the immediate vicinity of the tiger's slaughter-house. Our tents were pitched close by that deadly spot, a peaceful Arcadia now, whose turf for many days had been unstained by bloodshed. After nightfall a beautiful calm surrounded us, broken only by the occasional clanking of the chains that fettered Yule's elephants, or, while the camp was yet awake, by animated discussion among our followers on the enthralling subjects of rice and pice. And we in the mess-tent argued over our pipes about the merits of Mary Queen of Scots, or the Rent Act, or the perpetual settlement of Lord Cornwallis, or anything else that we could agree to differ about. And then, about midnight, silence and sleep descended upon us all.

"*Bagh! bagh!*" That was the cry that brought us back from dreamland, or the empty void of slumber, to the waking world, and we three Britons tumbled out of our beds and tents forthwith to learn who in the grey dawn shouted of tigers, and why. There stood the shouter among our tent-ropes, green with terror. Doubtless he would have been respectably pallid if the native Indian complexion permitted of that form of decoloration; but, doing the best he could according to his lights, he, after the manner of his kind, had turned green.

He had some reason for this and his excited cry of "*Bagh!*" He had just come out of the very jaws of death; his head was deeply scored by a tiger's claws, and the blood still oozed slowly from the wounds. He had been in the clutches of the terrible man-eater, and had succeeded somehow in coming out of that deadly embrace a living and quivering Hindoo. Being soothed and supported by brandy, administered under the guise of medicine, he told us his story while his wounds were being cauterised. Briefly, his tale was that he had made an early start from the village, had reached a spot on the road close to our camp, had there been brought to the ground by a tiger, and had crawled from under the beast, and got away, leaving his quilted coverlet with his assailant. The wadded *rezai,* which is the native's greatcoat and bedding in one, had saved him: he had wrapped this round him and over his head, as is the way of his people when they walk abroad in the chill air of early morn, and it had not only weakened the force of the tiger's blow upon his head, but had served as a shield from beneath which he had crept away.

And still was he being tended with caustic and bandage when his tale was done, and a pause occurred. Then, after an interval, it occurred to this Hindoo Caleb Balderstone to bethink him of his master. "Where was his master?" he asked. His master, he explained, had been walking just behind him when the tiger interrupted their march. He had taken no thought of his employer when he had rushed into our camp, his whole intelligence being absorbed in the one vital measure of taking to his heels. Where was his master?

It did not take us long to procure evidence that his master would not rejoin his servant on this side of the river of death. There on the road hard by we found very certain indications that this unfortunate had been carried off into the jungle by a tiger. There were the imprints of the tiger's feet, the marks of a brief struggle, and the trail from the road into the forest that marked where and how the master's corpse had been carried off.

Yule, Robinson, and I lost no time in starting on our quest for the man-eater. The elephants were got out forthwith, and off we went in as widely extended a line as our resources ran to. We had not far to go. In about a quarter of an hour I came upon it. There it was, within thirty yards of me, stretched in an almost open patch of scrub, with one paw resting upon the body of the man cruelly slain within the hour, calm and wholly undismayed by my appearance. Never did I interview a tiger so little disconcerted as was this by my abrupt intrusion. As its cruel eyes met mine they seemed to express no sentiment so strongly as languid curiosity. "*Que diable allait-il faire dans cette galère?*" it might have said, to render that look into appropriate and much-hackneyed words. Hardened by its long and unpunished career of crime against humanity, it had, I suppose, come to regard man merely as something to be eaten by hungry tigers, and I interpreted that look of its yellow eyes as signifying "You are not wanted now. Here is my dinner. Go!"

It never moved from that moment when our eyes met until I put a bullet into the back of its neck as it lay facing me: then it rose and charged, receiving a second bullet full in the chest from my left barrel and dropped, growling as it fell, into a clump of grass some half-dozen yards from me, where, only half concealed, it lay still growling.

And then a difference of opinion arose between the mahout who drove my elephant and myself. I was riding on a pad (not in a howdah), and had no weapon with me save a smooth-bore, empty now as to both its barrels. The mahout proposed to drive into the clump of grass forthwith. Stimulated by *ganja*, he was deaf to my suggestion that he should pause while I loaded, at any rate, one barrel. The *ganja* would not hear reason, although our tiger was delivered into our hands, and might have been left to yield up what life remained to it after its own way and undisturbed. "Don't be afraid, sahib," said the bedrugged mahout; and so saying drove on, and made his elephant finish off the dying tiger with a kick. So perished that notorious man-eater—an old tiger, as it proved, with worn and blunted teeth and mangy hide; but still capable, had it been spared, of killing men. I can imagine that a sigh of relief rose up as a pæan of rejoicing when the news of the creature's death went forth, and that many a wayfarer passed thenceforth with lighter heart along the road it had frequented.

There was danger then (and perhaps is now) for the foot-traveller in many parts of the Deoghur district. I substantially reduced that risk during my four and a half years there; but fifteen years after I left the district, I was told that tigers, panthers, and bears had increased in numbers to something like their old proportions. My successor in office had done nothing to keep them down.

Among those who encountered the maximum danger from tigers was the Government Geological surveyor, who, armed with no weapon more lethal than the hammer of his craft, had, in pursuit of formations and strata, to make his way right into the fastnesses of the forest kings. Poor Jo Medlicott, who for two years surveyed the Deoghur district for the Geological Department (and who was one of the brightest and best-informed men I have met), had as narrow an escape from collision with a tiger as can be well imagined. He went prospecting up a nullah, fringed and overhung on either hand by forest-trees and undergrowth, and for a few minutes turned from the bed of the main water-course (now a bed of sand) into a small subsidiary channel. When, having returned from that branch, he retraced his steps down the main nullah, he saw that a tiger had just preceded him. There could be no mistake about it, for this tiger's footprints often overlaid his of half an hour or less ago. He had, by a lucky chance, just missed a meeting with that tiger face to face, or, worse than this by far, the encounter that might have followed had he just preceded the tiger down the nullah and afforded the animal a chance of stalking him from the rear, over sand that would have given forth no warning sound.

Among the beasts of the Deoghur jungles an occasional cheetah was to be found. In Oudh and other parts of India this animal is domesticated and kept by sporting rajahs for the purpose of running down antelope: in the Deoghur country they kept themselves by running down the goats and sheep of the people. A curious animal is this hunting cheetah—a cat (*i.e.*, a small and much attenuated leopard) down to its feet, and at those extremities a dog. Twice in the course of my Deoghur career was I summoned forth from my cutcherry to shoot cheetahs. In both instances they had been imprisoned in a hut into which they had made their way after the goats of the hut-holder, and as to both I pursued the same tactics—that is to say, I rode gun in hand to the scene of action, from five to ten miles distant, climbed on to the thatched roof that covered the cheetah, and made a hole in the thatch in view to shooting the spotted thief where it crouched below. In both instances I failed of this purpose in consequence of the cheetah's anticipation of my plans; for so soon as I had displaced enough of the roof to make a hole through which I could look into the interior, the cheetah came out by it, and springing to the ground went off. On the second occasion, when, forewarned by previous experience, I conducted my house-breaking with a more jealous care as to monopoly of my skylight, the cheetah was still too many for me, and, bounding out from off a beam upon which it lay, swept me before it nearly off my coign of vantage. The first cheetah I killed within a hundred yards of the hut; the second was less summarily disposed of. I missed it with my right barrel (fired before I had regained composure and equilibrium), and my second shot, although it went home, did not drop my quarry or stay its retreat into a small patch of bush and grass close by. There it was speedily found cowering in cover that failed to conceal it, but how was it to be finished off? I had brought no spare ammunition, for two shots seemed more than enough for a creature that I had reckoned upon killing inside the hut that had become its prison, and there was no weapon at hand, except the spear of a village watchman—a spear lacking the keenness of Ithuriel's, a spear that, as to point and edge, was far less formidable than a ploughshare or the weaver's shuttle. However, this was the sum-total of our available armoury, and I attacked the cheetah therewith. The active resistance of the wounded beast was a *quantité négligeable*, but the passive hindrance offered by its slender and too lissome body constituted an insuperable obstacle to the spearing. I pinned the cheetah down with this rude halberd, so that an inch or two of its carcass only intervened between the spear-point and the ground, and yet was its skin unbroken by prick of steel. The wretched animal had to be finished off with a heavy stake.

Bears were plentiful in that land—black bears that, when they rose on their hind-legs, stood about six feet in height, powerful but clumsy beasts, that ordinarily employed their strength harmlessly enough. Now and again one of these would attack a man and maul his face and head with its cruel nails. One bear in my district was rumoured to be carnivorous; but, as a rule, these bears were strictly vegetarian, and lived upon the wild figs (the fruit of the *Ficus indicus*) and other products of the forest: and if they did not live in amity with man, their inclination was, I fancy, to preserve peaceable relations with him and other animals, by the simple device of having nothing to do with them. But perhaps by way of exceptions to a general rule, several of the Deoghurites wore on their heads and faces the scars of bear-wounds that they would carry to their grave or funeral pyre.

These bears furnished sufficient objects of sport where better could not be had; men on shooting expeditions in the Himalaya were glad enough to get an occasional bear, even though ibex and mark-hor were the chief objects of pursuit; and I fancy the bear of Santhalia did not merit the title of sloth given to those whose feeding-grounds are just below the snow-line. There was nothing slothful about those Santhalian bears when they pounded along, or up or down, the rock-strewn hills of Deoghur, but rather the speed and agility of the chamois: on the flat it was easy to dodge and get away from them, lumbering of gait and slow of turning. I have seen a coolie escape from a bear that pursued him on the plain, and have had similar experience myself; but on those steep and stony hillsides the bear was master of the situation.

It was on one of those rock-piles that I shot my first bear, unless the credit of shooting it has to be given to Robinson, or divided between us. The bear was in a cave formed by a solid slab of stone wedged into a cleft that intersected the hill for a horizontal distance of about 40 feet. This slab, fixed between perpendicular cliffs, formed a roof to the cave, and on the side next to the open country was some 20 to 24 feet from the ground—the path, that is to say, by which the bear was supposed to travel to and from its lodging. Robinson and I ascended the hill and climbed or crawled on to the slab, while Yule stood in the open at the end of the alley to receive the bear when it emerged. Our arrangements would have been perfect if the architecture of the cave had been what we expected: we should have cajoled or compelled the bear to come from under the slab, and if Robinson and I had not killed it in the passage below, Yule would have accounted for it when it reached the open. But, owing to our defective knowledge of the cave's structure, it was the unexpected that happened. The bear, rudely driven from its bed, did emerge into the alley,—so far the programme was carried out; but on the instant that I fired into it the creature turned in its course back under the slab, and before I could have cried Jack Robinson to my comrade, there was the bear entering our very restricted first-floor chamber by the opening we had come in by. That drop of many feet into the alley would have hindered flight had we inclined to the Parthian method. There was no course open to us but to hold that pass like a pair of Leonidases—not that we held any council of war or discussed in any way the action to be taken; we only fired into the bulky trespasser, and, as it chanced, dropped it dead on the threshold of our somewhat crowded apartment.

In my experience of bear-shooting chance was a peculiarly prominent element, if only because of the difficulty of aiming at a vital point in the fur-covered body: a good deal of that which loomed upon one as bear was hair only, and it was not always easy to judge where the hair ended and bear commenced. I recall one occasion upon which it seemed as though I were trying to make a maximum of misses, or to save my bear as a peripatetic target. I put the animal up in a narrow nullah, fired at it, and pursued it in its flight down that nullah for about half a mile, always within easy range of it, always firing when my gun was loaded, and never, as it appeared, doing any harm to it. It was for about a dozen shots a case of "ineffectual fires," and then a bullet went home, and the bear was rolled over like a rabbit.

But it was not always safe, when they rolled over rabbit-wise, to regard them as done for. Of the bears of my acquaintance several dropped to a hit, and affected to be dead, only to get up when the time was ripe for movement, and be off again.

One of my beaters learned something of this histrionic feature of our bears, as I shall proceed to tell.

Three bears were beaten out of the jungle towards me—a she-bear with two young ones, nearly fully grown. They came out close to where I stood, and presented fairly easy shots. I dropped the mother, and put a bullet into one of the others; and when I fired the second shot, the mother was up again and all three off. I turned to where my second gun should have been; but the bearer of that weapon was off after the bears, and the gun was off too, its bullets fired into the air, to fall he knew not where nor cared. Then came a stern chase and long, a chase made sterner by the necessity of loading my piece (a muzzle-loader) as I ran, and then up got those three bears again, and again the mother seemed to have received her deathblow, this time lying in the dry bed of a nullah; and an idiotic beater went on ahead of me to where it lay, and put his thumb into the bear's mouth, and the bear bit the thumb so that it adhered to the man's hand by a strip of skin and tendon only, got up and went off again beyond the nullah into a water-course begirt with bush and tree—we, except the too-confiding beater of wounded hand, in pursuit.

Then my two shikaris and I hunted about for the animal, and, after some time, one of them pointed into a thick bush and said, "There it is!" I looked and saw only greenery, and the gloom of heavy shade at the heart of it. The other shikari looked, and whatever he may have seen he saw no bear, and said as much. This latter was the one in whom I most pinned my faith—that faith which, in such circumstances as these, was so often blind —and so I sided with him. "There it is," said the former; "There it isn't," said the latter; and while the argument proceeded I stood there with my rifle uncocked upon my shoulder, acquiescing placidly with the noes. Then the first shikari, angry after the manner of some minorities, took up a good-sized stone without preamble, and hurled it into the bush, with the remark, "I'll show you that it's there." Sure enough the bear was there, but not for long. When the stone fell it was up and at us with angry growls, and we this time were off in front of it; but, going head down and blind as to our doubles, it soon let me place myself upon its flank, and then one shot more brought that much-dissembling beast to the ground, never more to go off on its own account. One of the orphaned bruins we got later in the day; the other was not seen again.

By way of contrast to this long and only partially successful campaign against three bears, I had a very brief and wholly triumphant affair with another triplet, all killed between dawn and sunrise. That morning's shikar also contrasted in a curious way with the long day's shooting that preceded it. I had expected great things of this long day, in that I had joined the Santhals in one of their periodical hunting-parties, and so was accompanied by a force of beaters some three thousand strong. With this formidable array of bowmen, I took the jungle in the early morning, full of ambitious hope that tiger, panther, and bear would be my spoil before nightfall; and when at eventide we gave up the chase I had not fired a shot,—I had not even seen of big game an animal to shoot at, or heard of one having been seen by any of my companions. Small game, such as pea-fowl, hares, and foxes, had fallen before the ruder weapons of the Santhals: now and again a peafowl rose within sight of me, and was accompanied in its rise by many of the short sticks with which the Santhals, after the manner of the New Foresters, assail some of the forest creatures; but these aerial Aunt Sallys were not for me, and my long day ended absolutely blank.

I slept that night in a tent close to the point where our army of beaters ceased to disturb the jungle, and was still sleeping when a villager brought into camp intelligence of three bears that he had just seen and marked down in a small patch of scrub a couple of furlongs distant. When this information penetrated my drowsy *sensorium*, sleep fell away from me, and I was up, clothed, and in my right mind, with a celerity that would have been creditable to the clown in an old-time transformation-scene; then with a score or so of camp-followers, chuprassies, &c., as beaters, I set out. The ground was very favourable to my purpose: the jungle, what there was of it, narrowed funnel-like towards the side upon which the bears were to be driven out, and a shallow water-course running through the funnel was the almost inevitable route the bears would take. I planted myself at a spot that commanded this exit, placed a brushwood screen in front of me, leaned my spare guns against the screen, and waited. Not for very long: as soon as I had settled down in my ambuscade the beaters commenced their drive, and in five minutes out came the bears within twenty feet of me, and again the bears were mother and adult offspring. Two of these I dropped right and left, the third I wounded as it turned; then the mother bear called for further attention, and I finally stopped her with a second shot; then, leaving two dead at the funnel's mouth, I went after the third, came up with it where it was pounded by the heavy soil of a rice-field, and finished it off. And the sun was only just risen when this third bear died, and I had had a good day's sport before I broke my fast with the *chota hazri* of the land.

Until I came to know Koodha Buksh (of whom more—much more—hereafter), and to enjoy his service as a shikari, I always preferred to have my spare guns placed ready to hand against a screen or tree or rock, rather than in the keeping of an attendant. I have mentioned one instance of many in which the attendant failed me. That man failed me in consequence of his pursuit of the quarry; others failed me for the opposite reason —they ran away, carrying my spare gun out of action. But I must do justice to one of my gun-bearers of that time, whose promptitude and steadiness probably saved me from a mauling. I was bear-shooting on that occasion, and, standing in a gully that intersected two largish rock-piles, had just killed one bear, emptying both barrels in the killing, when a second, upon which I had not counted, came rattling down-hill straight for where I stood. Time did not permit of my getting a loaded gun from my shikari, who was about as far from me as was the bear. The hilly and rocky nature of my environment made flight impracticable. The situation was critical enough, but my shikari was equal to it; for, not being able to hand the loaded gun to me, he fired it himself, with such effect that the bear, which had threatened me a moment before, came tumbling down the hillside and rolled over almost at my feet in the throes of death.

Thrice during those Deoghur days did I pursue a herd of wild elephants that occasionally, when the paddy was uncut, visited the district. There were twelve or fourteen of them, and they inflicted a considerable amount of damage upon the standing rice, &c., although, as far as my jurisdiction was concerned, they strictly confined their depredations to the night-grazing in, and treading-down of, crops. Sometimes, however, I heard of these marauders (I assumed that they were one with my herd) as being in the district—Doomka—that adjoined mine; and heard, moreover, of their attacking villages, killing people, unroofing huts and granaries to pillage the contents, and looting also from the carts the garnered grain which was the rent and sustenance of the unfortunate ryots. But the herd that crossed the border into Deoghur (whether that of Doomka or another) confined their operations within narrower limits.

I had never been able to sympathise heartily with the joys of elephant-shooting, until now that elephants had come to plunder and harass the people who, in a sense, were under my protection. I had hitherto regarded this form of shikar as peculiar to Africa and Ceylon, and the Indian elephant as a precious thing of higher destiny, that should be taken alive in the toils of the hunters (the *khedda*-men of Dacca or others), and domesticated to man's use. But what was I to do? I had no *khedda*, or anything connected therewith; no racing elephants that could run down these invaders of a peaceful land; no mahout, quick of limb and wit, who could in the twinkling of an eye shackle the legs of the fugitive when, being run down and hustled by its tame congeners, this was required to make its capture good; no well-trained behemoths of mighty strength, that could pound a captive elephant into good behaviour. I had none of these things, and therefore had to go after this herd with no better resources than those which nature and a gunsmith had supplied to me.

And on the three occasions that I went after them they led me a very thorough if not a pretty dance. I pursued them always on foot, always hoping that I should surprise them and kill a tusker or two in the leisurely way most pleasurable to all concerned, except perhaps the tuskers; and never did they allow me to drop in quietly upon their jungle encampment. Always I came upon their spoor; and for the greater part of each hunt I pursued them over hill and dale for many weary miles, keeping ever close in their rear, and, with one exception, never coming in sight of them. Once I outmanœuvred them by tactics of a brilliant but exhausting order, and, by making a detour among the small hills, came upon their flank and within fifty yards of them. There they were, of all sizes, a dozen at least, on the farther side of a ravine; but even then not for me was the tusker that bossed the herd. No shot that could be regarded as of a fatal character (to the elephant) was practicable from where I stood; not one of the herd offered a broadside target; and firing at their heads seemed an utterly useless expenditure of ammunition: there they were, however, the first wild elephants that I had seen, and I was bound to celebrate the new experience somehow. I chanced a shot just behind the tusker's shoulder that did not drop him — how, indeed, should it? That did not turn or stay him, but only urged him and his family to further and faster flight. I chanced a second shot, aimed at a point something farther back than was the first; and the tusker went away with his herd and three ounces of lead somewhere in his anatomy. That was the sum-total of my elephant-shooting, and I have never once regretted that neither that tusker nor any of its kind had to be added to my list of big game killed. Yule, I believe, on another occasion came upon this herd, and wounded one; but not even he — the champion tiger-shooter and pig-sticker—ever killed one.

Before leaving Deoghur and its wild creatures I may mention a curious superstition of the Deoghurites that, as far as I know, was strictly localised to that people or the people of Santhalia. They believed that an extraordinary animal with the voice of the fox and the horns of a goat went before the tiger as its *avant-courier*. They styled this mythical creature the *feksiari;* and when the fox at certain seasons uttered the cry peculiar to that time, the Deoghurites said, "There are the *feksiari* and its lord the tiger." No one of them professed to have ever seen this mysterious night prowler, and yet they all seemed to know everything about the physical characteristics of the beast from its horns downward. There are many superstitions that rest on no more solid foundation.

What number of animals I killed during my four and a half years at Deoghur I cannot say. I kept no diary or any record of my sport. At first I saved the skins as trophies, and had a fairly large bungalow carpeted with them from end to end; but they smelt objectionably in the rains, and tripped me up in the hot weather, and I got rid of them. Then I kept skulls ranged upon shelves until I made my house a Golgotha, and was driven to cast those osseous relics forth; and when I left Deoghur for Oudh I took with me no memento whatever of those four and a half years' shikar, and but a hazy idea of the number of heads of big game that had fallen to my gun.

Whatever the number was, it was of fair proportion, and obtained with only trifling casualties, caused by panthers. One beater was killed by a panther while I was beating through some light cover, but he died very much as the consequence of his own neglect. He stumbled upon the panther in the scrub, and the beast hit him one blow in the back and fled. I saw nothing of this or of the panther at any time; but when I heard of this accident, the wounded man, thinking little of his hurt, had gone off to his home. He died two days later of lockjaw; whereas, had his wound been cauterised and dressed at my camp without loss of time, he would in all probability have survived, as did several other beaters no more seriously wounded. Tigers were in my experience far less dangerous than panthers: even when wounded they fled from the line of beaters, and from first to last no beater of mine ever suffered hurt by these forest kings.

CHAPTER VIII.

THE ELEPHANT IN TIGER-HUNTING.

YULE IN THE TERAI—DANGERS FROM TIGER-SHOOTING ON ELEPHANTS—UNCERTAINTY OF ELEPHANTS—ELEPHANTS *FUSSING*—ELEPHANTS REFUSING—THEIR COWARDICE—BOLTING UNDER FIRE—MAD ELEPHANTS—PREPARATIONS FOR THE TERAI—THE CAMP LOST—SIR HENRY TOMBS, V.C.

HAT old Calcutta ambition of mine to get farther afield—to penetrate into the mysterious Mofussil—was adequately realised in 62, when I was transed to Oudh. At the esent time the distance know from Calcutta is, comparatively speaking, a mere stone's-throw, and may be travelled by rail without a break in about a day and a half. In 1862 it was a journey of many days, made laboriously in the barbaric contrivance known as the *palki*

ghari, except as to some 250 miles (Calcutta to Ranigunj, and Allahabad to Cawnpore) which could be done by rail. Day after day one plodded along from Ranigunj to Allahabad by way of the Grand Trunk Road, until one got heartily sick of that splendid engineering work, and could see no good in it whatever. To-day Quetta, or even Kandahar, is, by time, nearer to Deoghur than then Lucknow was. But time and the *palki ghari* run through the longest course at last, and in the early morn of an April day I reached Oudh's capital.

Yule was then tiger-shooting in the Nepal Terai—his last performance in the character of tiger-slayer—and I was not without hope that he would summon me to his camp, to talk "shop" with him in the moments that could be spared from shikar. There was some little excuse for this hope, in that I was called upon to organise a revenue department newly created by him, as to which his personal counsel would have been invaluable. But, unfortunately, he did not see eye to eye with me in this matter. No request came to me to join his forest camp, and while I constructed a departmental system out of Abkari (excise) and stamps at headquarters, my chief hunted through the swamps and jungles that lie at the foot of the Himalaya.

Very fortunate were the privileged few who were with Yule on that occasion. Herky Ross, the champion rifle-shot of India, and brother of the first English champion, Bob Aitken, the hero of the Bailey-guard of the Lucknow Residency, Colonel Towers, and another globe-trotter, were of the party. The tigers shot numbered forty — a record that has never been touched, I fancy, before or since, not even when tigers have been netted and imprisoned and put down for the shooters.

Yule's fortunate guests had a fair amount of excitement with their sport. One fighting tigress got upon the pad of a beating elephant occupied by a chuprassie, and was cut about by his tulwar until it dropped to the ground, and was there killed by gun and rifle shots of the party. On another occasion a tigress, more vicious, or of more effective vice than the other, got upon a pad ridden by a chowkidar, and seizing that unfortunate between its teeth, flung him to and fro as a terrier worries a rat, until life was gone — a murder promptly avenged by half-a-dozen bullets.

Then it happened that Ross, somehow or other, got thrown from the elephant he rode into a heavy swamp, and also in the immediate vicinity of a tiger, and had to be extricated from that doubly inconvenient situation; and (fourthly) it came about that in a scrimmage with a tiger in the forest, the elephant ridden by Yule bolted among the low-branched trees, with the natural consequences that the howdah was wrecked, and its contents, including the rider, thrown to the ground and scattered, Yule being so much bruised and shaken that he had to lie up for a day or two. But these *contretemps* and any other that occurred did not impair the general character of that expedition as a splendid success.

It will be observed that the accidents I have mentioned above were associated with, and two of them caused by, elephants. Now, people who cry out against the danger of tiger-shooting on foot are very apt to regard tiger-shooting from elephants as perfectly safe. I have often heard this view expressed, and never agreed with it since the time when I had seen enough of both methods to compare one with the other. My experience justifies my holding another opinion. My life and limbs have been jeopardised over and over again when I have shot from elephants, and never appreciably so when I shot on foot; and I believe that a man who has confidence in himself, care for the loading of his guns, and knowledge of what he is about, is safer when, confronting a tiger in the open, he has only himself to depend upon, than when he is largely dependent upon the humours and vagaries of a beast in which it is unwise to repose any confidence whatever. The accidents that occur to the man on foot are, I admit, more likely to be serious or fatal than those which befall the elephant rider; but there is less probability of any mishap arising. In some instances elephants are indispensable. This is the case when one shoots in the high and heavy cover of the Terai swamps or in the long grass of the Ganges valley and other tiger-grounds; and then only, in my judgment, is the elephant endurable.

Although my description of the elephant, if I gave it in the fullest detail, would not be as defamatory as was that written by Charles Reade, I entertain an opinion of that beast which would shock many thousands of the admiring friends of Jumbo and his successor in the Zoo. These admirers are apt to rhapsodise about the intelligence and docility of the elephant. What can be said of the sagacity of a gormandising beast that, after a light repast of paper bags, concluded the entertainment by swallowing a leather purse? This was recently one of the intellectual feats of a Zoo elephant. According to my observation, the elephant is intelligent in a diabolical way at times, but rarely up to the mark when its intelligence would be useful. So with its docility: that quality is prominent, no doubt, when the exhibition of it is convenient to the elephant; but one often looks for it in vain when it is needed for the convenience of any other living creature. Then the elephant is a revengeful beast: it is treacherous often, and, with few exceptions, an arrant coward.

How very uncertain the docility of an elephant may be, and how revenge may be substituted for that quality, was illustrated by an event that is fresh in my mind. A mahout tried to drive his elephant into the centre of a newly excavated tank. The elephant found out with its trunk that a hole of some depth was just before it, and would not move. The mahout persisted, and urged the recalcitrant elephant with the iron goad (the *gujbāg*), and, after a short conflict, the elephant seized the mahout with its trunk, dragged him off his seat on its neck, and placing him below its forefeet, trampled the life out of him. This animal had some reason for being annoyed by its driver; but there is nothing to be said in extenuation of another elephant that, *à propos* of nothing, tossed me with its tusk. I was feeding the brute in the eventide when the day's work was done, and this toiler with others had to be tended and encouraged: I was feeding it with delicacies dear to the elephantine palate, and without rhyme or reason the docile and intelligent creature butted me into the air, no doubt with a benevolent intention of impaling me, frustrated by my offering no resistance to the tusk, and by the bluntness of that weapon.

Much praise — in my opinion too much and undeserved praise—is lavished upon the elephant because of its clever detection of treacherous ground—bog or quicksand—lying in its path. It is true that the elephant, with that remarkable caution which is a part of its egotistical and pusillanimous character, will feel its way with its trunk when doubt occurs to it as to the security with which it may advance another footstep. But, unfortunately, its discrimination between what is and what is not *fussund* (bog or quicksand) often fails. It will obstinately refuse to enter a swamp that is perfectly safe, and it will, without protest of any kind, rush into the most treacherous place, where even the elephant's huge frame may be absorbed without touch of a sound foundation.

The *fussing* of an elephant was a not unfrequent incident in the tiger-shooting of the Terai. Instances have been known of an elephant sinking altogether in *fussund*, in spite of every effort to extricate it. Mr (afterwards Sir Charles) Wingfield, Chief Commissioner of Oudh, was, I believe, on one occasion occupied for two or three days in getting one out of the morass into which it had sunk almost out of sight; and I have more than once lost several hours in manœuvring these talented animals out of that particular difficulty.

Nor does the elephant, under these circumstances, exhibit that appreciation of the efforts made to aid it which might be expected of it by its admirers. As a fact, it then becomes more dangerous to man than usual—at least to any man rash enough to get within reach of the trunk which is now groping all round for anything that may be pressed under behemoth's feet to make some sort of foundation. For where branches or saplings are procurable, these are employed for the purpose of giving the sunken creature foothold, and are placed cautiously within reach of its trunk for that purpose; but the elephant is not too particular about its material, and will take its human ally, who is working heart and hand for its release, just as soon as a sapling. Sometimes a *fussed* elephant is hauled out by its comrades with tackle made up of the chains that are part of the elephantine gear.

Anticipating somewhat, I will now give an example of elephants refusing when there was no *fussund* to justify their hesitation. I was alone at the time, and, in the absence of any second gun, could arrange for no stops, or hope to kill the tiger I was after otherwise than by shooting it myself. The tiger had been marked down in a narrow strip of tall reeds on the forest side of a long swamp of about 40 yards in width. There was just room for elephants to pass in single file along the edge of the cover, between the swamp and a precipitous cliff, which descended from the stretch of forest 30 or 40 feet above. On the opposite side of the swamp, which was thereaway clear water devoid of reed or grass, was open country, where I should have placed a second gun if I had had one: the swamp was notorious for its dangerous character, and no attempt was made to put my elephants into it. Believing, from previous experience, that the tiger would, when roused, make for the jungle by one of the water-courses that formed approaches to it, I posted myself up there in a position from which I could command the swamp, and the Indian file of elephants slowly advancing along the edge; and before long the tiger broke, but not on the forest side. It made straight across the swamp for the open country, where was no man to hinder its retreat. It made its way through the cover below me without my getting a chance; but when it reached the open water I put a bullet into the back of its head (the only part exposed to me), and that turned it. Then it lay in the cover and roared its disapproval of the whole proceeding.

I descended from the forest by one of the ravines and took up my position on the swamp edge within 20 yards of the spot where last the tiger had roared or growled. Even from the commanding height of my howdah I could see nothing of the wounded beast,—not a stripe or a glimpse of black-barred skin was visible, only the feathery heads and tangled blades of reeds and grass. I urged my mahout to hazard entrance into the labyrinth that held the tiger: he protested in the name of *fussund*, but made a show of forcing his elephant forward. The elephant indorsed that protest, and stood immovable upon the edge, and there was a deadlock as complete as that of 'The Critic.'

Two hours or more were occupied with a siege of this enemy that never once was seen. Fortunately the tiger could not move far in any direction without exposing itself to view. It stuck to a small patch of cover, into which I fired a steady succession of bullets. At the outset it answered the shot of my first barrel with an angry growl, and I fired the second barrel at the growl. By-and-by the response became uncertain; then it ceased, and there was silence. At last my patience was exhausted, and I insisted upon hazarding entry into the swamp. The sagacious elephant protested, and hung back; but the mahout was driven into obstinacy by my objurgations, and in we went, to discover that there was no *fussund* there to trouble us, or tiger either, for the animal was lying there sunk below the water, and stone-dead.

As for the cowardice of elephants, I might quote examples by the score, and many of these would tend to demonstrate that fear in those animals far exceeds their vaunted intelligence. They will on occasion rush blindly from some imaginary danger into a real one. Whatever imagination they possess is apt to be employed in the conception of alarming things that do not exist in fact; and panic is contagious with them: a hundred elephants will tremble because one of their number has been terror-stricken by some air-drawn peril.

Very ludicrous, albeit exceedingly exasperating, is it to see a line of forty elephants turn and fly before a tiger that has been seen, perhaps, by barely half-a-dozen of the fugitives. Off they go, those white-livered monsters, at as near an approach to a gallop as they can accomplish, each one of them fancying tigers at its heels—

> "And though he posted e'er so fast,
> His fear was greater than his haste;
> For fear, though fleeter than the wind,
> Believes 'tis always left behind."

Nor can the mahouts stay them in their flight, or direct their course until the elephantine mind has grasped the fact that tigers innumerable are not pursuing. And in the meantime, possibly, the tiger has effected its escape, or has fallen to the gun of a stop placed in advance of the beaters. That is one of the chances of tiger-shooting, whereby the animal that promised to be the spoil of one man falls to another.

This is very much what occurred one day when three of us rode with the line, and the other two of our party went ahead to different points as stops. A tiger broke in heavy grass cover just in front of Shipton (13th Hussars), who fired at it. The tiger charged upon the head of Shipton's elephant, and when that and the others turned tail, seized hold of the tail of another elephant; then a stampede, in which the whole line unanimously joined, and the tiger was left master of the field. He sauntered off in the opposite direction, elated, we may suppose, and confident, but confident too soon; for thereaway Peters (13th Hussars) awaited it, with eye and hand as deadly there to the forest king as here they are to the harmless rocketer, and while we others were yet careering over the country with our backs to the scene of conflict, a shot or two from Peters settled the foe from whom we fled.

But a tiger, seen or unseen, is not required to affect an elephant in this way; very much less will do it. With many of their kind a gunshot is sufficient—witness the following by no means unique incident.

On one of my annual Terai expeditions, I arrived at the camp of rendezvous some hours in advance of the rest of the party, and found myself with an afternoon at my disposal for jungle-fowl or other shooting. Game, especially jungle-fowl, abounded in the jungle close at hand, and I ordered an elephant to be brought round to my tent to carry me and beat the cover. There were forty elephants available: one of these two score was brought, and on to the pad of that one I, with Khooda Buksh shikari and a little pet dog of mine, mounted. The dog was an unfortunate addition to our party, as it proved, but that we could not very well foresee. So off we jolted, and as we entered the jungle I asked the mahout if his elephant would stand fire when I shot from its back. The mahout replied in an eminently unsatisfactory way: he expressed a very decided fear that his elephant would be alarmed, and an unequivocal doubt as to its standing fire in the sense of standing still. To this I responded by the absurd statement that he, the mahout, had to make the elephant stand fire, inasmuch as it was for that purpose we had started; and the mahout, bowing to the inevitable as usual, said, "Very good, sahib," and "Whatever you order" —just as if he had been one of Canute's courtiers —and on we went.

Shortly a jungle-fowl rose, and I fired with considerable effect upon both bird and elephant. The former dropped, the latter bolted; but not yet was the elephant altogether out of hand: it seemed as if the mahout was holding it, and would in a few paces pull it up. Then my dog yapped, and then the elephant went off, full tilt, and wholly beyond restraint, straight through the jungle. There was a situation for a sportsman, whose aim had been to enjoy a quiet pottering ride, without excitement greater than that which comes of a rising jungle-cock or scuttling hare! ahead of me a forest of branches, any one of which might fulfil its destiny by impaling me—many of which, not to be avoided by agility of mine, hit me in every part of my body as I was hustled through them. That was what had to be faced to the bitter end, for if I had jumped down to the ground, there was every chance of the elephant imagining me to be an attacking tiger or what not, and kicking the life out of me as I dropped. Khooda Buksh and the dog were swept off the pad by those unsparing branches, that seemed to be playing the three-stick-a-penny game, with us for the cocoa-nuts; or, as it seemed to my heated imagination, that pad was as the deck of some foundering ship from which the crew are washed by furious waves. And being swept off on to *terra firma*, and not much damaged, those two would not leave well or me alone, but followed,—the man, after his own faithful way, to see what help he could render, the dog to yap its sympathy with its master in his trouble. I am afraid that my affection for the dog was at that moment converted into a feeling of antipathy. Once the idea occurred to me of turning round and shooting it as it pursued; but it was not easy to turn when one hand at least seemed to be required for holding on to one of the pad-ropes, and the notion was abandoned. Then Khooda Buksh caught the yapping pet, and dropped back with it out of the elephant's ear-shot; and eventually, after the bolter had established something like a record of a long-distance run, and smashed his way through enough timber to keep an army in fuel for a campaign or two, it suffered itself to be pulled up. I walked back to my tent carrying upon me as many bruises as if I had been engaged in a prize-fight.

But I have only thus far dealt with the elephant that is in possession of such intellectual gifts as may be his, and there has to be considered the case of the elephant that, being *must*, is for a time bereft of its senses. It is only the male that suffers from this affliction of insanity; but every male is liable to it some time or other, and unfortunately may be attacked by it without warning of any kind. Some men of long experience of elephant-keeping say that the *must* condition is preceded by premonitory symptoms, and if taken in time, may, by diet and treatment, be averted; but without presuming to contradict those better informed people, I can aver that I have known some of them to be taken by surprise by the sudden *musting* of elephants under their own immediate supervision.

Some elephants become demons of cruelty when *must*, as, for example, a commissariat elephant that, during my time in Oudh, broke away from the Lucknow lines and went over a considerable tract of country, killing men, women, and children wherever it found an opportunity of doing so. I do not remember the total number killed by that beast, but it was sadly large. And of course, valuable as the animal was to the Government, only one course could be pursued in regard to it. The sentence passed upon it was that of death, and the execution was carried out, not without difficulty and danger to the executioners, by several Europeans, who followed and shot it down.

But without rushing into such extremes, an elephant suddenly frenzied in this way may make itself exceedingly unpleasant, and not a little dangerous. Twice has it been my lot to ride an elephant that received the charge of another suddenly stricken with this madness. In the first instance, Yule, H. B. Simson, and I occupied the pad upon Yule's magnificent tusker, an animal of splendid proportions, and in first-rate condition; and seated there we awaited some development, for which Yule had called a halt. It was in the Mutiny time; but whether we were after mutineers or shikar at that moment I do not remember. All that I can recall is that we were there just outside a village, our tusker one of many elephants, and that suddenly, as a bolt out of the blue, Yule's big *mukna* (a male elephant with only rudimentary tusks) charged down upon our tusker, and butted it in the side with a force that would have overturned a less stalwart animal. And here was another illustration of elephantine cowardice. Our tusker, had it been of a mind to exercise its strength, could easily have mastered its assailant, but it never for a moment entertained the idea of resistance. Bringing its gigantic intellect to bear upon the situation, it may have regarded the onslaught as that of some irresistible and devastating force never yet encountered by it, not that of its familiar stable companion; and here may be the explanation of its immediate flight. At all events it fled, hotly pursued by the *mukna*, that bit the fugitive's tail, as if to resent the rudeness that presented that part of the tusker to an old friend. We were nearly knocked off our elephant when the charge and the hurried flight occurred, and then nearly unseated by the eaves of houses, as the tusker hurried through the village and turned corners without any allowance for our legs; but this untimely chase did not long endure. The elephant attendants, the mahouts' helpers, came spear in hand to our aid, and without much difficulty goaded the *mukna* into a more peaceable frame of mind and abandonment of its pursuit of the tusker.

Again, some years later, in the Nepal Terai, I was riding on the pad of a splendid tusker when a similar incident happened. My mount was one of the staunchest elephants that ever faced a tiger, one of the very few that are staunch invariably. Indeed it bore the reputation of erring in the other direction, for not only would it stand up to a tiger, but it would take the attacking business to itself, and fall upon the tiger with knee and foot, regardless of the claim of its rider to engage in the fray. It went through this performance once with Ross, I think, and with considerable confusion before the scene was played out. At the time in question this hero among elephants was in poor condition, which unfitted him for meeting the charge of another elephant as big as, and in better condition than, itself.

We were forming our line to beat a long stretch of grass cover for tiger, and my elephant was standing in the centre as still as an elephant can stand, while the others were being got into position. At the farther end of the line was a *mukna* (wholly unsuspected then of criminal intentions), which did duty as a beater, and carried no howdah. And while we halted thus, down came the *mukna* upon my tusker, and hurled it over. Rifle in hand, I then accomplished the biggest jump of my life. I have no idea how many yards I covered in my hurried descent from the overturned tusker to the ground. I could not stop to measure it, but I reached the ground safely, and out of harm's reach. Then I beheld the *mukna* kneeling upon the prostrate tusker, and prodding the fallen animal's side with its small but hurtful tusks; and the tusker's mahout, also clear of the *mêlée*, was adjuring heaven to destroy the *mukna* and its much-vituperated female relations of many generations, and appealing to me to shoot it: and in the excitement of the moment, and spurred on by the mahout's shout of "*Maro, sahib! maro!*" I went very near to killing 10,000 rupees' worth of elephant. But, with my finger on the trigger of the rifle, aimed at that *mukna's* most vulnerable point, I refrained; and the mahouts and attendants of many elephants came to the rescue with spear and goad, and the *mukna* was driven from the much-assaulted tusker, and so the matter ended. The tusker was much knocked about, and had to be laid up for some time: the *mukna* broke one of his tusks in the action, and the half of it that was broken off remains with me to this day as one of very few trophies of my Indian shikar.

If my views as to the nature of the elephant be heterodox, I think I have shown that I have some reason for the want of faith that is in me in respect of that animal's excellence. But, notwithstanding these antipathetical sentiments upon my part, I could not avoid seeing a good deal of them, and taking infinite trouble to enlist them in sufficient number for my annual Terai trip. The tiger season of that country may be said to commence in the end of April, when the land is sufficiently parched, and the sun sufficiently scorching to drive tigers from the forest into the swamps, and to end with the outbreak of the rains in June, when any grassy hollow in the jungle serves for the tiger's midday refuge, and when, also, the Terai malaria becomes absolutely deadly to unacclimatised man, whether European or native. For this season—*i.e.*, for April—it was necessary to begin recruiting elephants some six months beforehand, and, when I did not secure the commissariat elephants, this recruiting often involved much correspondence with rajas and nawabs, lavish diplomacy, and heartrending disappointments.

For the average raja or nawab, whatever his professions of friendship may be, is apt to measure the substantial tokens of his goodwill by the power of the recipient to benefit or injure him. As to elephant-lending, he is guided by a tariff which may be outlined thus: To a borrower of the first grade, his whole stud; to him of the second grade, one elephant of half-a-dozen —possibly a lame one; to him of the third grade, nothing but a polite refusal, conveying some fiction about other and previous engagements. The scale is more finely graduated than I have shown, but this will serve my purpose. For two seasons I occupied the premier position: I was then revenue secretary to the Chief and Financial Commissioners, and had much to do with matters of vast importance to the native magnates of the province. Thereafter, as the head of a revenue department that concerned those people little if at all, I fell straightway into the second grade, as far as most of the elephant owners were concerned. Mostly, however, I was independent of these fickle natives, in that I obtained all the elephants I wanted from the commissariat, and very good animals these were on the whole, well fed and carefully tended by respectable mahouts, who were satisfied with normal rations for their charges, while the attendants of elephants lent by natives would frequently demand, as a minimum allowance for one elephant, enough atta and ghee for a couple. One season the commissariat department did me the honour of lending me the Viceroy's state elephant—a giant amongst Gargantuan creatures: a tusker with but one tusk on ordinary occasions, that one being supplemented by an artificial tusk of wood when its wearer was fully caparisoned for its viceregal rider. I rode that giant once—only once. I found that quite enough. Any pride that I may have felt in my exalted position was shaken out of me in five minutes, and I was left with the abiding thought that however uneasily crown-wearing heads may lie, the wearer of a viceregal diadem must sit upon that one-tusked elephant with a degree of uneasiness that can be nothing less than torture.

There were many other preparations to be made, and made betimes before taking the field. In fact, so many details as to commissariat and so forth had to be arranged, that it might have been supposed our object was to wage war against the people, not merely the tigers, of Nepal. Organisation had to be thorough, lest we should starve in the wilderness or fail in our mission by reason of some requisite overlooked. For in the Terai human habitations are few and far between, and supplies, save occasional milk, a possible but rare batch of fowls, or a pot of wild honey, not to be counted upon. Of the few people met in those wilds the majority are herdsmen from Oudh, who bring their cattle up here for the summer pasturage; these herdsmen have nothing to sell, not even dairy produce: so it came about that arrangements had to be made beforehand for feeding ourselves, our animals, and our hundred or two of camp-followers, for a month or six weeks on end. How different all this from the shikar of my Deoghur days, that came any day of the year as chance directed, and was met without any preliminary thought even of twenty-four hours!

First, one had to get a permit from Katamandu to enter Nepalese territory, for in the matter of passports Nepal was theoretically as behind the times as Russia. But, as far as I saw, this permit was useless for practical purposes. I was never asked for mine, even though I passed by Nepalese guard-houses and through Nepalese villages over and over again. And some Europeans dispensed with this document altogether when they entered the Terai.

Then as the time for starting approached, one had to lay in stock of tinned and other eatables, and sheep and poultry as live stock, and many liquids for the Europeans of the party; and it had to be seen that the supply of soda-water especially would be adequate to the needs of men who, in the broiling heat of the Terai day, would be continually thirsty for about twelve hours, and rarely able to slake that thirst with fairly drinkable water. For the Terai fails in the matter of potable water, and even the tea that is made with such water as one gets there is frequently more vigorously flavoured with decomposed vegetable matter than with Pekoe or Souchong.

Ammunition had to be thought of, and a stock of gunpowder, shot, and bullets laid in, adequate to meet any possible demands. And *anars* (rude clay bombs filled with coarse bazaar powder) had to be provided in view to shelling tigers out of impenetrable cover or *fussund*—not that these explosive instruments were often, if ever, of any particular use. Peters has tried to remind me of one tiger that was thus driven out of its stronghold, but I cannot recall that or any similar incident. I can only remember these *anars* being lighted and cast into a swamp, where they mostly fell into the water, to be at once extinguished, or, where most successful, spluttered and expired with a feeble pop that would not have greatly alarmed a sheep. But, notwithstanding this frequent failure, *anars* continued always to be essential items of our paraphernalia, and were carted hundreds of miles before they were broken by the upsetting of a cart on land, or soaked and spoiled by the overturning of a cart in water, or feebly exploded in a tiger's lair as aforesaid.

Then a contractor had to be found who was competent to cater for the elephants and camp-followers, by keeping communication always open with the base, from which he drew a never-failing supply of grain and atta and ghee, and tobacco and ghoor, &c. These supplies had to be packed out to our camp, wherever it might be, on ponies, or where the commissariat officers were with us, on camels: and no little judgment and foresight were required on all hands to ensure the arrival of each caravan at that point where our constantly flitting camp might chance to be.

Indeed, when in that trackless land one made a march of any distance, judgment and forethought, as well as good beasts of carriage, were necessary to ensure the arrival before nightfall of the tents and other requisites of the new encampment. Nor is it by any means an enjoyable novelty when these things do not present themselves at the close of the day. I know this from bitter experience, for one evening when, after a long day's hunt, Benson and Martin of the 21st Hussars and I reached the spot selected for our camp, behold! not a sign of canvas was there; not a kitmutghar to hand the refreshing peg or brimming pewter; not a cook or any substitute therefor to prepare the reinvigorating dinner; not a sign or vestige of any sort of the encampment we had expected to find awaiting us. Then while the light lingered in the western sky,

"And Hope the charmer lingered still behind,"

we fired guns as signals of distress, and listened all in vain for answering shots or shouts from our belated servants. Then we sadly realised that for that night the canopy of heaven must be our sheltering roof, and the game we had shot that day, with any cold tea or other fluid left in our howdah-bottles, our dinner—and possibly our breakfast of the ensuing morn. But, happily, Khooda Buksh, the helpful and imperturbable, was then my shikari (as he was also my valet, factotum, and friend), and with me in this emergency. He it was who procured for us a dinner of some sort—a hotch-potch of venison and jungle-fowl that we had bagged during our march, and rice and ghee and condiments that he had begged from the mahouts. Good all round as he was, Khooda Buksh did not excel as a cook. He was not the artist to kill himself, after the manner of Vatel, because the fish had not arrived. He would not have been very much put out if nothing edible had appeared for us or himself; but edibles of a sort being procured, he did his best to convert them into a stew, and appetite doing the rest, we fared sumptuously.

Then sitting on elephant-pads we smoked our

pipes, and were filled with contentment, as well as victuals, until it came on to rain; and that rain was not the manifestation of a passing shower, but a steady downpour that might be expected to continue through the night: wherefore we took more pads, and piling one against the other, made a sort of lean-to roof, which kept out a considerable portion of the descending flood, and enabled us to get wet through by imperceptible degrees. So we weathered the night, and when the early morning came, were ready for more of Khooda Buksh's stew—and then the camp came up.

Not that, in one of these expeditions, anxiety and responsibility ceased with the completion of the commissariat arrangements. The work of that department being seen to, there remained the day-to-day duties of the general in command, the quartermaster-general, and the shikar staff generally. Information as to the movements of the enemy (known as *khubber*) had to be procured from day to day, and marches and countermarches made accordingly; details of a little-explored country had to be studied, in view to discovering practicable routes for carts, &c., *fussund* to be avoided, and other matters. And when the foe was at hand, strategy had to be exercised in the attack and in cutting off his retreat. Then, too, constant care had to be given to the howdah elephants, to prevent their being incapacitated by sore backs from carrying howdahs. Lastly, discipline had to be rigidly observed, and the orders of the man in command faithfully and promptly carried out.

It has been my good fortune to control the affairs of more than a dozen of these expeditions without any difficulty arising out of defective discipline, and men who were then commanding or have since commanded regiments or divisions have been amongst the most obedient to orders. Hume (now General Sir Robert Hume) of the 55th and Fane of Fane's Horse were prominent in this respect; as were Peters, who was promoted from the 13th Hussars to command the 4th, and is now a retired general; Gream, commanding officer of the 64th, and now one of the retired general host; and Combe, then a captain of the 21st Hussars, and now general commanding the cavalry at Aldershot. In naming them, I would place on record my lasting remembrance of the loyalty and good-fellowship for which I remain a debtor to them, and others of my companions that are mentioned in these reminiscences.

Would that I could include Sir Henry Tombs, V.C., among those who hunted the Terai with me. He was to have been of my party one year when he was general of the Lucknow Division, and I rode in from camp one day in March to talk over our final arrangements with him. He was then full of life and the idea of tiger-shooting in a month or so, and casually he spoke of going to see a dentist at Meerut about a tooth that was giving him some trouble. A fortnight later I heard that it was cancer, not toothache, that had to be dealt with; and when (had all gone as we hoped) he should have been joining me in the Nepal country, he was speeding home to undergo cruel operations and die in the flower of his manhood, when the British world had come to know him as a brilliant soldier, and a splendid career lay immediately before him.

CHAPTER IX.

A HUNTING CAMP IN THE TERAI.

SCENERY OF THE TERAI—BEES—HEAT—THIRST—EVENING IN CAMP—"BUFFALO" SMITH—CAMP SCAVENGERS—VULTURES—THE TERAI SHIKARI—KHOODA BUKSH—THE MAHARAJAH OF BULRAMPOOR—THACKWELL'S MISADVENTURE—KHOODA BUKSH'S COURAGE—ON A BORROWED ELEPHANT.

THE Nepal Terai came upon one as a delightful contrast to the monotonous succession of mango-groves, unhedged and unfenced fields, and stereotyped villages, that are the prevalent characteristics of the drearily level districts of Oudh. In the Terai wide stretches of forest were relieved by undulating glades studded with trees of noble outline and foliage, and emerald plains where in this season the cattle grazed. There was at every turn some fresh and unaccustomed beauty to admire in this sylvan world: a group of forest-trees that overarched the track and stayed the rays of a fiery sun; a park-like bit, the very home of Oberon's court, seen through an arch of greenery where, possibly, the feathery cane trailed overhead; a mountain stream meandering between its tree-fringed banks, deep shaded by the branches that kissed the flowing water and poisoned as they kissed; a lake that mirrored the steely blue of heaven, save where the wide-spreading lotus made a splendid harmony of green and white,—all these, and many another physical charm, were there abundant; and many an unfamiliar creature of the wilds was to be seen as one jogged along—spotted deer in the glades, now and again a sambhur or ghond breaking from cover, or the more frequent pig or hog-deer, or a porcupine, to say nothing of those animals for which we more particularly looked, the tiger, panther, and bear. And birds were there that were peculiar to the Terai,—the white bird of paradise; the night-jar, rising from and settling upon the ground always; the bronze-winged pigeon, darting in and out amidst the trees like a flying gem; the golden oriel, piping its chaste and Wagnerian recitative up in the tree-top; and another member of the feathered choir (whose name I wot not of) that whistled very correctly one-half of a music-hall refrain, and always forgot the remainder; and there were the more generally known pea-fowl, jungle-fowl, black partridge, and florikan, that were perhaps more admired when they came up to the table in a stewpan than in their natural condition.

Among the living things of the Terai forest were some that we could very well have dispensed with—the bees, to wit. Ordinarily these were harmless enough, or, at the worst, only became aggressive when their hives were disturbed; but then, as many hives were attached to low branches of the denser cover or to the trailing cane, it was no extraordinary occurrence for the elephants, in beating a jungle, to very much disturb several families of these insects, and then it was often enough a case of *sauve qui peut.* But for a time during one, if not two, of my Terai expeditions, the bees did not wait for any provocation whatever: they swarmed down from their hives in the upper branches of trees, and attacked us simply because we were in sight; and some trees carried hives (black and crawling on the surface, and each 3 or 4 feet in depth) enough to set up an extensive apiary, say from twenty to thirty. One day they fairly beat us out of the field. Jacky Hills, Combe, Benson, and I were carried off in different directions, and by a singular consensus of opinion we came together again, not at the cover-side, but in our camp. That day the bees would not leave us alone: wherever we went one lot of attackers followed, or a new lot relieved them.

And again that season the bees furiously assailed

us, and Combe unwisely jumped down from his elephant and took flight across a bit of open some 300 or 400 yards in width. His sun-hat fell off as he ran, and he arrived in the shelter of a clump of trees a pitiable object — his face like a cushion full of black pins, studded with stings, and he thoroughly beat by his run, exposure to the sun, and hundreds of pigmy spear-thrusts. It did not greatly console him to think that every bee that had left its sting in him had lost its life in doing so; comfort only came with brandy freely applied to his wounds, and even when the pain was reduced he suffered something for a day or two.

Because of these bees one takes a blanket as a part of one's howdah equipment. This is folded up and used as a cushion when not otherwise employed. When the bees attack one, it is put over and about one to keep the wretches off. A few get in at uncovered points, and them it behoves one to slay cautiously before they have delivered their sting, or leave alone. I do not remember having received more than seven stings in any one attack.

Wonderful is the pertinacity with which angry bees will pursue their object. Patiently one waits under the friendly blanket while overhead there is the buzzing as of a swarming hive; gladly does one hear this rattling of many wings die away in the distance, and cautiously does one emerge when there is reason to believe the bees have departed. Then, if a chance and isolated bee present itself within reach of any avenging weapon one may possess—a bough, or a hair-brush, or what not—it is in the greatest degree desirable that one strike with unerring and effectual aim; for if that chance bee be hit and not incapacitated for further action, it will to a certainty fly off and gather its fellows, and return with an angry host to avenge the insult of that unavailing blow. I know this from personal experience.

The bee is but one of several plagues that have to be set off *per contra* in the ledger of Terai joys. The fly is another—that common nuisance which infests the Terai country as an entomological anomaly—*i.e.*, a house-fly, where houses there are none. Wherever in those regions the camp of man is pitched, there do these dipterous insects—these minimised harpies—swarm. At night they are only moderately active, but when the day has warmed a little, they fill the air with their discordant buzzing, and every tea-cup, milk-jug, or other possible receptacle with their bodies. The only way of eating a breakfast in their company is to take that meal in an enclosure of mosquito-netting, and even then hundreds of them contrive to effect an entrance, and, being inside, dispute each mouthful between the plate or cup and lip. Then there are sand-flies, whose dimensions are such as preclude exclusion by any material that will admit the air, and whose stings are as aggravating as those of mosquitoes. And, finally, there is an insect that, as an amateur entomologist, I call the eye-fly—an insect that attacks one during the heat of the day, and particularly when one is open-eyed for tiger, with the set purpose of getting into one's eye. That villanous insect does not sting: it is satisfied with committing suicide, when the consequence is inflammation to the eye that crushes out its useless life; and it persists, in spite of frequent repulse, in finding a grave there. It is a nuisance when it dodges about within a foot of one's face, aiming now at one eye, now at the other. It is painfully so when it perishes triumphant.

The heat, too, is something to be faced and reckoned with; for the best season for Terai shooting is during the last six weeks of the hot weather, and as the tigers only descend to the swamps about mid-day, the hours for shooting are those when the heat is greatest. Not that one would be any better off if the shooting could be done in the cool of the morning, for a tent is an unendurable oven during the day, and the open air, however scorching, preferable to that canvas modification of the brazen bull of Phalaris, the tyrant of Agrigentum. But the heat in the open air is something that words cannot convey to the gentlemen of England who shoot at home at ease, and have never experienced the merry month of May as it is in Northern India and the Nepaul Terai. Seasoned as I was, I was often driven to various expedients to mitigate the severity of that blazing sun which beamed upon me out of what Anglo-Indians have styled a beastly blue sky. The large gig-umbrella held over me by my attendant in the back seat of the howdah, double-lined as it was, had little or no effect. A plantain or other broad leaf lining in my *sola topee* mocked me with delusive hope. The only thing that brought relief to aching eyes and burning skin was a wet towel, in which I enveloped head and shoulders, and through which I breathed a cooler air and saw nothing of the glaring light and wavering heat-gas that surrounded me. But one cannot shoot tigers or other game with a towel by way of veil, and I found that I could not do so while wearing tinted glasses; so when shooting was to be done, I faced the situation *au naturel.*

The handling of a gun after the sun had played upon it for an hour or two was sufficiently warm work when done in gingerly fashion, and with the least possible contact with the metal of barrel or trigger-guard: the sudden clutching of a barrel suggested collision with the wrong end of a red-hot poker. And the thirst! when once the man who is out in that heat yields to the temptation of his water, or cold tea, or lime-juice and water-bottle, he is thereafter for the rest of that day a lost creature, the slave of any fluid with which he can wet his parching lips and allay his insatiable thirst. Then would he drink kerosene, or ink, or sherry at eighteen-pence a quart, or any other abomination that possessed, in his view, the indispensable qualification of being liquid. So, too, will the natives—the mahouts and others—descend from the elephants and drink greedily from any fetid pool, though death be in the cup.

There is no little physical suffering to be borne by him who shoots tigers in the Terai season; but this is fully compensated for by success and the relief that comes with the eventide, when one returns to camp. Only a poet of the first order (say by the successor of the late poet-laureate, when he shall have been chosen) is worthy to sing the joys of the delightful twilight, the long cool drink that clears the heavy cobwebs from the throat and quells the torturing thirst, and that plunge into the depths of a tub whose brimming water seems to hiss as one's heated body sinks into it. And if that poet sing rapturously enough of the subdued heat of the twilight time, what shall be his song when it bears upon the cool air that descends from the Himalaya after nightfall, compelling the shirt-sleeved diners of the camp to don their coats for the conclusion of the banquet? Some minor songster, some mere poetaster, might chant a pæan of praise of the cool night that follows, and tell of the hunters' revel, which, in our case, was by no means of a rollicking order—nothing more, indeed, than discussion of that day's doings, future prospects, Shakespeare and the musical glasses, tobacco and the occasional peg. One year (and I think one year only) whist was included in this post-prandial carousal, but not with any great measure of success: we did not play scientific whist. It was not always recognisable as whist at all, and sometimes the question was not so much what were one's partner's cards as when he would be awake to play them. Poor dear Buffalo Smith was especially erratic in his game, and especially liable to fall asleep in the act of revoking or some other heterodox performance. He was a ripe scholar, distinguished among scholars as a Fellow of St John's, Oxford; he was a first-rate settlement officer, winning his way steadily to the forefront of his service; a good sportsman; a man of generous heart and open hand, and deft in keeping a long and complicated whist score,—but he had shortcomings in his play of that game, particularly when he was asleep.

I do not know why this member of the great family of Smiths was distinguished by the prenomen of Buffalo, except that he had to be differentiated from others of his name somehow, and poverty of selection may account for the adoption of this style. Smiths in India are generally treated in this manner, and I have met or heard of a score or so curiously prenomened men of that clan, from "Smith of Asia" down to "Cucumber" Smith, so called because it was alleged that he had never made the acquaintance of the cucumber until he went to the sunny East.

As for those enjoyable evening meals, whatever of luxury appertained to them was strictly confined to the fluids: wines and other liquors we had of the best, and these, cooled by swinging in a basket packed with wet grass, would have satisfied the most exacting; but of the solids, Apicius and Lucullus would have thought with mild horror. There was a terrible monotony about the day-to-day *menu* which it was impossible to avoid, and chicken was the inevitable foundation of the banquet, whatever variety might be introduced in the way of tinned provisions, an occasional joint of mutton, or the spoil of our rods and guns.

But when I speak in this collective sense about rods, I must not be understood to imply that I ever caught any fish. That was done by better masters of the gentle craft who were out with me—by Hume, Gream (then of the 62d), Jacky Hills, John Braddon of the 55th, and others. They went out in the early morning or late evening to whip the stream close by, when our camp was upon the bank of one of the small rivers that flow from the Himalayan snows: they brought back into camp goodly supplies of small mahseer, running from 1 lb. to 3 lb., and a spotted fish believed to be a trout, that averaged about ½ lb. in weight: and my only concern with the business was to assist in eating the fish they caught. In the larger hill-rivers, such as the Gagra, mahseer rivalling in size those of the Indus were to be caught by trolling with a spoon or live bait; but I never saw anybody but myself attempt to catch them, and as a fish did not respond to my spooning in less than five minutes I gave it up, and took a header into the deep clear stream, instead of trying further to get anything out. Ice-cold was that water, only just come from its source above the snow-line; and among the boulders that formed its bed, where the shallows were, we sank our bottles of many fluids, to extract them, thoroughly cooled, when wanted.

Game constituted an item of our *carte,* but this also became monotonous after a time. Florikan (a member of the bustard family), highly appreciated by the Indian *gourmet* when in season, was out of season in April, May, and June, and so was the black partridge. Pea-fowl, that lordly bird which, with its tail wide spread, adorns the regal and aldermanic board on state occasions, is no more to be eaten every day than the plebeian tripe or cow-heel. Indian venison and the flesh of the wild pig are only regarded as among things edible when there is absolutely nothing else to eat; and jungle-fowl, the only item of Terai game that was in season, and also fairly good to eat, did not greatly differ from the tame bird, the ubiquitous *moorghi.* But our *chef* overcame any difficulty arising out of flavourless or too flavourful meats by disguising them out of recognition in a common stew that was kept constantly going, and replenished with further supply of bird and beast, and tinned vegetables, and sauces, and jelly, and wine; a stew, in fact, that had the desirable quality of presenting several courses at once, and, ill-natured people might add, the attributes of the hog-wash tub.

Having said so much about our commissariat, I will only add that our supplies of bread, fresh vegetables, milk (except that of the goats which travelled with us), eggs, and butter were uncertain as to arrival and the condition in which they made their appearance. But who cared? We were out for shikar, and the pleasures of the table, such as they are, we could afford to postpone until we had returned to civilisation.

And before leaving the general description of our Terai camp, I think some few words should be bestowed upon the scavengers that were always with us and ready for their work, even though, far beyond the range of human vision, they swept the skies with their strong pinions in circling flight. The vultures were our scavengers, and often only they (for kites and jackals rarely, and carrion-crows only less rarely, shared this duty with them in the Terai), and the way in which they descended out of space on the instant when this work was to hand was amongst the most striking features of life thereaway.

Well does the tiger know the result of leaving its kill where the keen and far-reaching eye of the vulture can detect it. Some people hold by the fable that the vulture smells out its prey; but the tiger knows better than that—knows that if its kill be dragged beneath overhanging cover it will be safe from the vulture, and may be left accordingly with confidence. So does the tiger deal with the carcass of cow or deer or what not, when the jungle is adapted to the object of concealment, and then goes away to sleep off the effects of its first meal from the kill; but if it be not practicable to hide the kill, the tiger sits hard by and watches it, and the vultures swoop down upon the branches of the trees that overlook the tiger's shambles, and sit there waiting until the forest king shall be good enough to move away. That spectacle of many vultures seated almost motionless on the jungle trees is a hopeful one to the shikari, and he comes to understand with tolerable accuracy when it signifies that a tiger is close at hand: so does his experienced ear detect in a particular note of the carrion-crow and chattering of the monkey the warning that a tiger or leopard is afoot in the immediate neighbourhood. More especially is that cry of the monkey a tell-tale one, for the Indian crow is a mischievous blackguard and babbler, that may be expected to perjure itself at any moment out of sheer cussedness. Perjury comes cheaper, but not more naturally, from this bird than from the Indian professional witness, who hangs about the outskirts of the courts ready to swear to anything—a murder that has not been committed, or an *alibi* that is utterly false—for a remuneration of eight annas or less. But I do not know that there is much to choose between them.

The vulture is seen at its best when a dead tiger, brought into camp to be skinned, is exposed in the open. Overhead is a cloudless sky, and not a bird to be seen in that great void by human eye. The tiger's body is thrown from the pad on to the ground, and before the skin has been removed, there above one, and always nearing the earth, are the vultures circling; moving upon wings that do not seem to move; poising like things of air: now a dozen of them, in a few minutes a score or two, and then a hundred strong. Then, when the flayed carcass of the tiger is left by those who skinned it, the vultures descend: down they come like feathered thunderbolts with a loud rush of wings from out of the sky, and from east and west, and north and south. The very embodiments of power while they whirled aloft and in their quick descent to earth; and now, as they waddle round that carrion beast, misshapen ghouls, whose only apparent strength is that of the ravening jaws which tear and gorge the tiger's flesh, until within the hour nought of that splendid brute remains but a clean-picked skeleton.

Indispensable to the successful issue of Terai sport as the line of elephants, is the shikari who knows the country—the man who is acquainted with the tigers' haunts, their tricks and their manners, and who, looking at the *pugs* left by tiger or panther in river-bed or nullah, or even in the forest, can say with some degree of accuracy what time has elapsed since those footprints were impressed upon the ground, what distance the animal that made them might be expected to have travelled thence, and where, having these matters in consideration, it may be looked for with reasonable prospect of finding it. Shrewdness of observation and considerable experience are necessary to the acquisition of this branch of woodcraft: a neophyte will altogether fail to distinguish a tiger's footprint among the leaves that carpet the forest or on hardish ground; and as to the very obvious *pug* in river-sand, he will be able to form no opinion worth having that is not patent to everybody. When a tiger's *pugs* are seen in wet sand and the water is yet oozing into them, the neophyte knows that the tiger has just passed that way, as does everybody else; but in the majority of instances he cannot say whether they were made an hour ago or in the early morning or last night, and can deduce from them no useful information whatever.

So is the experienced and intelligent shikari of the Terai a man to be obtained as a part of one's establishment, and the two or three local men of any reputation in my time had to be engaged at a rate of remuneration that would have been ample for half-a-dozen B.A.'s of the Calcutta University.

Another reason for the employment of these experts arose from the fact that no information about tigers or other game could be got out of the few people one encountered in that sparsely populated country. In Deoghur every man, of whatever sort or condition, was glad to aid, with information or otherwise, him who sought to kill tigers. In the Terai there was to be found, outside one's immediate following, no man of that disposition. It has often happened to me, when I have been following up a tiger in the forest, to hear the tinkle of the cattle-bells, that told of cows or buffaloes grazing in an adjacent glade, and I have pushed on to where the cattle browsed and the cowherd watched or slept, hopeful of *khubber;* but never has the cowherd had information to give or a particle of interest to exhibit in the matter: always as supremely indifferent as he was ignorant, his apathy seemed to say, "Why ask about Terai tigers of me who am a lodger only?" A tiger might yesterday have killed one of the cattle in his charge, might, within the hour, have passed beneath the tree in whose shade he, the coloured Tityrus, lay; but what of that? Why because of a cow more or less, or a tiger nearer or farther, should he allow his thoughts to be distracted from the practical subjects of chupatties and pice? And because of the difficulty of acquiring *khubber* as one went from cover to cover, shikaris had to start from the camp in the early morning, and scour the country round about for *pugs* and kills.

As the years wore on I became somewhat independent of these Terai shikaris,—not so much because of the knowledge and experience I myself acquired, as for the prowess in the whole field of shikar of Khooda Buksh, my shikari, factotum, and friend for the last eleven years of my Indian career. I have known a good deal of many Indian natives, from the prince to the *murdofarash* (the pariah who looks after the ashes of the funeral pyre and prevents the defunct Hindoo from lingering on the banks of the sacred rivers). I have tried many of them in one sense to find them wanting; I have tried several in another sense to find them guilty: but never did I meet with one who, for good British virtues, was comparable with Khooda Buksh. He would deserve more than mere passing allusion in any work, and especially does he deserve it in a book that deals with sport, for no truer sportsman ever breathed than he. And so important a member of my *dramatis personæ* is he, that I shall bring him upon my stage with all the preliminary ceremony of prologue, &c., adopted in such cases by the playwright. Slow music must necessarily be dispensed with—would also that slow writing may be likewise banished!

The Maharaja of Bulrampoor of that time was one of the five loyal talookdars of Oudh—*i.e.*, one of the few who had stood by the English in the Mutiny of 1857, and had been the recipient of many honours and acres by way of reward for his support of the British Raj. He was a good shot and all-round sportsman, who, with a stud of about a hundred elephants and et-ceteras in proportion, lived largely for shikar. He killed his tigers and other game from his howdah, shooting indifferently from either shoulder. He kept hunting-cheetahs to run down the antelope; and he went out hawking after the manner of the nobles of Northern India, and few had better falcons than he. These were the pursuits he loved best, save only when he could pursue a titled Briton.

Bulrampoor's partiality for "lord sahibs" procured for me the benefit of his society on that occasion when Sir William Ffolkes made one of my party. The Norfolk baronet was the attraction, not I; but I came in for some measure of reflected glory—so much, indeed, that his highness volunteered to lend me a complete stud of elephants for my next season's campaign.

That is exactly what Bulrampoor did to poor Thackwell of the 5th Lancers, when he (Thackwell) was one of a party that had a "lord sahib" in it, and Thackwell listened and believed, and in the following season took a month's leave in view to using the thirty or forty promised elephants for tiger-shooting. Chaffey, a brother-officer, who has since commanded the 5th, accompanied him on this expedition, and Khooda Buksh went as his shikari.

When it came to the point, Bulrampoor lent them one elephant! and I shall describe later how he lent one to me, and what came of the riding thereof. With that one elephant Thackwell and Chaffey made no headway as far as tigers were concerned, and only when their leave was about to expire—when their last shooting-day had come—

did a chance of tiger-shooting present itself: a tigress and cubs were marked down in a ravine, and after these Thackwell and Chaffey went on foot. In that ravine Thackwell saw the tigress, and, firing from the bank above, wounded it: the tigress charged up the slope, and when it reached the top Thackwell pulled the trigger of his left barrel, the cartridge misfired, and the tigress, unchecked in its attack, sprang upon Thackwell, knocked him down, and began to maul him. Then Khooda Buksh showed the rare courage that was in him: the ordinary native shikari in such a critical situation as this might have been expected to take to his heels incontinently, or to climb the nearest tree whose branches were beyond a tiger's reach, and from that refuge shout for aid. Khooda Buksh did not give thought to his own safety, but to his master's peril only: he attacked the tigress with a stick and beat it off, and the tigress, cowed by his dauntless bearing, retreated into the ravine, slunk past the spot where Chaffey was stationed, and was killed by Chaffey there and then. The cubs were caught and presented to the London Zoo by Chaffey.

Thackwell was badly wounded in the arms, but, there were good grounds to hope, not mortally hurt. He was carried in a dhooli to the nearest district station (Baraitch), where three doctors attended him. Two of these three advised that one of his arms should be amputated, the third held that amputation was unnecessary, and poor

Thackwell naturally adopted the view of the minority. The temptation that way was too great: he was young, a captain in a cavalry regiment, passionately fond of his profession, and of shooting and all manly exercises, and to his view the loss of an arm meant the loss of many objects of living: so did he elect to retain his limbs intact, and take the chance that went with that decision. And at first it seemed as if he had chosen wisely. Day by day he appeared to be nearing complete recovery: he had so far improved that he was able to sit up and chat with the friends who surrounded him while he smoked his pipe; and then, coming as a surprise and shock to those who watched him, an artery burst beneath the healing surface of his wounded arm, and the brave spirit that had done no man wrong, nor ever thought or wrought evil, passed away.

Thackwell it was who told of Khooda Buksh's heroic deliverance of him from that tigress's jaws, not the brave soul that did the deed. Khooda Buksh was my servant and companion for many years. He and I used to discuss many things relating to shikar, and some few other matters that were not beyond his somewhat restricted intellectual horizon; but he never alluded to this —not even when he spoke of Thackwell's sayings and doings, those sacred memories of the master he had loved and served so well. Very faithful was he to that lost master: for a year or two after he entered my service he invariably spoke to me of Thackwell as his sahib. I was then to him an outsider, who by an accident of the hour chanced to be his employer, but I was not the master of his affections. *I* was not his sahib then, but I was to become that in the fulness of time.

Before I describe the virtues of Khooda Buksh, I may mention the one failing that I saw in him —viz., his imperturbability, or, as I have thought it in evil moments, stolid indifference. He was a thorough optimist, to whom whatever was was right, however unsatisfactory it may have been to other people. If the cart that carried my stores overturned in a river and destroyed the tea and sugar, or a camel came down with my camp equipage and smashed everything friable therein, he observed the disaster with philosophic unconcern, and mishaps that affected himself he regarded with similar equanimity. In short, he carried to an exasperating extent the generally wholesome maxim, *in arduis equam servare mentem.*

But he possessed a legion of good qualities to set against that one of doubtful merit. He was thoroughly truthful; and truthfulness is not an omnipresent virtue in Indo-Aryans. Indeed, to some observers it has appeared so rare, that these students of the native character have said in the most leisurely manner that all Indo-Aryans are liars. He was thoroughly honest also, and that is more than can be said for every member of his race. I would have trusted him with untold gold had the Indian currency permitted; I did trust him with untold silver—*i.e.*, with all the money that was expended from month to month in my establishment, and which, because of his inability to write or keep accounts, remained very much untold.

That he possessed courage as well as coolness of a high order his rescue of Thackwell proved. He had no opportunity of giving such another example when with me. He did not, I am glad to say, save me from a tiger's clutches, but I have seen him undertake risky tasks that many a man might have shirked; and on two or three occasions, when he and I were after tiger on foot, he sat by my side holding a spare gun while I stood at the cover's edge waiting for a tiger to be beaten out to me. And he was true as staunch, as faithful as he was brave. He did not, as I have shown, take a new master to his heart at once; but having so taken him, he would have given life itself in his service.

As a sportsman, he was untiring himself, although he sometimes went very near to tiring me. In camp, it was his task to see that the tents, &c., which went on ahead to the next camping-ground, left betimes—at 2 A.M. in the Oudh districts—and it was no light work to rouse sleepy camp-followers for the striking, packing, and loading of tents, &c. In the early morning he roused and valeted and chota-hazried me, and sent me off on the march, then packed my sleeping tent, &c., and followed. Riding the twelve or fourteen miles of my march in an hour and a half, I had time to do some work and eat my breakfast before Khooda Buksh came up. And he always "came up smiling," and willing, nay, anxious, to start off at once to a snipe-jheel, if there were one within reach; and his view as to what was reachable was always something more liberal than mine, as were his sentiments about trying yet another likely bit of ground ("Only half koss distant, sahib") when the sun was westering to its fall, and my lips were thirsting for the kiss of a brimming tankard. His heart was in all sport of jheel and jungle; and although he could shoot fairly well himself, he most enjoyed his sport vicariously. He was the only one of all the shikaris I have been out with who spoke his mind about my misses; according to the others I had never missed. If I had fired an 18-lb. shot at a titmouse, they would have pronounced it badly hit, albeit that bird continued perched upon a bough and twittered flat denial that it was touched. But K. B. (as he was familiarly styled) was an honest, perhaps even a severe, critic in this respect. He would not admit that a snipe was hit unless it towered or fell forthwith, and now and again a snipe would sell him by flying a couple of hundred yards, apparently unwounded, and then falling headlong to the ground.

Unique among natives in many ways, K. B. was most so in the matter of humour. He was the only native of my acquaintance who enjoyed a joke, and could perpetrate a hearty British guffaw. The educated Bengalis (not the Baboos particularly) have amused me greatly by tales of kazis and rajahs and courtiers, in which the vices and weaknesses of the characters were held up to scathing ridicule; but it was the grim satire that tickled me, not the fun or mirth. Those *raconteurs* were more sardonic than Swift, and had none of the great Dean's lighter touch. There was just a dash of mischief in K. B.'s joyousness, and when no other joke was forward, he was not superior to a practical one. I will give a brace of examples.

Once upon a time K. B. and I went by rail to one of the Oudh stations, and when on our arrival he was passing along the station platform a superior native Being in a first-class compartment beckoned to him. K. B. approached that superior person, and was asked who was his sahib (meaning me). K. B. could not resist the temptation to administer a snub to, and take a rise out of, the inquisitive bahadoor. He affected an air of mystery, and whispered that his sahib was the Viceroy and Governor-General.

But his better practical joke—a joke that was practical in a double sense—was perpetrated on another occasion of our railway travelling. He and I were starting for camp from the Lucknow station, and he was confronted with the difficulty of finding room for himself and a quantity of stores and luggage in a crowded third-class compartment. It was a physical impossibility to get himself and our belongings into that compartment while all the passengers already seated there remained. But how were these superfluous travellers to be removed? Cajolery addressed to them, or entreaty addressed to the station-master, would have fallen upon deaf ears. K. B., like a latter-day Wamba, grasped the situation and a ham that was among the stores in his charge, rushed into the compartment, and waving that ham aloft shouted, "*Haram! haram!*" (shame or desecration). As a matter of course, every one of K. B.'s co-religionists who possessed any religious sense had to fly from before that brandished pork, which was anathema maranatha to every pious Moslim. There was straightway a new Hejira, and K. B. calmly appropriated the vacated space for himself and chattels.

It must be admitted that K. B., good fellow as he was, had not a spark of religious sentiment in him. Nominally a Mahomedan, he had as little respect for that creed as for any other: he had no prayer-carpet; he said no *nemaz;* and though a poor Indian of untutored mind, he utterly belied Pope's view of him, and saw no deity in clouds or heard him in the wind. But if he failed in this particular, he entertained a healthy self-respect that became him well: once only during the many years that he was with me did I, in the heat of the moment, and when he had been more than usually philosophical about some vicissitude, speak to him in terms that he resented, and then quietly but resolutely he resigned his situation. But his affection got the better of his pride, and after absenting himself for twelve hours, he let me know through another retainer that he desired a reconciliation. Had he held out a little longer, I should have made the first advance in this direction; as it was, I jumped at the opportunity he offered, apologised for my misconduct, and never offended again. Nor did he presume upon this moral victory: he remained the same kindly, cheerful, and faithful servant, to the time of my departure from India, when there was a sad parting between us, that left him tearful, and me not altogether dry-eyed.

And now I will clear my stage for the Maharajah of Bulrampoor, by describing my experience of borrowing elephants from him. He lent me one, as I have said—a howdah animal of tolerable character, if only it had been sound; but it was not sound: it suffered from chronic lameness or weakness of one hip-joint, and this craziness of limb brought trouble to me.

I did not ride that elephant often; I am not sure that I rode it more than once. I am only certain that I rode it once too often. Anyhow, I was mounted upon this beast one day when I came upon the fresh footprints of a fairly large tiger. Those *pugs* were near the edge of a swamp, which was, for the most part, a long pond of clear water. In no portion of this miniature lake was there heavy cover, but it was fringed on one side by a narrow strip of high grass, in which I hoped to come upon the tiger whose trail I followed. Limited as that cover was, my hope was justified by the absence of any other from the environment of the lake, whether grass or reed or forest.

I had not gone far upon those tracks when I saw the grass ahead of me wave the signal that a tiger was afoot. Then I looked upon that tiger as mine —for what could save it? It could not break away on either hand without exposing itself to the batteries of the three gunners who were after it; it could not get away forward beyond our reach; I never dreamed that it could break back and so escape; so I pushed on, keen for the triumph that I had already discounted, Jacky Hills and Gream close following. Again and yet again I saw that signal of the waving grass, and might have shot the tiger without seeing it; but why attempt to kill my quarry, yet unseen, with a chance shot, when in a minute or two it would show itself either by flight in the open or by turning in defiance upon its pursuer? So, always close behind it, I drove it forward into the last patch of that strip of grass, when the alternative was forced upon it to fight or fly. It elected for the former, and charged straight for my—*i.e.*, Bulrampoor's—elephant. I had seen nothing of it until it was on my elephant's head, and then, again, I said to myself, this tiger is mine. Confident that the result would be such as it had been in my previous experiences of this situation, I leaned over the howdah, placed the muzzle of my smooth-bore close to the neck of the tiger, and pulled the trigger. This was the work of two or three seconds; but a performance of Bulrampoor's elephant, which synchronised with it, upset all my calculations, and nearly everything else of mine then present. The brute of an elephant thought fit to draw back from the tiger, and in stepping back its game leg gave way, and over it went sidelong with a crash, that spread the mahout, my shikari, myself, and all my paraphernalia broadcast upon the ground, and a good deal distributed us and ours among the legs of elephants pushed to the front by my comrades.

As that crash of matter and fall of elephant were exactly timed to the pulling of my trigger, the bullet aimed at the tiger's neck sped harmlessly heavenward. Perhaps that was as well for us, who involuntarily became the tiger's companions when we were all precipitated to earth together. A wounded tiger, of malicious nature, might have made it very unpleasant for some of us as we lay there unarmed, much shaken, and wholly unfit for fight; but this one was unwounded, and, being thrown from the elephant's head, did not stay to improve its acquaintance with us. It made no further demonstration of any kind; perhaps it was satisfied with a modest victory, and thought it not unseemly to march off after a first triumphant round, or discretion may have prevailed over valour: be that as it may, the tiger disappeared.

And of all the unexpected things that may happen in tiger-shooting, that disappearance was, I think, the most unexpected. The tiger must have escaped across the open within fifty yards of Jacky Hills and Gream, both of whom, gun in hand, looked down from their howdahs upon the scene, ready and longing to shoot the beast that had so upset the beat. But they looked down too closely: closing in in front of my prostrate form, they thought only of shooting the tiger when it threatened us fallen ones; they saw nothing of it —and so that tiger was lost to us.

CHAPTER X.

MIXED SHOOTING IN OUDH.

SNIPE—QUAILS—BLACK-BUCK—NEELGHAI—GHURRIALS AND MUGGURS.

DURING my fifteen years in Oudh I enjoyed a fair amount of sport other than that of the Terai. My official duties while I was in that province involved a six months' tour through the twelve districts into which Oudh was divided, and into every portion of them, where there might be an office or distillery to inspect or a jheel to shoot over. Every year I rode and drove a distance of about 3000 miles; and this nomadic life gave me opportunities of visiting all the best shikar country, whatever the distance from my headquarters might be. Unfortunately for me, I could not always ensure being first in the field at every point. It frequently happened that other men, similarly inclined with myself, arrived before me, and got the first and best of the shooting. These rivals sallied forth from every district *sudder* station, many of them from many quarters, and, single-handed, I could not cope with them in the race; so went the cream of the shooting to them, and the skim to me who followed.

But when fortune was good enough to smile upon me, I made fairly good bags of snipe between November and March while the season lasted. I did not expect to beat that Kanchrapara record of 51½ couple: 20 couple satisfied me, and when I reached 30 couple I considered that there was nothing left to wish for immediately in the way of snipe. And very frequently I shared the good things of the jheel with friends who came from Lucknow or elsewhere to join my camp; and a possible big bag for a single gun became a very modest one for three or four.

Fairly good quail-shooting was to be had in the wheat and grain fields, and in dry grass cover of a certain kind, from December to April; but in this branch of sport the shooter had to compete with the man of nets—the native who caught the birds alive for the quaileries of Anglo-Indians. And one may well pardon the purchasers of these netted fowl; for when in the summer solstice the Anglo-Indian is a close prisoner within the *kus-kus tattied* walls, and below an ever-swinging punkah; when his eye cannot bear the light of mid-day, and his jaded appetite cannot tolerate the gram-fed mutton or gun-bullock beef of his healthier days — the quail, round and tender, served in a vine-leaf wrapper, comes as an appetising delicacy, and saves a man from sheer starvation. The teal or wild duck, similarly kept and fattened in a tealery, is another possible article of food when the luxurious Anglo-Indian feels that without some tremendous tonic he is unequal to the consumption of a roast butterfly-wing. Oh, they are truly a luxurious people, those Anglo-Indians, as so many Englishmen believe! Even if they have not as everyday incidents of their daily life the plashing of cool fountains, the waving of fans by ox-eyed houris, and other delights of the kind commonly credited to them, they have quail and teal as aforesaid, and the splashing of the water upon the *tatties*, and much disturbance of moistened air by waving punkahs, and rheumatism incidental to that artificial moisture, and prickly heat, and mosquitoes, and white ants in that final stage of their existence when, rising from the floor on ephemeral wings, they knock against and fall upon or into everything, and shed their wings everywhere before they perish. All those delectable things, and others of much the same sort, are given to the Anglo-Indian, and yet he does not understand that his life is full of delight and sensuous joys ('Arabian Nights' *passim*), and allows thoughts of furlough and the decline of the rupee to cast their shadow upon him.

Those white ants, by the way, if not sportive themselves, are the cause of sport to others—the crows and kites, to wit. They are not sagacious things, even to the moderate level of the elephant, and in the absence of any restraining instinct they often swarm out of their earthen homes while it is yet light; and while they are fluttering in the air seeking for something to knock their heads against, the birds of prey assemble, and swooping hither and thither among the insect battalions, devour them wholesale. This comes by way of just retribution to the white ant, in that this insect shares with Time the discredit of being *edax rerum.* It devours the beams and roof, and walls and floor, and mats and furniture of the Indian household. It is said to have devoured the rupees in a Government collectorate—that is, the native treasurer alleged that this had happened when his balance in hand showed a considerable deficit.

Revenons à nos cailles. In Oudh the sportsman was satisfied with the moderate bags of quail that came to him in the ordinary course. He did not resort to the employment of call-birds, as is the fashion of the Punjab, where these decoy-birds are put down overnight to attract all the wild quail within earshot. Bags of 50 and 100 brace are the consequence of this practice: we in Oudh were satisfied with 15 to 30 brace that fell to us haphazard in the course of much patient beating of cover, and, after two or three years' modest shooting of this kind, I only shot quail when they rose from my path to a snipe jheel, or when, during the last hour of the day, five to ten brace were to be got out of the grain- or wheat-fields close to my tent.

Hares, black and grey partridges, and (in the Transgogra districts) florikan, were occasionally to be got in small numbers, and of larger game antelope, neelghai, and hog-deer.

Black-buck (antelope) shooting I found very fascinating for a time. It is a form of shikar that generally exercises all one's patience and accuracy of hand and eye, and frequently exercises all one's muscles. Native shikaris stalk them from behind a cow with eminent success; but it is not given to every European to be competent to manage an Indian cow, and I never tried that method. I have shot them from behind my horse, with rifle rested upon the saddle, but mostly I followed them on foot; and I think the more open attack, when made with due caution, is the more efficacious. My plan was that of oblique attack. When I sighted a black-buck at a distance, I walked straight for it, until it took notice of me (say at 200 yards' distance); then I faced slightly away from it, and walked for a point that lay a hundred yards to right or left of it: when for a few moments it resumed grazing, I made a crab-like advance that brought me something nearer to it on a direct line, but always with averted face; and when the black-buck started, I brought my rifle (hitherto held concealed behind me) to the present, and fired a snapshot, aimed, for choice, at a point just behind the shoulder. I found that I succeeded better with this snapshooting at a running buck than with the more deliberate sighting of a standing one; and, at any rate, I succeeded so well in my judgment, that I sickened myself of black-buck shooting on any large scale. I became *blasé* as to this form of sport after killing twenty-two buck in three consecutive days. I might possibly have escaped from this feeling but for the result of the third day of those three; albeit, on the second, suspicion whispered within me that I was converting myself into the meat-purveyor for the villagers round about. But on the evening of that third day, when the carcasses of eight black-buck and a doe (killed by a bullet that had first penetrated and killed a buck)—nine carcasses in all—were hanging from the branches of trees around my tent, I felt that I was a butcher undisguised, and that my slaughtering hand had converted that tranquil grove into a butcher's shambles. From that time out I never made a business of pursuing them, but shot them only, one at a time, when I or my followers wanted venison.

And however ardently the Briton's longing to kill something may burn in one's breast—however much one may "see red"—one may well be spared the pain of seeing some of the black-buck's death agonies. It is enough when the animal falls dead at the first shot; but when it flies before one on legs broken by ill-directed bullets, running on the stumps of those shattered limbs, the sight is apt to sicken one, and bring shame upon one's handiwork.

As for neelghai, I was wild to kill one when I went to Oudh, if only because I had never as much as seen one in Deoghur. But very little neelghai went a long way with me in every sense: as meat it was only a partial success when none other was to be had; as an object for the rifle it was only preferable to that domestic buffalo which I killed, in that it could be killed for nothing; as a creature to be ridden down it was—when, after its habit, it got into heavy tussocky ground and swamp, and the thick-growing reed—distinctly a disappointment, and, moreover, a disappointment that caused me one or two heavy falls. I gave up neelghai after killing two or three of them.

The animal known as neelghai (or blue cow) in Oudh, and deemed by Hindoos of that province to be sacred, as one of the bovine tribe, was known in Deoghur as Ghoraroz, and counted by the local Hindoos as one of the deer species, which it was lawful to kill and eat: as a fact it is, I suppose, one of the antelopes. This divergence of views, entertained by Hindoos of different localities, is nothing, as an anomaly, compared with the varying treatment extended by Hindooism universally to different members of the bovine kind: on the one hand, the veneration for the cow, which makes that animal's life something sacred, and only permits of the twisting of the venerated creature's tail; on the other hand, the general practice at the Doorjah Poojah, and on other occasions, of sacrificing buffaloes to the gods by beheading them before the altars.

Among the game (?) that I permitted myself to shoot, or shoot at, during my wanderings in the Oudh districts, were alligators—the ghurrial, or long-nosed saurian, whose prey was fish, and the muggur, whose prey was man or cow, or any animal that it could catch, with fish on fast days. Neither of these is of attractive appearance, but I think the latter is the most repulsive member of the animal creation. Of the muggur it may be said, indeed, *monstrum horrendum informe;* all the epithets signifying forms of ugliness may be fairly applied to this brute: shapelessness is the main characteristic of its blunt head, the bloated carcass, and those legs that, curtailed of their fair proportions, are merely flappers. When it lies stretched along the ooze or sand of a river bank, or by some stagnant pool, it may well be taken for a harmless if hideous and very dirty log, but it is not harmless or as useful as that derelict timber, and its disposition is evil as its body. Yet has that monstrous form something in it which is precious to somebody, even as the less ugly toad is said to bear a jewel in its head. There is a portion of the internal structure of the mugger which is greedily seized upon by natives as a charm, whenever the mugger is given over into the native's hands for autopsy.

When I corrected the term "shooting" into

"shooting at" muggurs, I did so advisedly, because shooting seems to convey the idea of bagging the creature shot, and this is by no means the ordinary result of firing at an alligator; for, as far as my experience goes, the alligator is never to be seen save in the water or on the edge of it, and even when it is lying asleep on a sand or mud bank some feet from the water, no bullet that does not paralyse it on the instant will prevent it from lumbering (the word gliding would convey the idea of too graceful movement) into its aqueous home. A bullet in that point where the head and body join, and where a neck would be if this saurian had a neck, will stop an alligator, and it is by such a shot that I have killed and bagged them.

Muggurs and ghurrials, with an occasional wild goose, were the only things I had to shoot what time I went down the Ganges in a small covered boat to visit certain trade registration posts on the Oudh frontier. Alligators abounded there: small ones were to be seen by the score on the churs and sand-pits, and every now and then a big one—a muggur of 16 feet, or a ghurrial of 20 feet—was to be observed, generally with noses pointed towards the river, and most of them doubtless much more wide awake than they looked. There, upon the sand, these reptiles basked in the genial warmth of a December mid-day sun, and there I now and again killed and landed one.

But the place for shooting at them was the bridge of boats across the Gogra, on the Baraitch road. I have stood on that bridge (not at midnight) and fired at twenty or thirty of them within the hour; but always I had to take them as they rose out of the depths, and when they presented only their heads as targets. Over and over again I have seen them sink in response to my shot, and the clear water of the river incarnadined by what might well have been their life's blood; but only once did I bag one in that way, and then I succeeded as a consequence of bad shooting. I hit a ghurrial on the projecting jaw instead of in the head: instead of sinking in the water to die, it emerged upon the bank, and there was disposed of by a shot in the vital spot.

CHAPTER XI.

RECOLLECTIONS OF THE TERAI.

SPORTING COMPANIONS—SHOOTING FROM THE HOWDAH—MAHOUTS—PADDING TIGERS—A TIGRESS AND THREE CUBS—A MYSTERIOUS TIGER—SMOOTH-BORE GUNS—JACKY HILLS—HIGHEST RECORD OF TIGERS—TIGERS CHARGING ELEPHANTS—A MONSTER PYTHON—THE PRESERVATION OF THE TERAI—FOREST FIRES—JUNG BAHADOOR'S ELEPHANT-CATCHING CAMP—PETS—THE MONGOOSE—SNAKE AND MONGOOSE FIGHTING.

BUT *the* shikar of each year from 1863 to 1876 (save 1869, when I was at home on sick leave), to which I always looked forward with the keenest interest and anticipation of enjoyment, was that of the Terai. Would that I had kept some sort of diary in those days, to which I could refer at this juncture, for my memory, challenge it as I may, utterly declines to serve me in some particulars that might be deemed worthy of mention. By a process of exhaustive analysis I can affirm that I made thirteen expeditions into that region, and I arrive at that positive result by a process which is as simple as exhaustive, for I went to the Terai regularly every season from 1863 to 1876—save that of 1869, when I was not in India. Then, as I usually spent from four to six weeks there, I make out with tolerable accuracy that I gave in the aggregate some sixteen months to the pursuit of tigers thereaway; but when I try to recall the total number of tigers killed on those occasions, I am utterly at a loss. I can remember that in 1863 I got ten, and I suppose that score remains indelibly fixed in my mind because at the time it seemed to me highly satisfactory for a novice in the Terai methods; but I cannot fix any total for any subsequent year, and can only say in that regard that the annual total was more than once below ten, and, indeed, as low as five or six.

Another point as to which my memory will not be jogged to any purpose is as to my companions in some of those thirteen expeditions. Two or three times I went out alone, but even as to ten or eleven occasions I cannot make up my parties; and in addition to those I have already named as my companions of the Terai, I can only think of Colonel M'Bean, chief of the Lucknow commissariat, E. J. Lugard, aide-de-camp to the General commanding the Lucknow

Division, Westmorland, R.E., and Mitchell (who was doing India with Sir William Ffolkes). But then some whom I have named were with me more than once,—Peters, for instance, three times, and Jacky Hills even more frequently.

My memory is green enough, however, when I think of the pleasant life and splendid sport that it was my good fortune to enjoy so often under the shadow of the Nepal hills; and although, doubtless, the more agreeable features of those jaunts are most prominent in my reminiscences, I can without difficulty recall those that may be regarded as drawbacks, and, having arrayed all the disagreeable characteristics before my mind's eye, I should even now be glad to encounter them all for the sake of one more month after tiger.

For many of the minor trials of Terai sport not yet mentioned the needle-witted elephant is directly or indirectly responsible. It is weary work riding one, whether on pad or howdah (pad-riding being the easier of the two), for eight or ten hours at a stretch; and starting from our camp at 10 A.M., it often happened that our home-coming was delayed till 8 P.M. Perhaps we had to travel eight or ten miles to reach the swamp where our day's work was to be commenced. Possibly we were drawn away from camp by a tiger's trail or something incidental to the business in hand which drove camp out of our minds; or, worst of all, it chanced now and again that we lost our way in the forest.

With what gruesome import the announcement fell upon my ear that the way was lost when, being benighted in those trackless forests, we were ten miles from our tents and dinner and bed, and some unknown distance from any other human habitation! But our guide would impart this intelligence with as full a measure of apathy as if he had told us that the day was Monday, or something equally immaterial. "*Rasta bool gya*" ("I have forgotten the road") would he say; and euphonious though that brief sentence be, it came upon one as sadly discordant when surrounded on every side by unmeasured miles of forest-trees that in their sameness mocked all attempt at identification, and by their denseness of foliage high overhead shut out the light of guiding stars. I have spent a night in one of those forests, and had an opportunity of learning that not going home till morning may on occasion be a very painful experience.

Then the howdah, that bed of Procrustes, in which one can neither sit nor stand with any approach to reasonable ease, and in which a recumbent attitude is impossible! Its advantages are—(1) that, standing in it, a man can shoot on every side of him: (2) that it is convenient for the carriage of the occupant's paraphernalia,—his guns on racks on either side; his ammunition in a trough in front; his other requisites in leathern pockets here and there on the sides of the machine, or, as to that bee-blanket, on his seat: and (3) that in the hinder compartment an attendant can sit or stand to hold a monster umbrella over his head, or, when quick loading is required, take from his hand the gun just fired and re-charge it. Those are the advantages; otherwise the howdah is an abomination.

The great merit of the pad is its easiness compared with the howdah; but seated upon that, with an attendant, one can only carry a second gun and some ammunition; one can only shoot on one side with any effect; and a lively tiger may possibly join the party seated there. This last objection to the pad is all the more probable by reason of the fact that the sportsman cannot shoot all round: for, supposing him to be right-handed and only able to shoot from his right shoulder, he would be unable, without shifting his position on the pad, to fire at a tiger close to him on his right hand; and if he hurriedly attempted to shift his position, he might very well fall to the ground, there to try conclusions with the tiger.

These considerations necessitate the employment of the howdah, in which it behoves one to stand as long as there is any chance of a shot. In my first season in the Terai I lost a tiger through non-observance of this ordinance. I had been beating down a long water-course in the forest for an unconscionable time, as it seemed to me, without seeing the tiger I was after. I had passed through the more likely cover in that narrow channel, which, dry as it was at that season, did not greatly promise tigers; and being in very patchy grass, I thought I might safely sit down. Hardly had I seated myself, when a tiger got up in front of me, and, before I was on foot to deal with it, the beast was away in the forest on my left, never to be seen again that day. I was alone on that occasion; there was no second gun on the alert to make up for my remissness; and so it was entirely due to my own indifference that my bag of that year was ten instead of eleven.

Laziness of this sort is palliated, if not excused, by the tiring effect of long standing in a howdah. Few howdahs are boarded at the bottom, so as to admit of any choice of foothold, and, even when they are boarded, he who stands in them finds it expedient, both for general comfort (or some approximation thereto) and accuracy of shooting, to stand, as a latter-day Colossus, with extended limbs and wide-stretched feet that rest (if there can be rest in a howdah) upon the plates or foot-frames on either side at the bottom of the howdah.

Then the howdah becomes a positive nuisance two or three times a-day, or perhaps all day long, by inclining over on one side, until it seems likely to topple off the elephant. When these symptoms make their first appearance (possibly half an hour after one has started) a halt is cried, and the whole strength of the company is enlisted to restore the howdah to its equilibrium, but mostly in vain;

mostly it is as obdurate as Humpty Dumpty in regard to being set up again, and proceeds to cant over within five minutes of the operation that aimed at its rectification. Another halt, and another wrestling with ropes and inexorable fate; another ephemeral balance, and another diversity, and so *da capo* until the inevitable final step, when a man hangs on to the upper side of the howdah as a compensatory balance, and stops there. Sometimes two men are required for this service, when they are suggestive of those footmen who hung on at the back of the state coach of the early Georgian era.

And this erratic conduct on the howdah's part is encouraged by the elephant's action when labouring through heavy swamp. When the elephant is up to its girths in tenacious mud, it heels over on its right side to extricate its left hind-leg, and that gymnastic effort being completed, heels over on its left side to get its right hind-leg clear: so it rolls heavily from side to side, like a Channel steamer in a choppy sea, with frequent disarrangement of its gear. The effect upon its passengers may be left to the imagination; but, in order to pile up the agony of the situation, I may add that sometimes one or more tigers may be skirmishing around the swamp-disabled elephant, and much more on a level with the riders of that animal than would be the case on firmer ground. But any disadvantage arising from this, and from any unusual difficulty of shooting, must be regarded as fully compensated by the elephant's inability to bolt. As for shooting from an elephant, there is, in my opinion, but one way of doing this—viz., to sight one's object clearly, let the eye direct the hand in levelling the gun or rifle, without looking at sights or barrels, and pull the trigger on the instant that the weapon touches the shoulder. It is impossible to take deliberate aim at anything from an elephant, because that beast is never still by any chance: even when it is standing at halt there is about it a continuous motion—a sort of ground-swell—which is just as certain a hindrance of a long aim as the rougher jolting that characterises its lumbering progress.

Lastly, as connected with the trials of the flesh and temper that come with elephants, let me say a word for (I mean against) the mahouts. Many natives with whom the Anglo-Indian has to do are aggravating, more especially in the hot weather. The punkahwallah who, on a sultry night of June, having clutched the punkah rope with his toe, stretches himself out at length in the verandah, and, lulled by the vain imagining that so he will pull the punkah, goes to sleep, is of this class; so is the cook who strains his master's soup through a much kerosened lamp-cloth or some more obnoxious medium; so, too, is the bearer, or other custodian of a master's property, who, in regard to some indispensable chattel lost within the last twelve hours, swears by all his gods that no such chattel ever existed, or that it was satisfactorily disposed of years ago,—all these people, and others of their kind, are very irritating at times, but none of them so persistently so as mahouts of an inferior class.

Some elephant-drivers take an interest in their work, even in the task of beating tigers out of their lairs, but they are the minority. The majority are inspired by the one ruling idea of shirking all work that can any way be avoided. Because it is less toilsome to sit on the pad and drive with a casual touch of their heel, they will sit there, although they lose all control over their elephants that they possess when, sitting on the neck with their feet in the stirrups and their knees pressed against the elephant's ears, they urge their mounts forward. Because it is less troublesome to spend the day without encountering a tiger, they will break line at the most important juncture, and possibly allow a tiger to head back and escape when a few minutes more of persistent effort in close line would have seen that tiger driven into the open and probably killed. Because it is easier driving in the light cover where the tiger may not be expected, they will scrupulously avoid the denser patches in which it should be looked for. And for these and other reasons, the task of controlling these undisciplined men — keeping them in something like an effective line and getting them to beat in likely places—is one of frequent strain and travail that may well try the most Job-like patience and drive the meekest of masters to objurgation. I always endeavoured on these expeditions to enlist the sympathies of the mahouts in my cause—to give a co-operative tinge to it, by the promise of so much per tiger head in addition to the ordinary buksheesh; but this did not seem to affect their conduct in the slightest degree.

And as to any risk to be run, the mahout who sits in his proper place on the elephant's neck is a good deal safer than appearances might lead one to imagine. As long as his elephant keeps upon its feet he is secure enough: a tiger cannot reach him from the front over the elephant's head, or ordinarily on either flank, because the elephant's ears cover his legs. It is true that one of Yule's mahouts had his leg smashed by a tiger that charged from behind his elephant's shoulder, and caught his leg when the elephant's ear flapped forward for an instant; but this was a quite unique incident, as far as my experience is concerned, and I know of no other exception to the general rule above laid down.

When, in spite of many obstacles presented by elephants and mahouts, a tiger is killed, there yet remains a difficulty to be coped with—viz., that of padding the tiger. There lies the beautiful monarch of the forest shorn of that mighty strength that animated him an hour ago, and harmless now as the bleating lamb: a *gujbag* or some such missile has been thrown upon the stretched-out body, and the dull thud it made upon the corpse was unattended by any sound from, or motion of, that stricken form. It is dead; and, in order that it may be stripped of its black-barred robe, it has to be carried into camp upon one of the pad elephants,—so now descend from your elephants, you mahouts and attendants of the more stalwart sort, and pad that tiger.

Hoc opus, hic labor est. A full-grown male tiger requires a good deal of lifting. I have seen fourteen men putting their shoulders to this work, or pretending to do so, without immediately placing the tiger high enough for the two or three men mounted on the pad to secure it. I remember how, with one of these larger brutes, Gream, the athlete, and Jacky Hills, the robust, and I were prominent among the workers, and how, taking up my position on the pad, I hauled vigorously upon the rope which we had passed round the tiger, and continuing to haul with too persistent vigour when the tiger had slipped from the noose I hauled upon, went over headlong on the off-side; and even now I can recall the heat of that operation.

When one comes to lifting a dead tiger, one becomes fully aware of its weight; so does one arrive at due appreciation of its strength after once feeling that fore-arm, which is one splendid mass of steel-like muscle. Then one understands how the tiger in his prime can throw a bullock over its shoulder and canter away with it. Then, too, one may well come to pooh-pooh the claim of the lion to be styled the king of beasts. But however interesting may be the study of the tiger in this particular phase once or so, it palls after a time: lifting it is peculiarly hard and hot work, and it is dirty work also, and is sometimes made particularly exasperating by the *lâches* of the elephant selected for the carriage of the tiger. For that intelligent beast is required to kneel to receive its freight, and to kneel long enough to allow that freight to be hoisted on to the pad and fastened there; and, as often as not, it will rise at the critical moment, just when the tiger has been raised to the edge of the pad, and tumble the tiger and some of its lifters on to the ground, and so bring about the *status quo ante.* The elephant has wonderful shrewdness in some utterly useless directions. It will, for example, pick up a pin with its trunk, and, I daresay, with sufficient encouragement would swallow the pin, and convert its interior economy into a pin-cushion; but I have never known one direct its talents to the simplification of tiger-padding, although I have seen many devote their minds and bodies to the unnecessary duty of adding to the difficulties of that operation.

And when at last the tiger is padded, the elephant has to be reckoned with; for as likely as not it will for the next hour or so, after seeing that tiger hoisted and tied, imagine tigers in everything it sees and every sound it hears. It is well at such a time to approach an elephant with considerable caution, and from the front, lest it make itself disagreeable. Poor K. B. found this out on one occasion, when, after helping to pad a tiger, he ran after my elephant to mount by the tail; for the elephant, hearing him coming from the rear, necessarily assumed that he was a tiger, and kicked out at him with such force and precision as sent him flying for some yards.

This tiger-padding was such a nuisance to my mind, that when I could have my own way and it was practicable, I left a man with a spare elephant behind to remove the skin and bring it into camp, leaving the carcass where it fell.

The shikari who hunts the tiger in the Terai has to be prepared for many blank days—not a few days, indeed, so blank that not a shot is fired; for while there is any chance of a tiger in the neighbourhood the signal to shoot at anything is withheld. Many such days have I spent in driving through swamp or stretches of dry grass, or the broken cover of forest-glades and nullahs, when sambhur with magnificent heads and fine horned cheetul have got up at my elephant's feet to tempt me; and the black partridge and jungle fowl have flaunted around me to beguile; and at every turn game seemed plentiful as never they were in the most favoured spot when I might shoot at them. On many a day have I resisted these temptations with a stoicism that would have set up a dozen of those old-time philosophers with St Anthony thrown in, and without any reward in the shape of tiger or panther. From before noon till nightfall I have pounded along through every sort of cover, always hoping, but hoping vainly, and never once relaxing the iron rule, "cease firing."

Very curious are the chances of tiger-shooting sometimes. In my first season in the Terai, Lugard and I marched, shooting as we went, for a camping-ground on the edge of a swamp wherein tigers had been often found. We reached our tents in the evening, and ill tidings, always quick of travel, met us before we descended from our elephants. The Nawab Musumudowla (uncle of the ex-king of Oudh) had that day beaten our swamp thoroughly, and got nothing. It was melancholy news, and a poor appetiser for our dinner. But when the next day dawned there was nothing for it but to try that swamp again, on the off-chance that the tiger which had not come into it yesterday might be there to-day; and so, after breakfast, and an hour or two of office work for me, we started. The swamp was as to the greater part clear water, surrounded on three sides by open country; but along the edge next to the forest there was a strip of heavy grass, and that we beat from end to end without a glimpse of tiger. Then, acting upon information received (as the mysterious police-constable observes), I formed the elephants into a crescent-line and made a cast through the jungle that aimed at beating down a certain nullah towards the swamp. It was not a very hopeful business, for up in the forest a tiger when started may just as well go one way as another. There was, however, the possibility that the thick grass that was standing in the nullah might tempt a tiger to seek shelter there, and that possibility resolved itself into a certainty. There was a tiger in it: more than that, there were four tigers in it, all of which were driven out into a comparatively clear space, where cover of any kind was slight and scattered. Four—a tigress, and three cubs more than half grown. How the tigress got away immediately upon our sighting it I cannot say now, any more than I could then. It was as phenomenal an object to me as was young Joe Willet to his father. I looked at it, and there it was; and I looked at it again, and there it wasn't. Nor can I understand why it so promptly deserted its offspring—for mostly a tigress will fight for its cubs as long as they are with their mother, even though they be fully grown. But the maternal instinct was weak in that tigress: clannishness it felt nothing of. It disliked the situation, and left the scene and the cubs before a shot could be fired at it. The cubs did what they could to make things lively: they never attempted to follow their mother, but sought with creditable courage to defend their ground. Charging an elephant here and there, they fought while life and strength were in them, and died with their faces to the foe. That day my record of two tigers was broken, and one of three substituted.

Again, in that same season, it happened that Westmorland and I were encamped by the edge of the same swamp, and while we were making leisurely preparations for a start, Musumudowla's host descended upon our ground and beat over it. They beat it in vain, and not a shot was fired by their party to rouse the forest echoes or the forest king; so Musumudowla came and went, he and his, and we watched his line of elephants until, tigerless, they disappeared from view. What was to be done? As we were there primarily to try that swamp, it was evident that we ought to give time to any tiger that might be of a mind to come down out of the forest; so we gave time and delayed our start. Then we started, and when three-fourths of the cover had been beaten a tiger was seen moving ahead of us. It was going for the forest as fast as it could, but I managed to head it off, and inside of a hundred yards it stood at bay. One shot full in the chest killed it—a fine male tiger, too heavy for rapid flight through the thick grass, and too summarily disposed of to give it a chance of fighting. So had that swamp given to me four tigers in the year, and of the remaining six, three were killed one by one on three separate occasions in another swamp.

I have mentioned how I lost a tiger during that first expedition, as the consequence of being seated in my howdah when I should have been standing. Some years later I lost another through a misfire of my gun. Those tigers that I might have shot, but did not, naturally dwell in my mind more fixedly than any of those I killed; and the two just referred to, and that one which upset Bulrampoor's elephant, have always been remembered by me as the largest by far of their species.

There was something else to think of in respect of that tiger which a misfire lost to me. It was said by local authorities to be a creature of infinite wariness—almost, I may say, of mystery. Rumour had it that no strategy would avail against the cunning of this beast, and so, when I set out for its particular haunt, I was put very much upon my mettle, and brought all my mind to bear upon the method of attack. Its favourite lair was at the junction of a large swamp with a strip of heavy grass cover and a nullah that ran at right angles to it. The forest came down to the edge of the swamp everywhere, save along the valley through which the nullah meandered, and unless the tiger made for the clear water of the swamp, it was bound to take a line for the forest, either up the grass cover or more directly.

I laid my plans with infinite care: Peters, Shipton, Smith, and Maunsell I posted on every line of retreat, save that by which I approached the swamp from the forest. I emerged with half-a-dozen elephants in line exactly at the right point, and immediately saw the tiger move from the swamp edge up the grass valley, that promised now to be the valley of death for it. I pushed on after it, full of confidence, and after a burst of a hundred yards or so, saw it just below me: there it was in a place where there was no cover to conceal it; missing it was an impossibility. It was hardly probable that, being hit, it would move twenty yards farther, though it might make a fight here or there about this spot. Presto! the trigger was pulled; there was no report; before I could try the left barrel the tiger was gone: then a shot or two came from Maunsell at the head of the valley, and the tiger was away into the forest.

When a tiger was killed in this swamp in the following year, it was assumed that it was this one, and that Maunsell had hit it, because there was a bullet-hole in the tiger's ear. But when that crafty tiger, favoured by fortune, escaped from beneath my gun, and from before the guns of my companions, there yet remained untried a considerable portion of the swamp in which it had been found. To deal with this in the most effective manner, I formed a line which should sweep through a long stretch of forest, and, emerging at the far end of the swamp, drive into the open any four-footed animal that fell in our way. It was possible, I thought, that the tiger we had just lost might be so circumvented, or, if not that, then another. Smith I posted as "stop" in the open on the far side of the swamp, and he was sent off to his post by way of the chord before we started with the line by way of the arc. Then we dived into the labyrinth of trees and undergrowth, Shipton at the end of the line farthest away from the swamp and somewhat ahead of the rest of us, so that he should, when the proper time arrived, debouch upon the open as a second stop. Smith, left there to solitude and his own reflections, might well have thought that tiger-shooting, as I was conducting it then, was a snare and a delusion. For about an hour he neither saw nor heard anything of us: during all that time no gun-shot came from the forest to bid him hope that a tiger was afoot or give him assurance that we were yet in the neighbourhood. Then he saw the elephants emerge from among the trees, spread across the grass and reed cover of the swamp at its far end, and beat with crescent line towards him. Not long had he now to wait in uncertainty as to the nature of our sport. When the line was yet some eighty yards from his post a tiger broke immediately in front of him, and was neatly—too neatly—killed with one shot. So did it come about that he who saw nothing of the beat, in the sense of taking part in it, shot the tiger, and we who saw all the beat, saw nothing of the tiger until it lay stretched dead upon the ground before the elephant of the more fortunate stop. But, after all, I believe that I found quite as much pleasure in the successful crowning of my tactical efforts by another, as I should had I killed that tiger myself. Mine was the glory of putting Smith in the right place, and so beating over a mile or two of country that the tiger was driven out in front of him as I had designed. This second tiger of that swamp was, like that which escaped, a male, but younger and of less massive proportions than the first.

I have spoken of my preference for a smooth-bore as the weapon with which tigers are most effectively dealt with at close quarters. I shall now give an illustration in point. It happened one afternoon that, as Jacky Hills, Combe, Benson, and I were returning to our camp after a blank day, we sighted a tiger quietly strolling across a plain ahead of us. There was no cover on the plain except a few scattered bushes, none of which would have effectually screened anything larger than a hare; but half a mile beyond, a small hill rose *à propos* of nothing out of the plain, and on that hill and round it there was shelter for bigger game. The tiger, catching sight of us immediately after we viewed it, made for the hill at an amble. We pursued at the best pace of which an elephant is capable when it isn't bolting — my companions following it in a direct line, I making for the right, where the hill sloped into tall grass cover. I chose my line wisely; for the tiger, avoiding the steeper portion of the hill, and scared by those who followed in his track, came out upon a low unwooded spur on my side and gave me an 80-yard shot. For this shot I used a light rifle about the size of a carbine, and hit the tiger hard just behind the shoulder; but no second shot was practicable to me then, for the tiger rolled over on the farther side of the spur into a patch of long grass that screened it from sight. Then, my companions having come up, we invested the cover, drove the tiger to bay, and killed it. I think all four of us fired at it then, certainly three of us did, and lo! when we came to examine the dead animal there were but two bullet-holes—one of my rifle-shot, the other full in and not behind the shoulder, which had to be credited to one of us four. It was apparent that only one of us had dealt the tiger its death-wound. Two or three must have missed it. But the question was, Who had hit it?

Jacky Hills promptly decided that it could only be he who should bear this palm. "There is no other weapon in camp save my express," he said, "that could so have smashed the shoulder and summarily killed the tiger." He confidently anticipated the verdict that should be given upon the inquest, and we postponed argument until after the post-mortem. We were still seated at dinner, while K. B. directed the autopsy, with special instructions from Hills to look for pieces of a shattered copper tube in the carcass. We had just lighted our pipes, when K. B. came to us with his report, and that report gave unequivocal contradiction to Jacky's theory. No copper tubing had been found anywhere in the tiger; but in the ghastly shoulder wound they had come upon a flattened spherical bullet, and the only spherical bullet fired was that of my smooth-bore, a very old friend, with barrels worn to the thinness of notepaper.

Not but that Hills' express was on occasion effective enough, with his accurate eye and hand to direct it. I particularly remember how he killed a tiger with one shot, and that a very long one for tiger-shooting, say 150 yards or more. His express rolled the tiger over like a rabbit.

Hills, as became an officer of the Royal Engineers, brought a certain amount of science to bear upon our Terai expedition. He reported to somebody (I think his gunsmith) upon the behaviour of his express and ammunition, and he devoted himself at odd times to the preparation of a sketch-map that should have been a perennial joy to him, inasmuch as, by frequent alteration of its topography, he was continually improving it as a work of art, if not as a guide. In that variable chart the many nameless swamps and lakes and camping-grounds of the Terai were differentiated by a nomenclature that was of a historical turn. That chart was a diary of events as well as a record of localities.

My highest record of tigers killed in one beat was four, and that was achieved when I was the only shooter present, and had no companion to act as stop in flank or front or rear, or protect any but the one point that I commanded. From the *khubber* (intelligence) that had been brought in there was every reason to believe that two or three tigers might be put up either in a long narrow stretch of tree and reed and cane jungle in the forest, or in the grass cover of a light swamp which, continuing the former, extended into the open country. Obviously, the course to be adopted was to carefully beat the forest strip into the open grass, so that any tigers in the former might be sent forward into the latter, where I might reasonably expect to give a good account of them. Of course, if they broke right or left of the line, and took to the forest, they would be irretrievably lost; and in view of circumventing a flank movement of that sort, I posted shikaris on high trees on either side, with instructions to shout at any tiger that headed their way. It was questionable whether this shouting would have had the desired effect; but, at all events, the chances were in favour of my scouts seeing the tigers escaping into the forest, and letting me know the worst betimes.

Then I formed line to beat the jungle, and as the jungle abounded in cane as well as sundry other thorny flora, I took the centre, so that I could the better see that the line was kept; so, also, that my example might encourage the mahouts on either hand to force their way through the heaviest patches. Then followed a bad half-hour, during which my time was fully occupied in objurgation and entreaty addressed to the mahouts, and tearing my way through interlaced sprays and branches that bristled with countless barbs. There are British boys who have realised that the cane can be painful in its application, but they only know it in its dried state, when freed from the fish-hook-like thorns that grow upon it when it trails its long stems about its forest haunt. In its natural state it seizes upon the man who comes in contact with it, and rends his flesh and his clothes, even though the latter be an ordinary thorn-resisting material such as I used to wear. On this occasion there was a good deal of rending after this fashion; but if our line was not mathematically correct, it happily did not become wholly disorganised, and so we swept along until more than three-fourths of that cane-brake had been traversed. As yet, no scout to right or left had signalled the "gone away." Then I came upon fresh footprints in the moist earth that told of a tiger afoot, and heading for the grass cover, as had been designed. Now I began to look confidently for an interview with at least this one tiger, and, spurting the line through as much of the forest cover as intervened, we came out upon the open with every reason to believe that a tiger was in the grass that fronted us. Rallying the line so as to sweep this cover from side to side, I started. There was no *fussund* to disconcert my plans. There was every chance of that tiger holding to the grass, if I could only intercept its retreat by the way it had come there. It might very well break back, but would hardly take to the open on ahead or on either hand; so I looked to the organisation of the line, and took up my position in the centre of it. Then forward, the thirty elephants making thirty tracks in the long grass as nearly parallel as could be managed, and, after five minutes' steady advance, a tiger afoot within twenty yards of me. The waving grass told me so much, although the tiger that caused the motion remained unseen. But scarcely had I realised this when it became obvious that more tigers than one were making the grass wave above their paths. Two there were certainly, possibly three. Then I felt that I had my work cut out, and must be prompt of action. I did not wait until one of the tigers showed itself: I fired at the nearest of them, or at the spot where the long grass said it was, and fired with effect. For a moment it seemed as if the grass swarmed with tigers. That at which I had fired blundered forward and away from me, evidently hard hit; another charged for the elephant, a tusker, next to that I rode; and two others seemed to threaten an attack upon different points of my line. All was hubbub and commotion; elephants trumpeted, and prepared for immediate and precipitate flight. Fortunately my elephant (which was unattacked) stood reasonably firm, and enabled me to turn the tide of battle. The tiger, or I should say tigress, that charged the tusker, I dropped before it brought its charge home; then I went for the two nearly full-grown cubs that were careering hither and thither in a lost sort of way, albeit they drove the elephants before them. Those I settled with three or four shots, and then I re-formed my line, and followed the trail of the first tiger; but not far had we to go in pursuit of it. There, within a hundred yards of the spot where it had received my first shot, it lay in the throes of death. So were the four—the whole family—killed in what was indeed a *mauvais quart d'heure* for them. It took very much longer to pad them.

As regards a tiger's charge upon a line of elephants, it was a matter of frequent observation in my experiences that a tiger would, as a rule, select a tusker for this purpose when another selection was not forced upon it. I suppose that the white tusks make their wearer prominent among his fellows, and so distract the tiger's attention from the untusked animals. It is also noticeable that tigers, when roused in detached or semi-detached covers such as I have described above, will frequently hold to their ground after being disturbed, with equal obstinacy and stupidity. At such times they will as likely as not break through or charge a line of elephants over and over again rather than take to their heels, and the only explanation that I can find for this imbecile behaviour is that they have been caught napping, and, as it were, have got out of bed on the wrong and unreasoning side.

But the shikari profits by the tiger's unreason. Hume and his two companions of the 55th may remember how, in about the last beat of our expedition of 1868, we killed either two or three tigers in cover such as this; and Peters will not have forgotten the last tiger that was killed when he and I were out early in the season of 1876—killed as it was through its stubborn attachment to the cover in which we found it.

And there was no adequate reason for that tiger's objection to move on. The stretch of grass in which we found it was of such extent that a tiger could easily have emerged from it into the open at several points without being observed, or it could have retreated by way of a blind nullah that ran athwart the cover. Nor was there any consideration of the sun's heat to bid the tiger pause, for it was on a February day, or early day of March, we found it, when yet awhile there was no whisper in the air of that passionate warmth which should embrace all North-West India in two months' time.

In fact, all the ordinary chances favoured that tiger. The weather was cool; the nullah was a covered way to a sanctuary. The area of thick grass cover was equal to a beating capacity of fifty elephants at least, and we had seven. Good strategy, and, still more, good luck, turned the scale in our favour.

It was only upon the off-chance of finding a tiger that we had attacked that broad plain of grass; no *khubber* had led us there any more than to any other locality; no footprints guided us or bade us hope: there was the high grass in which tigers are sometimes found, and might be this time come upon, and so we entered it, our line of seven elephants making a ridiculously inadequate show as it spread itself out to do the work of seven times seven.

Not far had we advanced in this skeleton formation when an elephant trumpeted: not that it had seen the tiger yet awhile perhaps, but because it had smelt a tiger just ahead, where a cow not long since killed lay stretched upon the ground. Clearly a tiger had been here very recently, and the certainty of this cheered us on our way. But no amount of cheering could give such solidity to our line of seven elephants as would ensure the tiger being kept in front of us, if it was minded to break back through our scattered units. We did our best to cover the ground, the mahouts working with some approach to earnestness; and when we had advanced with infinite caution about a hundred yards beyond the "kill," we were rewarded by the view-halloo that told us the tiger was afoot, and, so far, ahead of us. But it was nowhere near Peters or myself, and did not remain in front of us any longer than suited its convenience. When we were nearing the end of the heavy cover the tiger turned and went through our line, still unseen by us who hoped to shoot it; and then for about an hour the beast dodged us backwards and forwards through the cover, giving no chance to either of the guns, and never, I believe, showing itself to anybody. And thus, evasive, cowardly to the last, it died when it was making for the nullah, whereby, in all probability, safety and freedom were to be won. Luckily, I was guided by signs made by mahouts to the left of our line when the tiger headed nullahwards, and was in time to intercept it. There, some ten yards from me, and about the same distance from the nullah, the waving grass told me where the tiger was sneaking through the cover. I fired the right barrel of my smooth-bore, aiming where I judged the tiger to be, and was sure I had hit it, although the only apparent result was that the tiger slackened its pace, that had been little better than a crawl when I fired. Then I gave it the benefit of the doubt, and my second barrel and the second bullet killed it stone dead. I never saw it until I looked down upon it lying dead at my elephant's feet, and it had died perversely mute, and without one single sign of standing upon the defensive from first to last. It had not even uttered a grunt or moan when hit by my bullets, and yet it was a healthy, well-conditioned tiger, rather over than under the average as to size.

That was the last tiger that fell to my gun, and my gun very nearly fell to the tiger — that is to say, it went very nigh to bursting in my hands, as a consequence of a bullet having slipped out of its cartridge some distance up the barrel, when the barrels were held downwards from my howdah. I was unaware of what had occurred, or that anything had occurred, to the weapon, until, in the following month, I took it to an English gunsmith to be cleaned up. He told me that the barrel had bulged almost to bursting-point, and that, if I had continued shooting with it in its then state, it must most assuredly have burst.

This chance of a bullet slipping is the one objection that has to be set against the advantages of a smooth-bore for tiger-shooting at close quarters. Experts in the matter of ball ammunition hold that you may not put a wad over a bullet as one does over shot, or turn the top of the cartridge over to secure the bullet. The only method they approve is that of pinching round the cartridge just above the bullet — a half-hearted expedient that is by way of a compromise of the turning-down method, and which, when the operator who pinches is a native Indian, is apt on occasion to have a result as unsatisfactory as that above noted.

In the course of those thirteen Terai expeditions I assisted in the execution of many panthers and bears; but although these animals helped to swell the annual bag, and so were acceptable enough when they came in one's way, we never made a business of pursuing them. Indeed I have on more than one occasion allowed bears to go scot - free, when they might have been shot easily enough, because firing at them was remotely likely to scare a tiger, and so lose to me the nobler quarry. In fact, panthers and bears which provided me with excellent sport in those Deoghur days when I met them on fairly even terms—they and I on foot—were, I found, very tame shooting from elephants. A tiger, assisted by the imbecility of one or more elephants, did now and again make things lively for a time, and introduce a quite sufficient leaven of danger into the amusement. But even when a panther showed fight, as on some occasions a panther did, it could hardly persuade the elephants to take it seriously; and as for the bears, they behaved in the presence of the elephant with the pusillanimity of buck-rabbits. Our average bag of panthers was about five, of bears three.

Nor did we, to swell our season's record, give ourselves up to python-shooting. I shot two or three in my thirteen years, and so many or more I could have shot on one day in one particular locality — a dismal swamp where trees of the mangrove habit cast their gloom upon the water, and rank grass and sedge festered in the slime; an unwholesome and eminently uninviting spot, foresworn of tigers, but dear to the python, which were to be seen there of great size and unusual number. There it was that I witnessed from a coign of vantage the imperceptible movement by which the snake makes its progress. As I stood in my howdah, I saw a monster python uncoil itself from a large fallow-deer just below me; then, as I brought the gun up to my shoulder, the python's head was lost to my view in dense reeds, while its tail was yet concealed in the cover where the deer lay, and as much of its body as made an imperfect S curve was exposed. I could have shot it in that exposed part easily enough, and fully intended shooting, but the python appeared now to be stationary, and therefore it seemed that nothing was to be lost by my waiting and watching. I was making what might prove to be a valuable observation in natural history, so I waited, with my attention never relaxing for one moment, with my eyes glued to that massive coil of sheeny mosaic and marvellous colour-harmony; and while I watched, with eyes agape, behold! an empty space where the python had been. The reptile had been gliding onward always while I watched it, and only when its tail vanished into the reeds where I thought its head still rested did I become aware of this. I avenged myself and an outraged natural history directly afterwards by killing another python, upon which I wasted no scientific observation. A smaller python this, but still large enough, when slung across a fair-sized elephant, to dangle on both sides nearly to the ground.

Wild elephants abounded in the Terai, as did they throughout the long stretch of forest and hill and valley lying between the Himalaya and the North-West Provinces. But while in the Dhoon Terai (which is British territory) elephant-hunting was permissible to British subjects upon licence, no one but Jung Bahadoor or his agents was allowed to hunt elephants in the Nepal Terai. The permit that sanctioned one's entrance upon Nepalese territory stated this disability in very succinct terms. The holder of the permit, however, was not only cautioned as to hunting elephants, he was enjoined not to molest or annoy them in any way. And so one went there at first in fear and trembling, lest some beast of a wild elephant should abuse its privilege, and force upon one a breach of the peace and the permit which might lead to the exclusion of British sportsmen from the Terai thereafter. It was not my evil fortune to stumble across one, although over and over again I came upon fresh traces of them.

As a fact, the whole of this Nepalese Terai was a close preserve, into which Jung Bahadoor would have preferred that none but himself should enter. It was rigorously preserved in regard to elephants, and closely conserved as to its timber; and economic developments other than these most primitive ones were discountenanced, if not prohibited. Now and then the splendid forests yielded a fair revenue. In one season I was told that a million sterling had been realised. But the timber was not sold every season, and the Nepal Exchequer would have come off very badly in the lean years of the Terai when the forests yielded next to nothing, if it had not drawn upon internal and more permanent supplies.

It was no doubt Jung Bahadoor's policy to discourage human settlement, and even temporary human habitation, as well as commercial and industrial enterprise: in short, his design was to restore the Terai entirely to its primeval state. Such a restoration, however complete, would not have been an operation of very striking magnitude at any time, and would have been barely noticeable in the days when I knew the Terai, and when, as I have already observed, that country was mostly an unpeopled wilderness. A portion of the Terai that I knew only as Nepalese territory had formerly belonged to Oudh, and had attracted some amount of settlement, but the scattered hamlets ceded to Nepal decayed under the blight of Katmandu rule, and for the most part had been long since abandoned. In the broad belt of country between the hills and the Oudh frontier cultivation was conspicuously absent. Here and there an isolated patch, hoe-turned for seed, suggested Crusoe's agricultural method and much of Crusoe's solitude. But nowhere had civilisation gained the slightest advantage in the contest with primordial forces. And the inhabitants (when there were any) seemed to be as utterly miserable as the denizens of Martin Chuzzlewit's Eden. Poor joyless wretches, life had for them no lingering hope, and but one desire—medicine! They came, the halt, the lame, the blind, and the sick of many maladies, and asked us white men to heal them. They demanded of us immediate cure of chronic and deep-seated disease, restoration of sight to empty eye-sockets, and prompt relief from the palsy of age. Unhappy sufferers from many ills, they confidently regarded the sahib as a mysterious combination of the Pool of Bethesda and the Fountain of Rejuvenescence. They believed in us, who were at the best only amateur physicians, as though we had been so many Galens; and Shipton, as a trained doctor, was as a veritable Æsculapius to them, and enjoyed quite an extensive practice that brought him the only guerdon he sought—the consciousness of having somewhat relieved the pangs of suffering humanity. I always carried a medicine-chest with my camp equipage, but my attempts at healing had to be restricted to the commoner forms of disease of which I understood something.

Jung Bahadoor's objection to people in his Terai preserve was logical enough. Elephants are shy of man; and man—the Indian cowherd especially—makes the conservation of forests more difficult than it need be, by his habit of setting fire to the dry grass in view of hastening the aftermath. So that his cattle may obtain the young grass, sprung phœnix-like out of the ashes, he will destroy millions of seedlings and saplings, and do infinite damage to the larger trees; for when in the hot weather the careless herd starts a fire of this sort, neither he nor any other can say whither it shall stray, or when or where it shall burn itself out. One of the frequent incidents of a forest beat in April and May is that of stumbling within the circuit of a forest fire; and it is one that gives the elephant another opportunity of exhibiting its intelligence. When it happens that the line of fire intercepts the line of advance, there is but one satisfactory way of meeting the situation—viz., to mark a weak spot in the line of fire, and push through that point into the blackened and cooling tract over which the fire has passed. It is useless retreating in front of it, and may be just as vain to retrace one's steps in the hope of turning its flank, so it remains to make a dash through the blaze. There the line of fire creeps rapidly along the ground, licking with fiery tongues the grass beneath and the leaves and branches within its reach; and there is a crackling as it advances like unto that of rifle and pistol shots, and clouds of smoke that dim the sun; but the blaze is not of equal volume through the line: here and there are breaks where the combustible material is scantier than elsewhere, and by one of these less ardent passages one heads one's way. Then it is that the "cussedness" of the elephant occasionally makes difficulties that reflect discredit on its intellectual capacity; and one is thoroughly well pleased when the gauntlet has been run with no worse contingencies than a smashed howdah and half-a-dozen contusions caused by various boltings of one's sagacious mount.

The forest fires, particularly those on the hill-sides, are at night magnificent spectacles. Seated in the open, after dark, to enjoy the cool breezes from the Himalaya, we were occasionally treated with pyrotechnic displays not unworthy of the Crystal Palace. Ravines and gullies coursed with lambent flames from crown to foot of far-off hills; outlines of distant ranges were traced as by myriads of lights from point to point; and, nearer at hand, the forest trees rose out of a crimson sea. It was a gala sight to look upon, but bad for the timber that Jung Bahadoor prized.

I do not know that this Mayor of the Nepal Palace took any interest in tiger-shooting himself, or objected to the sahibs killing such tigers as his territory provided. I never heard of his being out after them,—possibly he found it tame work after relation killing, of which folks said he had done enough to satiate Saturn himself; or he may have put it aside because of its interference with elephant-hunting. It was said that one of his regiments had tiger-skin facings, and another facings provided by the panther, but I never heard how or by whom the tigers and panthers required for this sartorial purpose were obtained. They may have been netted as were those which Jung Bahadoor laid down in the path of the Duke of Edinburgh, and, later on, of the Prince of Wales.

Once I came upon Jung Bahadoor's elephant-catching camp, and discovered what training by the Kheddah mahouts could do in the way of developing an elephant's speed and brute force. The first sign of this camp that greeted us was a flying squadron of young elephants that rapidly overhauled us as we jogged along towards our tents, and passed us as though our elephants had been standing still. Those were the greyhounds of the Kheddah, whose work it was to hunt down and ring in the wild ones; and until I saw them there, I dreamed not of the possible agility of the elephant. But a more phenomenal animal of the Royal stud awaited me in Jung's camp when we came to it,—one of the fighting elephants employed to coerce the captured wild ones—a very nightmare of a beast, fitted only for a zoological Inferno. There it stood, heavily fettered fore and aft, with its brow resting against the trunk of a tree, and I fancy the brow of that elephant and the trunk of that tree were of equal intellectual capacity. Not in the direction of pin-lifting had this giant been trained: its mind had been left untutored; every effort had been directed to the development of its muscles, and there it stood, leaning against the greenwood post, as different an animal from the ordinary elephant as is the champion dray-horse from the rocking-steed of the nursery, or as Sandou, the trained athlete and lifter of grand pianos, elephants, and similar unconsidered trifles, from the fat boy of the caravan. I felt some respect for the animal: there was nothing pretentious about it; no one claimed for it the wisdom of Solomon, or any wisdom whatever. With becoming modesty it confined its limited mental power to the solution of the only problem that presented itself—*i.e.*, was that object against which it had leaned for several hours another elephant, or was it, the leaner, really another tree? I respected it for that retiring virtue, and, considering it physically, was lost in admiration of its strength and symmetry. Jumbo was as a corpulent Berkshire hog compared with that warrior of the Terai.

We just missed a share in one of the elephant hunts of Jung's foresters, and perhaps it was as well we did, for the man who joins in an expedition of that kind can form no idea when or where the chase will terminate. Nor is there any attempt to give ease to him who rides. Howdahs, footboards, soft rugs, umbrellas, and the rest of the *Persicos apparatus*, should be hated and avoided by the elephant-hunter, who has, indeed, to scorn delights and live laborious days if he would be in at the capture of the quarry. Clinging on to a small pad by his eyebrows, or elseways as he can, he has to belabour his elephant with a mace whenever the pace slackens; and the holding on, and the urging along, occupy his time and attention so fully that the meal he carries in his wallet becomes a movable feast in a double sense, and the pipe he would fain fill and light is forbidden by uncongenial circumstances, and the last condition of that man is worse than the first, in proportion to the square or cube of the distance travelled. And the hunt, when finished, may come to an end dozens of miles from everywhere. Then it may well be that the novice in elephant-hunting exclaims against the cruelty of fate, and arrives at a drivelling condition in which he would give any number of kingdoms for a restaurant—ay, even for a beerhouse!

By arguments such as are here given, I have always sought to console myself for that disappointment in regard to our going after wild elephants.

I did not set any particular store by skins and horns as trophies of my Terai shooting, but one living trophy that I brought away with me I valued exceedingly. This was a tiger cub, one of three that I came upon in a patch of grass cover, and the best tempered of the party, as far as I could judge by a few minutes' inspection and handling. The mother of these three got away unseen just as I entered the grass, but the elephants soon winded the cubs, and I approached the spot where they were marked down, full of hope that one or two fair-sized tigers would present themselves. But there were only the two-month-old cubs deserted by a mother that proved to be utterly insensible to the most ordinary maternal obligations. For when I came upon those cubs, I counted upon the tigress mother as mine. It seemed as if I had only to exercise due patience and strategy to secure this result. I retired from the field leaving the cubs intact, leaving also scouts to watch the tigress's movements if it reappeared. I gave the tigress ample time to recover its nerve and maternal instincts, and, finally, I attempted by cautious approach and circumvallation to catch the whole family together—but in vain: there, when I returned to the spot, were the three cubs only. I repeated this performance again and yet again, with the one unvarying consequence; and then, as the day was closing in, I made my selection of the amiable cub, and carried it off in my arms, leaving the other two for their parent. Next day I returned betimes to the scene, and having carefully cut off the tigress's retreat, closed in upon its lair. Alas, only emptiness was there! The tigress had carried off its two remaining cubs into space, to be seen no more by me that year, at all events.

The cub that I carried off grew in strength and grace for some months as the pet of my household. Never but on one occasion did its amiability fail it, even for a moment, and then we had our first and last struggle for supremacy. My pet was about five months old when this crisis occurred, and a sofa-cushion was the bone of contention. My pet, stretched at length upon a couch, was bored for want of a plaything; it took the cushion and worried it, and it worried until its own temper suffered as much from the rough treatment as my cushion, and then I intervened, and my pet and I had a short encounter, in which the victory was mine. Thereafter, that splendid tom-cat gave no trouble to anybody: always loose about the house, it was my constant companion and my first-born's plaything; and there was reason to hope that thus it would reach maturity—tractable and trustworthy even as a full-grown tiger. But this was not to be: when it was about ten months old it died of some mysterious ailment which proved incurable, in spite of all the healing art of vets and doctors.

I tried a panther as a pet, with less success on the side of amiability and more on the side of health. The beast grew to be tame enough by fits and starts, but suffered from occasional lapses into savagery; and when it fought with me or any visitor of mine, it had no gentlemanly instincts in favour of fair-play. It would stalk any of us, coming upon us by surprise from behind the chairs or from under the table, until it became a matter of surprise when it did not stalk us, and that pet stood generally regarded as an unmitigated nuisance. Then I gave it to a rajah for a small zoological collection, and saw no more of it.

My Indian menagerie included two or three bears; but these animals, however sweet-tempered they may be, are not adapted to the home-life of the ordinary pet. I am aware that children have warrant for believing that bears can be accustomed to the use of chairs and beds and tables, and so forth. Thus are they and we instructed by the tale of the three bears; but, though it be rank heresy to question this teaching, I must say that I regard the presence of one bear (let alone three) in a domestic interior as incompatible with the survival of any furniture whatever, unless it be of cast-iron and the strongest of metal work. This much I say, speaking from experience.

As for deer and antelope, &c., I suppose I did no more than follow the Anglo-Indian fashion made and provided in regard to the keeping of these animals. The average Anglo-Indian domicile is, as often as not, a partially equipped Noah's ark. In the compound are to be found, as a matter of course, goats and sheep, and the sahib's dogs, and the mangy foundlings of the bazaar, and cows from whose milk the memsahib fondly hopes to draw supplies of cream and butter, and horses and poultry of sorts, and teal and quail and pigeons. And to the ordinary collection there are frequently added pea-fowl and monkeys, and deer and cranes of sorts, and other of the commoner creatures of the wilds, and, more rarely, a wolf (chained up to an empty cask) or panther, or any other beast of the forest or fowl of the air that the collector can get hold of. One enthusiast I remember rejoiced in the possession of an Ornithorhynchus paradoxus (or duck-billed platypus), which was very precious to him as such, although it was really quite a different creature. And to all the live-stock, domestic or otherwise, collected in the Anglo-Indian compound, have to be added the inevitable crows and kites and mynas, and other birds of Indian station life.

Very full of life—animal, reptile, and insectivorous—is the average Anglo-Indian household. In the north it is not an everyday incident to find a cobra or centipede or scorpion domiciled in one's bed or boots, but otherwise the northern provinces are bountifully provided with creatures of sorts—

many of which could be very well dispensed with. The cat only, among domestic animals, is conspicuously absent. That does not thrive in India, and is rarely to be seen in the Anglo-Indian establishment; but rats and mice abound, and knowing no fear of their feline enemy, make themselves thoroughly at home, mix freely with the family, and share the family meals, either discreetly by picking up crumbs below the table or audaciously by plundering the stores upon the sideboard. The purblind musk-rat (that shrew which is so admirable as a parent, and would be so harmless but for its harpy-like faculty of poisoning every edible or potable thing it touches) goes chortling round the room. The nimble squirrel darts in and out. In the verandah caged birds—canaries, doves, and the rest—discourse with the vagabond myna, that, being at liberty, makes itself free in every sense; and overhead the circling kite, watchful of scraps thrown from the kitchen, sings a treble to the hoarse bass of the carrion-crow. Then, when the too vigorous summer threatens, and when anxious mothers and wives, not quite unwilling to be grass-widows, commence their packing for Simla or Naini, there is to be heard too much and too often that bird-note which dominates all other pipings of the feathered choir, and says with damnable iteration, "We feel it" or "Brain-fever," as those who hear may render. Poor Trotty Veck interpreted in various ways the chimes that were so large a feature of his life and story; but as to the awful song of that Indian bird there are only two known renderings—"We feel it" and "Brain-fever."

Among the occasional visitors of the Anglo-Indian home is the mongoose,—a worthy animal enough when regarded as a pet, a predatory scoundrel when it finds its way into the hen-roost, and, I am afraid, a fraud in respect of that snake-killing prowess which is commonly attributed to it. It is said of the mongoose that it will relentlessly pursue the snake wherever it comes across one, that it will engage with the most venomous of the snake tribe, and that, being bitten, say, by a cobra, it rushes off to apply the vegetable antidote only known to the mongoose family, and suffers no ill consequences from that poisonous bite, which causes almost instantaneous death to other animals. One of the tricks of the snake-charmer's trade is the display of a mongoose (probably toothless) and a cobra (certain fang-drawn), which, if they can be cajoled into it, affect to go through a gladiatorial performance; but the whole affair is a sham quite in keeping with the snake-man's pretence of charming out of the sahib's verandah or *babbichi-khana* or garden-path a snake that he lets loose, at the proper moment, out of the hollow bamboo he carries concealed beneath his *dhooti*.

It happened to me once to see what might have been a splendid snake-mongoose fight if the mongoose were half as prone to do battle as is believed. Walking quietly along a path, within a dozen yards of me I saw a cobra and two mongooses actively engaged in looking at each other, and too much occupied that way to notice me when I passed and watched them. The cobra, erect and with outspread hood, turned now to this mongoose and now to that: the mongooses seemed to divide their attention between the cobra and consultative matter between their two selves. So did the three conduct themselves for some moments while I watched them; and then the mongooses sidled off on other business than snaking, the cobra dropped his hooded front to the ground, and glided off elsewhere, and that ended the battle.

I suppose the Anglo-Indian who becomes an amateur Jamrach does so very much for the sake of occupation, or to extend the narrowly restricted horizon of his home-life from May to October. Monotony hangs pall-like over his environment during that term, and the dead level of the plains that surround him is exactly typical of the flatness of his daily life outside the work of his kutcherry. Nor can it be truthfully said that the average official life, the preparation of the sacred *nuqsha*, the report on the Gangetic dolphin, or the annual statistics of the how-not-to-do-it department, is always deliriously varied. Children who call him father may not continuously gladden the heart and make endless variety in the life of this unfortunate—the climate forbidding that they should share his exile. So do Anglo-Indians take an interest in animals that are not exactly what they see everywhere, and every day, and every hour of the day: I have known them wildly excited by the first appearance of the bull-frogs that come in with the burst of the monsoon, and absolutely intoxicated by the *début* of the water-wagtail—the herald of the cold weather. And for much the same reason one does curious things in the way of time-killing: thus, for two years I acted as secretary of the Lucknow Race Club, and for a much longer time as manager of an amateur theatrical company, and I cannot understand that any sane man, being free to live his own life, would have accepted either of those honorary situations while any other employment—stone-breaking or otherwise—was open to him. My experiences as secretary of the Lucknow Race Club were in some sort of a sporting nature, as were my experiences as an owner or part owner of race-horses; but I do not desire to recall the latter, and for the former—well, they are another story.

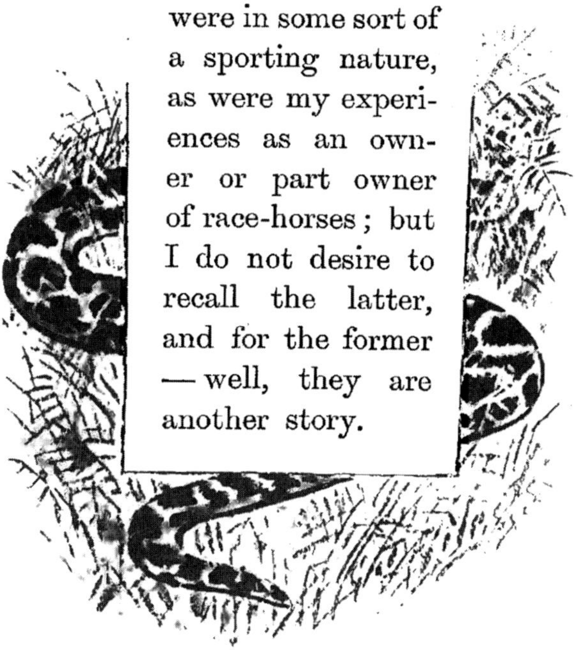

CHAPTER XII.

STATION LIFE IN OUDH.

WHIST-PLAYING—GAMBLING—DERBY SWEEPS—LORD WILLIAM BERESFORD—NAUTCHES—INDIAN JUGGLERS—PUPPET-PLAYS—A *MACHAN* INCIDENT.

GREAT always are the pleasures of anticipation, and more especially so were the prospective joys of station life that thrilled me when I turned stationwards from the Terai. I was leaving behind me the sweltering heat, the plague of flies, the daylong sun-glare, and that exacting thirst which had to be denied or to be barely assuaged with tepid and too partially cooled drinks; and before me was the prospect of darkened rooms, in whose kindly shelter I should escape from every ray of sunlight and breathe an atmosphere chastened by thermantidote and punkah to a mere summer heat—cool and dusk day-refuge, where air should be rendered odorous by the *kus-kus*, while the splash of water upon the tatties, suggesting the drip of perfumed fountains, made sweetest and most soothing music. Then before me was the promise of abundant ice, and unstinted draughts of cold fluid, and the diurnal plunge into the waters of the Chutter Munzil swimming-bath, and racquets and whist, and all the other delights of civilisation—delights that, while yet afar from me, seemed bewilderingly perfect, yet that came to be infinitely uninteresting after a few weeks' enjoyment of them. After a while followed satiety and a longing for jheel and jungle.

Not that whist ever staled in its infinite variety in those Lucknow summers of many years, even though occasionally the variety ran into extremes, and was distinguished by revokes and other pranks trying to human patience. We had a whist club for afternoon play, and we played after dinner at mess or the United Service Club or elsewhere, and not unfrequently we played until the break of day, when the soldier hurried off to morning parade and the civilian to his couch. For three summers I effectually avoided the sun by systematically turning night into day, and, although hypercritical people may pronounce this a dissipated habit of life, it had its hygienic advantages and was attended by satisfactory results. I lived mostly at the 55th mess during those years, played whist all night, did my day's work at dawn, and slept through the sunlit hours until the time arrived for racquets.

India has produced some admirable whist-players, if none quite equal to Da Costa and Lewis of the St James's. Colonel Drayson (I suppose he is now a General, like everybody else), who has written a book on this subject, or given his name to (or had it taken by) a Melbourne club; Hornsby, the gunner; Peters, and one or two others, made fame for themselves in Anglo-Indian whist circles; and many others played a game far above the Portland average, albeit that club counts among its members the mighty Cavendish, who in the world he lives in is known by a less aristocratic name. I have played a good deal at the St James's, and seen there infinitely worse play than that of the Tasmanian Club, Hobart, to say nothing of India. At the St James's I met with an experience that is unique in my card career — that is to say, when on one occasion I lost a rubber, one of my adversaries offered to pay me, he not having grasped the fact that he had won.

In Lucknow our ordinary points were rupees and chicks (four rupees), rising exceptionally to chicks and gold-mohurs. At the hill stations gold-mohurs were the ruling standard, and a goodly number of these would sometimes change hands at the end of a rubber. There was in those days some heavy betting both by players and outsiders, and whist came very expensively to some who indulged in it. But they were mostly good gamblers who played at Simla, Naini, or where not on the slopes of the ice-crowned Himalaya: they took their beating kindly, and kept their heads and tempers whichever way their fortunes trended. I have seen an outside bettor lose a heavy stake because the two players he was backing failed to count their honours and so score the second game of the rubber. He made no sign, that interested onlooker. He did not scold when, whist unforgiving, the rubber went against him: he paid and looked pleasant.

If the play was heavy at those hill clubs, it was mostly engaged in by men who could afford to pay what they lost, and was carried on as amicably as honourably by those concerned. At rare intervals the ordinary harmony of these meetings was disturbed—as, for instance, when the following highly dramatic incident occurred. A difference of opinion arose between two players, and one of them, rising angrily from the table, went to the door with the intention of leaving the room; but having opened the door, he changed his mind, slammed the door to, and was still inside. The other belligerent, sitting with his back to that door and hearing it close, concluded that his opponent had gone out, and thought it safe to unbosom himself of some highly uncomplimentary matter regarding him who should have been absent but was unfortunately present. Then that one who was inconveniently within earshot of those unfavourable comments seized by the throat the utterer thereof and nearly throttled him; and I do not know that society would have been injured in the slightest degree if the throttling had been effectual.

Although India has been discredited with an evil reputation as to gambling, I do not believe that play has been at any time as dangerously high there as it has been in England. It has been more general, perhaps, because Anglo-Indian society is more homogeneous than English, and more likely to indulge collectively in any amusement. It has been more widely known, because everybody in India knows at least as much about his neighbour as the neighbour does about himself, and because for the Briton in Hindostan there is no Monte Carlo to fly to for a good and unnoticed flutter. But India has never known any equivalent of Crockford's, and the almost universal tone of the Anglo-Indian world is such as would make an imitation of Crockford's difficult, and the deliberate fleecing of some pigeon to the tune of thousands impossible.

Many, many years ago a case of such pigeoning occurred in Calcutta. A young fellow just about to come of age and into possession of some £10,000 was pounced upon by a genial rascal whose possessions were a minus quantity, and who, if he had come into what he deserved, would have enjoyed the hospitality of No. 1 Chowringhee[1] for a lengthened period. This hawk was of the bluff and jovial order, a bibulous bird withal, and the poor dove saw in him only the boon companion ready at all hours to cast his years behind him and frolic with youth: a dangerous man for the unsophisticated to associate with, in that he wore his heart upon his sleeve, and that heart was stone to break the beak of the daw that pecked at it.

This mature scoundrel led his young dupe on in a friendly *écarté* match that lasted for some days; lured him on to always increasing stakes; and finished him with an all-night sitting in a private room with doors locked. From that *séance* the pigeon emerged a clean-plucked bird, the hawk with an I O U for the £10,000. But the latter had not reckoned with public opinion and the dupe's guardian: both were too much for him, and in the end he was only too glad to forego his claim to realise upon that £10,000 document and get himself out of the way.

That is the one case of the kind that came under my observation, and I saw a good deal of such gambling as went on. Where change is so limited in pursuits peculiar to Englishmen, and outdoor amusements impracticable for months together save in the sunless hours, it may be excused that cards in some form or other—whether as instruments of scientific or Bumble-

[1] The Calcutta jail.

puppy whist, or innocuous and solitary patience, or other games less scientific and innocuous—are largely employed. It may be deemed creditable to the Lucknow men of my time that they wearied so utterly of all card games except whist (which, however funnily played at times, cannot be converted into a round game), that in sheer desperation they took to roulette.

But promising as was this new departure, it proved an abject failure in the course of a week. The table was not true, and after very brief trial it became generally known that the odds were greatly in favour of some four numbers. There were numbers that never turned up, but one of those four was continually in evidence, and the player who backed those frequently recurring numbers was absolutely certain to win. It might have been expected that we should have abandoned roulette as soon as this discovery was made, but we were loth to relinquish our new plaything in that summary fashion, and we adopted the expedient of keeping each player in the bankership for a time limited to fifteen minutes, or such shorter period as was sufficient to break him. But even that would not work satisfactorily: each player, as his turn came to take the bank, knew that he was going to his ruin, and he who took it last was bound to be the heaviest loser, and might possibly be the only one. Never was there such a travesty of the Monte Carlo game. *Capita aut naves* was preferable.

One notable, and, I think, harmless shape assumed by the gambling spirit in India was that of the (English) Derby sweep. Born in the Bengal Club, Calcutta, the sweep travelled northwards, growing as it advanced. It was of respectable dimensions at Lucknow, in that it gave a first prize of from Rs. 50,000 to Rs. 60,000, and having reached and become domiciled in Umballa, it assumed such Gargantuan proportions that the first prize was over a lakh when that lakh represented much more of its nominal value (£10,000) than it does at the present time.

The Umballa sweep became an institution patronised throughout the civilised world much more freely than those of Homburg. Great Britain, Australasia, and every British possession in the East, took chances in this great lottery. People of every class and creed throughout Hindostan invested in it—generals and subalterns, commissioners and constables, nawabs and nobodies, paid their Rs. 10 for their turn at this wheel of Fortune; and all sorts and conditions of men came out prize-winners usually on a single ticket, as was the case with a station-master on the G.I.P., who one year took first prize—a fortune for his Rs. 10; as was the case also with a Lucknow man who won a handsome prize on a ticket, half of the price of which he had borrowed.

I took many tickets in these sweeps without any considerable advantage to myself, unless hope enjoyed for an hour or two be such. On the morning of the Derby of 1876 I received a telegram from India (I being then in London) to the effect that I had drawn Petrarch and Skylark in the Lucknow sweep. Petrarch and Skylark were first and third favourites, and nothing remained but that I should go down to Epsom and see those two romp home in their proper order. Peters and I went down together in a hansom, happily unconscious of the fact that in addition to the two horses above named we had between us drawn four others (mostly or all non-starters) in that sweep. What did I know or care about the mineral colt to be known from that day as Kisber? No more than for mineral waters! I thought the first prizes of the Lucknow sweep, equivalent to £5000 or £6000, as good as banked to my credit, and with reluctance laid a modest fifty off. I took only a languid interest in a race which I regarded as a foregone conclusion. I saw Petrarch lead round Tattenham corner without emotion: he was only then by anticipation where I had placed him, and then that mineral beast forged ahead of him, and yet two others owned by England's present Prime Minister, and Petrarch came in fourth—Skylark nowhere! It is a curious coincidence that a certain bookmaker who laid heavily against Petrarch for the Derby which it lost, backed it heavily for the Guineas and Leger which it won. Superior knowledge of form and condition may be the natural explanation of this, but ill-natured people found explanation of another kind.

Among the more prominent supporters of the Umballa Derby sweep were that good sportsman Lord William Beresford, more generally known as Bill Beresford, and Colonel (now of course General) Harris, whose popular *sobriquet* was "China Jim." These two were, I believe, members of a small confederacy that made a corner as to the Umballa sweep, and by adventurous purchase of likely horses drawn by others cleared some handsome profits. But I seem to remember hearing how one year, as a consequence of some telegraphic error in the instructions sent to their English agent, more was laid off than the occasion required, and the firm's annual balance was on the wrong side of the ledger.

But when the Umballa sweep had reached its zenith the Punjab Government interdicted it, and set the law in motion to suppress it. The Government was stronger than the Sweep; and now the Derby sweep of India has reverted to its old home, the Bengal Club, where it flourishes like a green bay-tree.

Possibly with a view to showing that life in India is worth living, an extraordinary glamour has always been cast upon all things Indian by travellers of the Sinbad the Sailor order, and I do not know that the many philanthropical and Indophilist globe-trotters who have recently "done" India have materially improved matters in this respect. In some particulars they have, I think, made bad worse, and superinduced profound darkness where they found only the twilight of ignorance.

Among the generally accepted fallacies, whose name is legion, were (and I fancy are) the two following: (1) that the Indian nautch is a graceful and brilliant spectacle of peculiar fascination for the lovers of the beautiful; and (2) that Indian conjuring is marvellous and beyond comparison with any of the achievements of Houdin or any other Western prestidigitator. As the nautch and conjuring happen to be the two most prominent of Indian indigenous entertainments, I will say something about them by way of showing the extent to which the Anglo-Indian may depend upon them for amusement during his term of exile.

I remember that my first conception of the nautch was that it was performed by earthly houris known as Bayaderes. I had this on good authority, as I believed; but I regret to say that I have since come to be sceptical as to whether Bayaderes have any existence in any part of this planet, and certain that they no more exist among Indian nautch-girls than does the griffin or unicorn in our zoology.

As to the Indian nautch-girl and her circumambulations, it is possible to the imaginative writer to say a good deal about her lithe form and her sensuous, voluptuous, &c., evolutions in what, for want of a better term, I will call the dance. So, too, being inspired sufficiently, he may speak of her imitations of the screech-owl as singing. None but the morbidly accurate people will greatly blame him, even though they know that he is ludicrously wrong, whereas a good many ignorant folk will believe him, and for that section of the community he will have established the Bayadere myth.

I have seen several nautches (and some of these were of the best) given by magnates of Cossitollah, Durrumtollah, and elsewhere in Bengal, where is the stronghold of the nautch, and the most lasting, and not the most offensive, impression that they left upon me was that effected upon my sense of smell. The strongest point of the nautch, and that which was all-pervading of it from find to finish, was its wealth in stinks, that commenced with atta of roses and ended with the rank exhalations from expiring *chiragh* wicks fed with mustard-oil. Think of the intermediate smells,—the overpowering jasmine perfume of the nautch-girls' chaplets and necklaces; the reek of Calcutta's open drains; the smoke from a hundred hookahs; the general nidor of cocoanut-oil and ghee and greasy humanity,—the awful combination of all being an Inferno compared with which a Seven Dials cooking-shop is Elysium itself. Nausea and headache were the invariable consequences of a nautch to me.

About the very best of them, as far as I saw, there was much of dirt and squalor; and I suppose they are very much the same now as probably they were when Clive and Warren Hastings were spectators of them—for fashions change slowly, if they change at all, in Hindostan. In spite of agricultural shows designed to improve native husbandry and implements, the ryot uses to-day the plough first employed for the cultivation of the soil; in spite of the example of Europeans and Bengali Baboos, the people clothe themselves to-day as did their predecessors in India when Alexander and Porus crossed swords; and in spite of the brilliant spectacle, the coloured calcium light, and the latest thing in skirt-dancing seen by many an Indian student at the Alhambra or the Empire, the nautch remains the old unleavened abomination that prevailed when Suraja Dowlah sat on the throne of Moorshedabad.

The nautch of my experience may be briefly described thus: Scene—the courtyard of the host's house, covered in temporarily by an awning of some sort which has no pretensions to be water-tight. In the place of honour the host smoking a hookah, and all round the yard a dusky crowd of hookah-smokers, squatted upon the ground for the most part, but as to a few honoured with chairs. Behind the host and guests a score or so of retainers, whose mission it is to purvey *pan supari* when the entertainment shall be concluded, or to sprinkle diluted atta upon the more important of the people present, or to bring *gools* or *chillums* for the hookah, &c. In the centre of the courtyard, which is carpeted or matted for the occasion, the nautch-girls, with their attendant orchestra, find their stage. In front sit the girls when the exigencies of the dance do not claim their services; behind them the three or four makers of noises, who by a pleasant irony are described as musicians, and where the instruments (old-time as the pipes of Pan and Apollo's dried-up turtle) consist of a stringed affair that rudely burlesques a Lowther Arcade fiddle, a reed arrangement potent of discord, and the tom-tom that a poet has dignified under the style and title of the Indian drum. The girls — the Bayaderes of romance — are unprepossessing females who would be menials in some household if they were respectable: some of them fat and middle-aged; none of them remarkable for beauty. The musicians — save the mark! — are scoundrels to a man, and would be convicted by a jury of physiognomists of any crime charged against them.

The smoke of a hundred hookahs rises and hangs as a pall over the throng. The musicians make hideous sounds, which have a sort of rhythm about them because of the time-beating of the constant tom-tom. A nautch-girl rises and proceeds to jingle music from her anklets by a monotonous shuffle round the stage, while she sways hither and thither and waves her arms, until she is relieved by another girl, who shuffles and sways and waves in the approved manner, and so *da capo*. Or, by way of change, a siren rises and emits vocal sounds of such power that when she brings out a high note (and she is as full of high notes as a confidential bank clerk) one sees the muscles of her throat throb again. And so the intellectual sport proceeds for hours until the regulation quantities of discord, smoke, and smell have been enjoyed. That is the Indian nautch.

As to Indian juggling, travellers have told marvellous stories, and are telling them even to this day. Sir Henry Yule, in his account of Marco Polo, mentions how that early wanderer described a quite miraculous feat that he had heard of or seen. I think he said he had seen it, and I can only hope that he will be forgiven for this statement, seeing how little chance there is of his being generally believed. This feat is thus described: The performer threw a ball of twine into the air, and that ball, unwinding as it went, rose out of sight into celestial spaces; then continuing to ascend, the twine drew up a rope until that was lost in the void above; then a boy (the inevitable boy of many conjurings, whether in Asia or at the Surrey end of the Westminster Bridge) ascended the rope until he was lost to view; then a man followed into the same nebulous regions; and then the boy's head came tumbling down to earth. That ended the performance. I daresay there are plenty of people who would swallow this, just as there are people who think India can do without its opium revenue, or be fitly governed by an exclusively native executive; but the majority would, I believe, prefer to discredit this traveller's tale.

Turning to more recent narratives, let us consider that mango trick of which so much has been made by truthful but too credulous visitors to India. This feat has been described to me by Anglo-Indian friends as something marvellous: according to them, they had seen the mango-stone planted by the conjurer, and had then witnessed all the processes of nature by which, this stone having germinated, the nascent sapling developed into the bearing tree. Well, I can only say that, having seen this trick performed many times, I witnessed none of these natural operations. As I saw it, the conjurer acted on behalf of nature, and with laudable modesty performed the necessary offices out of my sight. The mango trick as I have seen it was performed as follows: The conjurer erected a light scaffolding over the spot where the mango-stone was planted; over that scaffold he cast an all-enclosing blanket; then he disappeared, as to his head and shoulders, under the blanket; emerged in due course, drew the blanket aside—and behold, a young mango-tree, or a branch which answered the purpose, and which, as the mango-tree is an evergreen, may be obtained in every season: so ended Act 1. Then ensued another furtive performance behind the blanket, and another disclosure—behold the fruit upon the tree! and of course one should not be too particular about the composition of that fruit, or make intrusive inquiry as to its attachment by thread or otherwise to the tree; and so the trick goes well enough, albeit it does not astound one by its incomprehensibility.

As for some of the feats of Indian jugglers, they are totally destitute of any element of conjuring. Take, for example, that which is possibly best known to fame—the sword-swallowing performance. No sleight of hand or artful machinery is exhibited in this ; there is literally no deception : the juggler throws his head back so as to obtain a reasonably straight course of some eighteen inches from his thorax downwards, and then, employing so much of his internal economy as a scabbard, inserts therein the instrument that is accepted as a sword —that is to say, an instrument closely resembling the pointless and edgeless cutlass of the British sailor or bandit of melodrama. The performance is, in short, an uncomfortable one for all concerned, but not otherwise remarkable.

Lucknow used to boast of its special swallowers—unpleasant people who could gulp a billiard-ball or half-a-dozen birds of the avidwat order and reproduce them on demand. Once I witnessed this performance and was more than satisfied. I saw the birds pass through the hideous and gaping entrance to the juggler's maw, and anon come forth fluttering from that human cavern and spread their wings in flight. I saw a turkey's egg travel the same darksome route and return to the light of day; and the only emotion, besides disgust, that I experienced was envy of that juggler's capacity for taking pills.

The Indian juggler, when an expert in his profession, deftly acquits himself in sundry efforts of sleight of hand, and performs some few tricks that are not so decidedly overt as that mango-tree swindle, but at the best he is a feeble entertainer.

More amusing than Indian conjuring or the nautch is the *kutpootli*, or puppet-play, that in Northern India is the especial treat of European children, and the frequent joy of the adult native. It is true that the comedy played by the *kutpootli* dolls is mainly a procession of rajahs, who enter two and two (after the manner of Noah's beasts), and range themselves silent and motionless in durbar; but there is an undercurrent of farce which gives some life to the affair, and much delight to British children. A wayfarer is robbed by a thief and bullied by a policeman; a sweeper and his wife are prominent upon the scene in the prologue, and as comic as circumstances will permit; and although the farce of these minor characters had for me no particular meaning, it is quite possible that the initiated saw in it something of a distinctly edifying and satirical character.

Sometimes this oriental Punch and Judy travesty was elaborated for older audiences by the addition of a ludicrous caricature of the Anglo-Indian. This uncomplimentary rendering of the white man's peculiarities was given, not by dolls, but by the men attached to the show. Dressed in odds and ends of cast-off European clothing, and wearing masks designed to represent the European countenance, these dismal mimes presented their view of the average Briton's demeanour. As far as I can remember, the Britannic character thus portrayed was singularly circumscribed. The sahib in mask and scarecrow apparel was a creature of three emotions and no moral. He got drunk, he said d——n frequently, and he thumped his native attendant.

Only in one district of Oudh (in the Transgogra country) did I see *machans* used for tiger-shooting, and there the idea seemed to prevail that any branch of a tree that would carry a man was good enough for a *machan*, however close to the ground. I only saw one tiger killed in that district by *machan*-shooting, and on that occasion, a lady being of the party, the *machans* were ten feet or less from the ground. There were four guns out (Mrs A., who shared her husband's *machan*, being a spectator only); and a tiger, if so inclined and not prevented by a bullet, could have reached any one of the occupants of the four *machans* erected for us. The only sense of using those raised positions was in the fact that so there was less chance of the tiger seeing and being frightened off by one of us to the detriment of another. It was with rather the guilt-laden consciousness of the assassin that I, as one of four, lay in wait for a possible tiger.

But mine was not to be the assassin's hand. At first, when the line of coolies had shouted and drummed and horned their way into earshot of our ambuscade, it seemed as if the tiger would head my way; but the procession of wild things flying before the beaters included not the forest king. First, with wary step and safety-seeking eye, the jackal emerged, crossed the glade in front of me, and was gone into the jungle behind. Then patter,

patter, upon the fallen leaves, what is it that approaches so noisily—an elephant? No; a peacock! Clumsy of foot, as harsh of note, this worthy attendant upon the Olympian shrew followed the jackal. Then a heavily antlered stag stepped forth, and sniffing danger in the air, sped on. But the tiger came not; and then, bang, bang, and a roar on my left, told me that another gun than mine had opened fire upon it. But we all shared in the finish when, on elephants, we pushed the tiger out of the patch of heavy undergrowth into which it had taken refuge, and killed it.

And again I went after tigers in that district when the native shikari in charge of affairs, ignoring *machans*, sought to place the shooters upon the forks of saplings and upon low-hanging branches where security was not to be dreamed of, and shooting was an impossibility. Once, in our several beats, I permitted myself to be located in a sapling fork, but only to immediately quit that coign of disadvantage as soon as the shikari's back was turned. My position would, indeed, have been unendurable for more than a few minutes. I could only stand on one foot at a time. I could only remain upon my perch at all by holding on with at least one hand; and if I had had occasion to fire my gun, it must have been fired pistol fashion, with the one hand not immediately employed in keeping myself aloft. And all this torture and crippling for an elevation of about half the height that a full-grown tiger can reach from the ground without jumping. I came down from that perch forthwith, and for the remainder of the day ascended no other. It has to be added that, as far as tigers were concerned, no *machan* or substitute therefor was required on that occasion, for from first to last no tiger made an appearance to any of us.

And now, reluctantly enough, I bring these reminiscences to a close. It required something of an effort to commence my narrative. It calls for a greater effort to write "Finis," to drop the curtain and put out the lights. Memories that had long slumbered have been awakened, and will not at once be lulled to rest again. Delights that had been put away as unattainable have returned to my imagination as temptations difficult of resistance. The good sport and the good-fellowship that went with my shikar of thirty years challenge me to renew that past and live the old life again. What a good time it was! What good fellows were they who helped to make it so! But to talk of living that life again—that way madness lies.

L'ENVOI.

IT is mid-winter,—that is to say, it is the 15th July,—and as I am writing these lines in Tasmania, my statement that it is mid-winter is locally accurate to the letter. It is mid-winter, then, inasmuch as it is middlewards of Tasmania's apology for a hyperborean season, and looking out from my study-window, my eye ranges over a garden where roses, geraniums, chrysanthemums, nasturtiums, and other flowers are all abloom: looking beyond these witnesses as to the good character of Tasmania's climate, down the sloping paddocks that are bounded by a willow-fringed beck, and beyond to the broad waters of the Derwent, I see a sunlit river gay with a score of centreboard yachts; and looking farther yet afield, I find the scene closed in by hills of varied form that, tier after tier, exhibit tricks of light and shade that would delight the artist and drive the prosiest writer into poetry.

This, by the way, is written in Hobart, where my home is not, and the room that I call my study is not a study any more than it is mine, except temporarily. I am in Hobart, and there fronting me is a scene that has more of summer than winter in it. But I am, nevertheless, within sight of snow, if I choose to go round to the back of the house, for I live under the shadow of Mount Wellington, that towers over 4000 feet above the sea-level, and bears upon its crest and upper slopes a snow mantle that, if the sun be less conspicuous than usual, lasts more or less from June to August. A most picturesque mountain is this from every point of view, as is Hobart the most beautifully situated city of the many cities that I have seen in three quarters of the world. Constantinople, the splendid capital of the Byzantine empire, I know only by repute, and I am therefore unable to compare the two cities that are mirrored in the Bosphorus and Derwent respectively. But I can speak from personal observation of Delhi, Lucknow, Cairo, Rome, Naples, Florence, Moscow, and St Petersburg,—all more or less famous for their beauty,—and say without hesitation that Hobart, because of its magnificent environment, eclipses them all.

Unique as are its physical charms and climate,

Hobart possesses social and other advantages that should make it peculiarly attractive to retired Anglo-Indians and others of small independent means who desire to live economically and yet enjoy the pleasures of society and improving influences of civilisation; and for him who would live a retired life among his books or flowers there is ample choice in the country of places upon which nature has showered her gifts with prodigal hand, access whereto has been made easy by rail or road, and everywhere he shall find the most perfect temperate climate in the world, cheap living, and a kindly people; and in some parts he will find also such sport as I shall proceed to speak of.

Before I decided finally to settle in Tasmania I made inquiry as to its merits as a game country; and from men who had been there, or had belonged to regiments quartered in Hobart when that place was an Imperial garrison, I gathered satisfactory information as to Tasmanian possibilities in the matters of shooting and hunting. This information was decidedly delusive in one respect: I was told that men of the Hobart garrison had been wont to go out hither and thither to shoot snipe, and had habitually made bags of twenty to thirty couple, and I promised myself that I would do likewise.

Now, having been eleven years in Tasmania, I am in a position to state that I have not only never shot one, but that I have not seen one alive. I have seen three defunct snipe, these having been brought into the railway carriage I occupied by a sportsman who got in at the Epping roadside station, but never a living one. Not but what there are some snipe in the colony from September to the end of November, but they come in much smaller numbers than they used to, and come to fewer feeding-grounds. I have only just discovered one or two places where they may be looked for in September next, and I have made my arrangements to be at those places at the right time.

On one occasion only have I gone forth to shoot snipe in Tasmania, and then I went under the most favourable conditions except as to season. I was the guest of Sydney Page, then owner of the Stonehenge property, and a snipe-swamp was among his possessions. He had religiously preserved this for the admirable sportsman Charles Agnew, the Squire of Waverley (owner and rider of some of Tasmania's best racers); but Agnew had not come, and the cream of the year's shooting was to be mine! Now, I thought, as we started for the ground, I am about to see the swift-flighted long-bills rise to right and left, singly, doubly, and in wisps. I imagined the air thick with snipe, and my only doubt was that we were not sufficiently provided with cartridges. We reached the swamp that should have been, and found it dry and caked brickwise, and we flushed no living creature out of it but a harmless snake.

During one year three snipe were kept for my gun by the friendly owner of Mount Ireh; but I was charged during that season with heavy political duties, and could not make an opportunity for interviewing those birds. However, hope of better performance is before me. Snipe still visit this garden island elsewhere than at Stonehenge and Mount Ireh. I have heard of nine couple being shot by a shepherd Avoca way, and on the river Nile they are said to be plentiful.

Tasmanian nomenclature is every way erratic. The river Nile is not very far from the Jordan and the towns of Jericho and Jerusalem, but it is also in the neighbourhood of Brighton, a township remote from the ocean and in no particular representative of its namesake London-on-Sea. Similiar eccentricity prevails in respect of our *fauna*, and especially of our fish. A species of grayling that has its habitat in our hill-streams—a distinctly fresh-water fish—is styled herring in the North, albeit known to Southerners as the cucumber-mullet, by reason of some dim notion that it has a cucumber flavour about it. *Per contra*, our perch is a denizen of the sea; our Tasmanian tiger is a marsupial (as are all Tasmanian indigenous animals) in no way related to the feline tribe, which presents much of the appearance of the Indian hyena, and is known at the Zoo as the Tasmanian wolf; our badger, or wombat, only resembles the English animal of that name in as far as it is quadrupedal.

There is no particular glory about shooting our tiger beyond that of coming upon a beast that is peculiarly wary and shy of intercourse with human beings. It avoids man and the snares that are laid for it, just as if it knew that a price was set upon its head by the Government—a price equal to that paid in India for the more noble animal; for this Tasmanian tiger is the deadly foe of sheep, and every year many a merino falls a prey to this scourge of the flock-owner. Few and far between are the tigers shot in the lower pastoral runs, but up in the Lake country, where snow sometimes lies upon the ground for two or three days together, they are tracked down like the moose and killed in greater numbers.

Another marsupial peculiar to this colony is the Tasmanian devil, an evil-minded creature that plays havoc with poultry, and is more retiring than the native tiger. I do not know any animal that is more successful than this in the art of keeping out of sight. Dick Swiveller would have given a good deal (if he had had it to give) for this power. Jack the Giant-killer, having this, would not have needed an invisible cap. The brute will not even allow itself to be seen when caged; at any rate I have tried to see those of the London Zoo and Launceston (Tasmania) Gardens without success, although they were there to be viewed, according to the labels on their cages.

Of course we have opossums—the grey and the

beautiful black opossum, the latter being also, I believe, peculiar to Tasmania. But these do not offer what may be styled legitimate sport, for the method of hunting them is a good deal that adopted by the British poacher in regard to pheasants. 'Possuming is a nocturnal pursuit that may be followed any moonlight night by him who has a dog broken to the business, and a gun that will carry a charge of shot forty yards. It is the dog's duty to "tree" the 'possum—*i.e.*, to drive it from the ground where it is feeding into the branch of some tree hard by—and then the 'possum-hunter's easy task is to bring the quarry down with a pot-shot aimed at the poor crouching thing, whose dark outline, brought out in strong relief by the moonlit heaven, offers an easy mark.

Thus from off an overhanging bough of eucalypt or acacia do we—or some of us—shoot the wattle-bird (glaucopis), that joy of epicures, if not of sportsmen. Gourmets swear by this colonial delicacy, and hold it to be superior to quail, or snipe, or duck; our legislators seek to protect it from the too greedy pot-hunter by enforcing a close season of two years, as once was done in regard to quail; our rabbiters leave bunnies for a time to shoot the more remunerative creature of yellow wattles,—and yet to the shikari this bird is a failure unworthy of consideration in our Game Laws.

But then our Game Laws are in keeping with our antipodean topsy-turvydom. They have casually recognised quail; for a brief period the Game Act's protecting ægis was thrown over the hare; but, generally speaking, they have devoted attention to that jovial and mellow songster the black-and-white magpie, and other feathered creatures equally excluded from the game category proper.

The hare was abandoned to its fate because it abused the confidence showed in it, and devoted an excessive portion of its energies to the barking of fruit-trees. It became the subject of petitions to Parliament, and being relinquished to the just fate of its ill-doing, dropped from its lofty position in the game list to the level of its poor relation the rabbit in the list of pests,—for as pests do we know the rabbit, the codlin-moth, and the Californian thistle, and we legislate for their eradication accordingly.

Unfortunately, several of the British *fauna* and *flora*, introduced into Tasmania to give this colony a home colour, have not shown that discreet moderation which was expected of them. The blackberry, imported at some cost in care and coin, nurtured in the tenderest manner while it was being acclimatised, grown in one instance under glass, and prized at the outset as a splendid acquisition, promptly proceeded to misconduct itself by an extravagant growth wholly unknown to the parent stock. Blackberry-plants developed from modest bushes into trees, and instead of confining themselves to hedgerows, ran riot over the fields.

Blackberry-pickers nowadays use ladders to mount the Brobdingnagian brambles that bear the fruit they seek; blackberry-avenues have succeeded hedgerows; and the exuberant growth of the plant is hardly compensated by the excellence of the berry, which is as superior to that of England as are hothouse grapes to the crop of a vine grown against the wall of a London suburban detached villa.

Thus has the rabbit misconducted itself. It was imported for the sake of sport, reared with some difficulty in artificial warrens, and, as far as possible, preserved. In the absence of any Game Laws such as are known in England, or any restriction as to possessing or using guns, or any limitation of the people's right to shoot any undomesticated creature, the law of trespass alone presented means of preserving rabbits; and the tale is told of a man being fined £1 for going upon the estate of a large landowner in pursuit of rabbits. Now the interest of the landowner is all the other way, and the man who pursues the rabbit with gun or trap is paid by the skin for his work.

While the importation of the blackberry has proved a not unalloyed blessing, that of the rabbit has come to be an almost unmitigated curse, except from the sportsman's point of view. Throughout the pastoral country splendid shooting is to be had for the asking, or without asking, by him whom rabbits, with an occasional hare and quail and plover, will satisfy; but for the farmer in infested areas, who is always waging an expensive war against this rodent, and for the legislator, who is every session worrying over new Rabbit Bills, this animal is a nuisance.

The above exception in favour of the sportsman must include the professional rabbiter — the man who earns his livelihood for several months of the year by trapping and otherwise encompassing the destruction of the pest. But there is a method about his way of doing business. He kills a sufficient quantity of rabbits to keep him going, but he is by no means at one with the landed proprietor as to their extermination: they are his stock-in-trade, and he preserves them as strictly as does the English keeper his pheasants. Many of them he saves from destruction by the wholesale slaughter of their natural enemies—the domestic cat run wild, the native and the tiger cat, all of which are rigidly protected by Act of Parliament, and all of which are ruthlessly done to death by the professional rabbiter. Indeed it is a byword as to this person that he regards a day well spent upon the killing of one native cat, and infinitely prefers finding one of the cat tribe in his trap to catching a rabbit.

The fecundity of this imported member of the Lepus family is such as should make Malthus turn in his grave. The rabbit in its English habitat is prolific enough, in that it has as many as seven litters a-year, with as many as eight in a litter;

but that is not sufficiently rapid work for the Tasmanian rabbit, which, being of the feminine gender, begins its domestic cares when three months old, and thenceforth bears a litter of ten or a dozen for every moon, or at least for every month of the twelve. It is simply bewildering to think of the family that a healthy pair of Tasmanian rabbits may gather round their burrow after a year of domestic bliss uninterrupted by the trapper: no less than five generations would be there, exclusive of the first parents, descending to the great-great-great-grandchildren. M. le Comte de Lesseps considered as the head of a French family cannot be mentioned in the same breath as the Tasmanian rabbit; not even in Brigham Young can we find a human being who in this respect can be cited by way of comparison: one has to go to the finny denizens of the water, or to those fashionable but inconvenient organisms the microbes, for a parallel.

Speaking of microbes, I would ask if it has ever occurred to any scientific believer in them to explain how it comes about that, increasing with such monstrous rapidity as is attributed to them, they have left room on this planet for any other form of life? Some sort of explanation is to be found in the apparent fact that they are of modern invention, and this deduction is justified by the omission from the 'Imperial English Technological and Scientific Dictionary' (published in 1854) of both the microbe and the bacillus—to say nothing of the germ which is there treated as a thing innocuous, and not as the baneful propagator of disease that it is now held to be.

But, returning to our rabbits, I would invite the British globe-trotter of sporting proclivities who does Tasmania, to devote some of his time to a trip into the Ouse country, and away beyond to Marlborough and the source of the Derwent at Lake St Clair. If he be a fisherman, all the better and more complete will be his sport; for the streams thereaway are well stocked with trout of a fair size, if not with such monsters as are to be caught in the Great Lake some miles north of St Clair: and if he have also an eye for the picturesque, his outing will be something to look back upon with pleasure all his days.

From Hobart to St Clair the way is almost unbrokenly beautiful, albeit of beauty that varies. To Bridgewater (eleven miles), where the globe-trotter may catch a salmon or two or shoot a wild duck that have their frequent home in the sedge-lined shallows, the road—*i.e.*, the railway—runs along the right bank of the Derwent, and the wayfarer glides past a series of bays whose clear waters mirror now a group of overhanging eucalypts and anon the trees of some orchard or homestead paddock; and over on the farther side of the river (distant here some one and a half to two miles) he sees the nobly outlined hills — Mount Detention and the rest — that serve as a pendant to the Mount Wellington range upon his other hand; and from Bridgewater, where the river narrows and the hills creep in closer, as though they loved the companionship of this beautiful stream, to New Norfolk, the scenery is such as the Rhine presents to the enraptured tourist between Koenigswinter and Biebrich. It is true that the Derwent does not boast of the beetling crags, the ruined castles of medieval barons, and the legends of nymph and siren peculiar to the Rhine. How should it have those ruins, seeing that the aborigines, whom we dispossessed only ninety years ago, never built any sort of habitation, or recognised the desirability of a better mansion than that provided by a hollow tree? And how should there be legends of a poetic character in view of the fact that, if our predecessors possessed any (which is highly improbable), those unimaginative people were allowed to die out without communicating any of their myths to their British successors? They were a poor race, lower in the human scale than the Australian aborigines or the Aztecs—so low, indeed, that the mere propinquity of civilisation seems to have been the main reason for their very rapid disappearance from off the face of the earth. If there had been amongst them that proud spirit of despair which made the defeated Roman fall upon his sword, one might contemplate the idea of this race going to a self-sought death with a dirge paraphrasing Olivia's sweetly touching ballad; but no such spirit was there of that kind or any other, save so much as enabled the men to make the women do all the hard work of the *ménage*.

There were no rights for those poor gins: theirs was the duty of diving for oysters or mussels, and beating the bush for kangaroo and wallaby, and cooking and such other menial work as was to hand; and if they were spared from such toil as ploughing and reaping and pot-scouring, it was merely as the natural consequence of the absolute dearth of all implements whatsoever, except a light spear or javelin and a waddy.

Even with the beetling crags wanting, the reaches of the Derwent between Bridgewater and New Norfolk have a beauty of their own, less arrogant, perhaps, than that of the Rhine, but fully equal to it. This much will any discriminating tourist recognise if he be guided by his own judgment rather than by Murray's or Baedeker's handbook; for your handbook tourist admires to order, sees nothing save through the pages of his printed guide, and would, if so directed by this authority, pronounce the lower portion of the Rhine, from Cologne Rotterdamwards, to be infinitely more picturesque than the hill-clasped stream that flows past Lorelei and the Drachenfels. Such eminently receptive tourists have I encountered in various cities of Europe, what time they gaped their way through picture-galleries, or where not in the mill-round performance of "doing" this place or that, only varied by their being done on all hands. Murray or Baedeker open before him, paterfamilias bids his following admire the drapery of this Rubens while standing in front of Raphael's masterpiece of Madonnas at Dresden; and he and his go the round, always clinging to that volume, and return to their virtuous homes in Clapham or Tooting full of edifying matter relating to their foreign travel, which they might have drawn from its original sources without journeying five miles away from London.

But we shall shortly be ready to receive this order of tourist with the guide-book necessary to his enjoyment of a country new to him. Tasmania's ex-Premier, who is a fanatic upon the subject of our "beauty spots" (a term, by the way, that seems to indicate the patches worn on lovely woman's cheek rather than choice bits of scenery), and discourses about Nature's assets in this connection until a weary House of Assembly would, for mere sake of change, like to hear of Nature's liabilities—this ex-Prime Minister has, as far as words are concerned, started the local Murray, and it only remains for some one to do the work instead of talking about it. Then shall we have a modest tome that shall give word-pictures of our lakes and falls and rivers, our marvellous stalactite caves at Chudleigh, our museums and art-galleries, and all the lions of the island, and the proper and improving guidance of the gaping tourist shall be assured.

But we are at New Norfolk, the honeymoon town in which the newly-wed Southerners spend their early days of married life, and glean their first practical knowledge as to whether marriage is a failure. Enfolded on all sides by orchards and hop-gardens, New Norfolk seems like a bit taken out of the Weald of Kent, save that the Derwent flowing at its feet is of too bold and emphasised a beauty to be Kentish. Just below the town, where lofty poplars and willows come down to a point on the right bank, there is on the opposite side a bluff, and standing apart from this as Nature's sentinel (not asset) is the Pulpit Rock, that, still a beetling crag, beetled much more before a slice of it was taken off by the Derwent Valley line of railway. Up-stream from this the Derwent for a mile or two above New Norfolk is not unlike the Thames at Pangbourne, and then as one goes farther towards the source it assumes the character of a Highland stream, and flows over rocks and boulders in the manner of the salmon-waters of Scotland.

From New Norfolk to Macquarie Plains we pass through an agricultural country, here and there meeting a tract of bush-land, and beyond Macquarie we enter the land of rabbits. Thence to the Ouse there is a wide stretch of pastoral country given up to sheep and rabbits, and beyond the Ouse rabbits and sheep again for miles. During one drive of twenty miles I amused myself counting the rabbits—reached three hundred and stopped; and during that drive I met about three human beings upon the road. That is the country for the man who wants to shoot rabbits, and if he push his way farther yet he may shoot kangaroo even unto the border of Lake St Clair—a lake twenty-five miles in circumference, and surpassing in beauty any lake that I have seen, and I have seen Como, Maggiore, Lochs Katrine and Lomond, in the course of my wanderings. Lake St Clair, with its many bays and tree-fringed promontories, stands in an amphitheatre of hills, and towering above it are the splendid peaks of Mounts Ida and Olympus. No words can depict the glory of the scene that confronts him who stands upon the pebbly beach of St Clair. There might a poet live, and need no other inspiration than that of the glorious panorama round him; there might the artist spend his life, and need no other subject for his brush than St Clair in its different moods and aspects. But as things are at present, none but a man who has infinite resources in himself or a hermit would care to spend a lifetime there, inasmuch as there is no human habitation there except a resthouse, and no society of any sort within three or four miles. The poet, the artist, or the recluse might, even under these conditions, make an all-satisfying home of that resthouse, but not the average man. However, this is not likely to be St Clair's lasting state. The time must come when its shores will be lined by villas and casinos and clubs, when St Clair will be the summer resort of Australasia. Already thousands of Australians fly from the summer heat of the mainland to Tasmania, where the climate is temperate in the hottest season; and still more should they seek refuge at St Clair or Lake Crescent, where the air is bracing and delightfully cool, even when in the Tasmanian plains people find it a few degrees too warm.

The fisherman who desires to capture monster trout has only to betake himself to the Great Lake. There are in the Tasmanian Court of the Imperial Institute eleven trout that averaged 18 lb. in weight, and in the Agent-General's Office there is a photograph of a catch of fifty-three fish that scaled 470 lb. Or he may catch salmon, as I have said, in the Huon, where of an evening I have seen these fish rising in every direction. It was from out of the Huon waters that Sir Robert Hamilton, ex-Governor of Tasmania, and a good fisherman like Lord Gormanston, the present Governor, drew the largest salmon yet caught in Tasmanian waters.

Some doubt has been expressed as to whether Tasmania really possesses the true salmon,—the veritable *Salmo salar*,—and authorities have differed as to this widely, as is the wont of authorities in other instances. Sir Thomas Brady of the Irish Fisheries Board, and an expert, saw that salmon which I have referred to as the spoil of Sir Robert Hamilton's rod, and gave it as his opinion that if that was not a salmon he had never seen one; but even this *ex cathedra* judgment has been questioned. And I must confess that I have been dubious as to authoritative opinions on the *Salmo* tribe since an experience I had at Sir

James Gibson-Maitland's salmon, and trout-breeding establishment at Howietoun. There Sir James endeavoured to enlighten me as to the features that distinguished a salmon from a salmon-trout and so forth. He had a good-sized fish drawn from one of the ponds. He held it in his left arm while with a dexter finger he pointed out the number of scales between the jowl and nearest fin; then, having counted so many (but how many I found it unnecessary to remember), he said, "Because this fish has that number of scales between those two points it is a true salmon;" and then, by way of frustrating my search for knowledge, the keeper said, "No, that isn't a salmon;" and Sir James agreed that it was something else, and I remained ignorant of the distinguishing characteristics of the noble fish as I was at the outset.

There are some points in regard to the acclimatisation of salmon in Tasmania that are beyond any doubt whatever: (1) That some thousands have been expended in the introduction of ova; (2) that Sir Thomas Brady went out in charge of one batch of 400,000 eyed ova, and saw the fish hatched out in the salmon and trout breeding-ponds at the Plenty; and (3) that fish are caught from time to time that, as to appearance, colour, and flavour, are so like the true salmon that it is immaterial if they are something else.

And good sport is to be had by the disciple of Izaak Walton in Tasmanian waters, whether he fish for this salmon of questionable identity or for trout or herring. Alas! that is not for me. I did make one attempt to whip the Forth river for herring. In an evil moment I conceived the wild idea that I could make a cast that would serve to beguile this innocent fish to take my fly; and I armed myself with the necessary apparatus (which includes gentles that, one at a time, have to be fastened to the hook) and set to work. The obvious result was a dismal failure as far as filling my creel was concerned. I never got a rise, much less a fish, and I hooked nothing except the overhanging branches and the logs submerged in the river: boughs and logs I was continually hooking, until my patience gave way and I left the water.

But other and more expert people can fill *their* creels in an hour or two when the Forth is at its best. Twenty and thirty dozen have been caught out of that river by a single rod in a day. Fishermen from Hobart, and even from Australia, come to try conclusions with the Forth herring; and I, who live on the bank of that river, cannot hope to draw any finny creatures from it unless it be the eel of the creeks, the black fish in the waters above the bridge, or those handsome denizens of the sea, the mullet and salmon-trout, which come into the estuary; and I do not know that I am equal to the capture of the black-fish, even if I tried that department of fishing. I have caught mullet and salmon-trout by spinning out of the stern of a boat, and I might catch rock-cod if my seamanship permitted of my going outside of the Heads. Rock-cod is not a cod, nor, as far as I know, has it anything to do with rocks; but it is, as an edible fish, equal to the Tasmanian flounder (which is not a flounder), trumpeter, and trevally, and that is saying a great deal. I ought to add that neither the mullet nor the salmon-trout above named justifies its name; but as to Tasmanian nomenclature generally, that is the rule, and things Tasmanian are seldom what they seem by name.

A day spent up the Forth is by no means deficient in delight even for him who cannot angle. It is a beautiful river above bridge, much after the fashion of the Highland stream. Its course lies through a series of hills that are timbered, for the most part, from crown to base, and over a bed of gravel, pebble, and boulders, with here and there a rocky formation that breaks the flowing waters into a miniature waterfall. On either bank there is ever and again a fringe of greenery wherein may be found the most beautiful Tasmanian shrub—the native laurel and the Christmas tree, and many others pleasant to the eye. On either bank, too, there are pleasant copses, where in the shade of forest trees one may enjoy an *al fresco* meal; and away in the distance, raising its crest above the lower hills, one may, looking up-stream, see Mount Roland, that giant among the local mounts, and sole wearer in winter of a diadem of snow.

I have had some very enjoyable days after the

brown quail in the Forth country; not that thereaway are to be made such bags as are to be shot in other parts of the colony. From forty to fifty brace have fallen to one gun in the Chudleigh neighbourhood, and big bags of the grey or stubble quail have been made in the southern part of the island; but twenty brace constitute a good day's shooting about the Forth, and with the adjuncts of picturesque scenery and invigorating air full of ozone, twenty brace are a sufficient return for a four hours' tramp.

But a good dog with a special aptitude for brown-quail-hunting is essential. It is not sufficient to have a dog that will point or set to its game. The game has to be roused sometimes by something more than the eager glance of pointer and the footfall of the approaching shootist. Sometimes the dog has to worry into a thicket of branches after this evasive bird, and it does not occur to every dog to have a day when it cares to scramble about such cover as that of the Tasmanian blackberry. I once shot nine quail, roused one by one, out of one bush.

Hares are to be found in goodly numbers in the northern districts, where they are hunted with a pack of beagles, coursed, and shot. It was my lot to be one of a party that shot the Quamby country one winter day, and we killed between seventy and eighty hares, besides sundry wild duck, quail, and rabbits. The object of that expedition was to thin the hares down, not to exterminate them.

There are good sportsmen in the Quamby and Longford neighbourhoods—men who ride and shoot straight; and a grand patron of every form of sport is to be found thereaway in the Squire of Entally, the Hon. Thomas Reibey, one time Premier of Tasmania, and now a member of the Administration of the day. Mr Reibey kept that pack of beagles for many a year. He is as good a whip as there is in the island, and he has bred and owned, and still owns, some first-class race-horses.

Once a-year the beautiful grounds of Entally are the scene of a cricket-match between a Launceston and some local eleven; and on most northern sporting prospectuses, whether of race-meetings, chopping-matches, or what not, his name is to be found as patron or vice-patron.

There are stags in Tasmania,—the descendants of imported fallow-deer,—and these are hunted by hounds, as are also the indigenous kangaroo. It cannot be said that the country to be ridden over is such as would commend itself to the hunter of Leicestershire: hills of the Cornish pattern have to be negotiated at a flying pace by him or her who desires to keep in with the hounds, and in some parts there are frequent post-and-rail fences of formidable strength that must be cleared or involve trouble. At one steeple-chase in Tasmania, every jump being post-and-rails, I saw three jockeys heavily thrown, one of whom was killed on the spot and another seriously hurt.

I here quote a cutting from a Tasmanian paper

which gives an account of a day with a southern pack:—

Hutton Park Beagles.—On Monday [30th ult.] Hutton Park pack met at the top of Spring Hill. Starting, we take a brier-and-deadwood fence out of the main-road on to Sandhill property. A cast is at once made, and the hounds draw forward as they fly through all the most likely country to the westward in quest of the wild deer.

After drawing for our game for some four miles, and crossing several deadwoods, we find ourselves at the back of the Hutton Park "tier run," in the midst of ferns, rocks, and wattle-scrub—a rough enough spot to be in, without the rain, which now comes down heavily and wets us through; but we are evidently on the right spot at last, as old Signal picks up a "trail." The pack are with him in a moment, and immediately a fine stag breaks cover away through the thick scrub in front. The hounds swing on to the trail at a great pace, over two fences away to the top of Savage's Tier. Doubling, the stag takes us back over the same country and fences, thence along a boundary wire-fence, over a big deadwood, and the hounds lead us straight up the rugged face of Jones' Tier at a terrible pace. Three horses alone reach the summit in time to see the leading hounds disappearing over the top of the next range. Every effort is being made by those still in it to get on closer terms with the leaders, but it is extremely difficult to keep at steeple-chase speed up the face of hills one after another, the sides of which are almost perpendicular. However, mile after mile at such a pace, and over such a country, must bring the deer back to us, is a comforting thought; and it is evident from the energetic working of the hounds, as we reach the top of the highest tier for the third time, that our game is not far ahead. Such persistent tactics in taking a bee-line to the top of every rough hill far and near, with the hounds behind him, forcing the pace without a check, begins to tell at last; for, making down the south side of the tier, he takes us over a fence into more thick scrub, on and down to a gully, where he is sighted as he plunges into the centre of a water-hole, and out again, with the hounds close at his heels. He now takes to doubling at close quarters and laying up, which makes it a very hard matter to force him in the thick bracken; but ultimately at this game the hounds prove too much for him, and at last he is captured, after one of the hardest and fastest runs the writer has ever taken part in. The distance covered must have been fully fourteen miles, and the hounds ran practically without a check from start to finish.

Six horses alone have struggled to the end. The master (Mr E. O. Bisdee) on No. 6, Miss French on Circassian, Miss B. Pennycuick on Frank, Miss B. Butler on Barbette, Messrs T. G. Bisdee on Doctress and A. Munnings on a roan.

Kangaroos and wallaby are reckoned among Tasmanian game, and are, for the purposes of the table, as good as, if not better than, hares; but as objects of sport I confess that they have not appealed to my shikari instinct. Both touch my sense of humour—they are so distinctly comic of appearance, save for the gentle and melancholy eye, which appeals to my more merciful side. Neither kangaroo nor wallaby can be strictly regarded as a quadruped. It is true that both have fore-legs, or rudimentary limbs that occupy the position of fore-legs, and that occasionally they put their fore-feet to the ground; but so may a man do with his hands, and it is as hands that these marsupials use their fore-feet. When they want to travel they hop upon their hind-legs, and then, as also when they are seated, the tail comes into play, and the kangaroo or wallaby becomes a tripedal creature. The Tasmanian kangaroo is the small brush variety, not to be confounded with the "old man" or "forester" of Australia that, as the boxing kangaroo, made its appearance at the Aquarium. Only once have I been tempted to go out after kangaroo, and on that occasion I posted myself, unwittingly, upon a bull-dog's nest—*i.e.*, the nest of a monster ant known as the bull-dog—and at the moment when my dog had roused a kangaroo my attention was distracted from the same by what I took to be a bayonet-thrust in my leg. I left the dog and kangaroo to finish matters as they chose.

I cannot pretend that Tasmania is another India in respect to shikar; but it has, in addition to many charms that are distinctly missing in India, such a fair show of sport as I have mentioned above, to say nothing of cricket, yachting, boating, polo, racing wherever men and horses do congregate, and even golf in one place. A sportsman need not perish of shikar inanition in Tasmania, and I am better able to compare the one country with the other in that I have been during the last six months in both. For since I wrote the preceding chapter it has chanced that I took the Indian route from England to Tasmania.

When I left India in 1878, I shook the dust of that country off my feet. It did not occur to me then that I should ever revisit Hindostan, but fate arranged matters otherwise than I had foreseen, and after an absence of fifteen years I found myself in October last landing once again at the Apollo Bunder, and doing battle with coolies and Customs officers, and eating prawn-curry in the gregarious Esplanade Hotel, and going through the old old routine of the newly arrived Englishman.

India is too rigidly conservative to change its habits and customs much in three lustrums, and I found it very much what it was when I left it in 1878. No alteration was to be observed in the fashion of native costume, or in the agricultural implements, which are in this year of grace very much what they were when Cain tilled the soil; the smells were the same, and full-bodied as ever; and there in front of Watson's was the familiar crowd, made up of jugglers, money-changers, gharrie-wallahs, and other predatory people, who are in India not peculiar to the neighbourhood of the Esplanade Hotel.

The first change of which I became distinctly aware was that of the Customs arrangements. I was importing a gun that twice before had entered India duty free—an ancient but serviceable weapon that had killed hundreds of snipe and several tigers—and upon this the Customs people pounced and levied duty, in spite of my assurance that I was only on a short visit to the country, and should in the course of two or three months be off to Tasmania, taking my gun with me. If they had levied duty such as it was straight away, I should not have felt as much aggrieved as I did; but everybody in that Customs department seemed to be bound hand and foot by red-tape, and it occupied about an hour and a half to clear that gun, and occupied also about a dozen officials, none of whom seemed to have the vaguest idea whether he or some other fellow was responsible. At the first blush of this enterprise it appeared as if I was to get away with my gun (duty duly paid) within five minutes. A European officer, inspired by the idea that he was the final authority to be dealt with, made an entry of what I understood to be my release; then a native understrapper intervened, and I was carried off to another block ot buildings for the purpose of interviewing a superior native being, who, after discussion, discovered that he could do nothing for me; then I was taken to an official (also a native) in another room, who was besieged by a small force of gun-owning Britons, some of whom were exceedingly angry, while those of weaker spirit were despondent. Here in a very babel I was required to produce the entry made by that European, and I had it not; and a native official of the lowest rank being sent for that document, returned without it or any intelligible explanation of its non-appearance. Then I went after it myself, and lo! that European had forgotten all about the entry and myself, and had to shake his intellect together to grasp the situation. Eventually I got the necessary document from that bewildered person, and laid it triumphantly before the presiding genius of babel, who took it into his consideration in leisurely fashion, and demanded of me a declaration of value and an autobiographical sketch, which I furnished; and then he demanded the key of my gun-case, and of course I could not find this where I thought I had placed it—*i.e.*, in my pocket—but had to hunt for it in the handbag I had left in my gharrie, where I found it. Then the case being opened, the official inspected the gun and made elaborate notes of marks and name and number; then I was transferred in a feeble and perspiring condition to yet another official, who with marked deliberation made out a portentous receipt in duplicate; and then, having paid the duty and received my receipt, I was free. Oh, those dreary hundred minutes! Will the Indian Government reform its Bombay Customs system by at least simplifying it, if not by abolition of the duty on guns?

I discovered another change, but this time for the better, when I visited the Bombay maidan, particularly that near the railway station, in the afternoon. India had evidently adopted cricket as one of its national games. Baboos (B.A. and others), padded in orthodox manner, stood up upon that plain and faced the deadly yorker and bumpy balls delivered by other Baboos, with marvellous stoicism. Not always was the ball "*telum imbelle sine ictu*"; now and then it hit a mark, if not the wicket, and a Baboo winced but flinched not. From end to end Baboos and other coloured people played at the practice-nets, bowling and batting vigorously, but with indifferent pretence in the way of fielding. I did not observe a single Baboo, however youthful, to move out of a walk. No, fifteen years could not be expected to effect such a metamorphosis as that; and if during the next two or three centuries the Baboo is to play serious cricket, matches must be decided by some other criterion than the score of runs, or the running must be done by hirelings or in palanquins, or, when the Baboo energy rises to that pitch, on ambling ponies.

Striking alterations in the manners and customs of the people saw I none. But it did occur to me that the gharrie-wallahs and railway station coolies of Bombay had hardened in respect of extortion. There is, I believe, some sort of tariff prescribed for the charges made by these banditti, but that tariff is a dead letter. My first gharrie cost me a full day's hire (according to the *nirig*) for an hour's drive, and about 50 per cent of the capital cost of the whole turn-out; and to meet the demands of the railway porter I should have been a two-anna-bit drilling-machine.

But the troubles of Bombay were only purgatorial trials preceding the Elysium of the snipe-jheel. Arrangements had been made to preserve for me some of the best snipe-shooting in India —in Saharunpore, Moradabad, and Allahabad. There was I to spend December and the Christmas of 1893, after a preliminary month in Oudh.

In one of those districts was I to have a last chance of beating that $51\frac{1}{2}$-couple record. What were the temporary annoyances of my brief agony with the customs, gharrie-wallah, and railway porters, when beyond was that land of promise?

It was another instance of the vanity of human wishes. The snipe did not come in during November, or during '93-'94 at all; and the early dissolution of the Tasmanian Assembly forced me to be off out of India before December arrived. I had two or three hours' shooting in the vicinity of Lucknow with H. B. Mulock, and our greatest achievement was a bag of $25\frac{1}{2}$ couple shot in two hours one afternoon, and of those $25\frac{1}{2}$ couple 25 couple were jacks and only one a full snipe.

So ingloriously ended my Indian shikar.